Matthew Bennett

Programming with Oracle Developer

A Division of Pearson Technology Group
201 West 103rd Street, Indianapolis, Indiana 46290

Programming with Oracle Developer

International Standard Book Number: 0672321106

Library of Congress Catalog Card Number: 00-110296

Printed in the United States of America

First Printing: August 2001

04   03   02   01   4   3   2   1

Trademarks

Warning and Disclaimer

Executive Editor
Rosemarie Graham

Acquisitions Editor
Angela Kozlowski

Development Editor
Kevin Howard

Managing Editor
Charlotte Clapp

Project Editor
Heather McNeill

Production Editor
Michael Henry

Indexer
Aamir Burki

Proofreader
Teresa Stephens

Technical Editor
Bruce Kostival
Jeff Rowan

Team Coordinator
Lynne Williams

Interior Designer
Anne Jones

Cover Designer
Alan Clements

Page Layout
Lizbeth Patterson

Contents at a Glance

Table of Contents

Dedication

To Larry Ellison, the vision behind a company that took a chance on hiring me in 1986 when I was still in high school. Oracle has continued to pay my bills and for that I am grateful.

Acknowledgments

I would first like to thank my wife for encouraging me to write this book. Although she probably would have preferred that I finish the already-started crown molding project, she was very supportive in helping me get this book written.

I would also like to thank my children Katey, Davie, Amanda, and Nathan, who would have much rather spent time sailing with Dad than waiting for him to finish one more chapter. They were very patient and often stood by my side encouraging me to write.

The people at Sams Publishing were very helpful in helping me complete this project. Angela Kozlowski was very easy to work with, and I appreciated her understanding as I continued to push dates back due to other time commitments. Kevin Howard and Heather McNeill were also great to work with during the editing process. I am sure there are many other people at Sams who helped to put this project together, and I appreciate their help as well.

Finally, I would like to thank Bruce Kostival, the technical editor for the book. He was responsible for making sure all the examples worked, as well as making sure that I didn't leave anything out. He had some good additions and added dramatically to the overall quality of the book.

Tell Us What You Think!

As the reader of this book, *you* are our most important critic and commentator. We value your opinion and want to know what we're doing right, what we could do better, what areas you'd like to see us publish in, and any other words of wisdom you're willing to pass our way.

As an Executive Editor for Sams, I welcome your comments. You can fax, email, or write me directly to let me know what you did or didn't like about this book—as well as what we can do to make our books stronger.

Please note that I cannot help you with technical problems related to the topic of this book, and that due to the high volume of mail I receive, I might not be able to reply to every message.

When you write, please be sure to include this book's title and author as well as your name and phone or fax number. I will carefully review your comments and share them with the author and editors who worked on the book.

Fax: 317-581-4770

Email: feedback@samspublishing.com

Mail: Rosemarie Graham
            Sams
            201 West 103rd Street
            Indianapolis, IN 46290 USA

Introduction

In January of 1986, I was working in a ski shop in San Jose, California, when I got a call from Oracle Corporation asking me to come in and interview for a job. I liked skiing and tuning skis, but I could sense that Oracle had a much better job in store for me. It was one of the best choices I could have made.

I started out doing data entry for the telesales department. One night I got caught playing on the system by Ada Lai. Rather than disciplining me, Ada sat me down and taught me the basics of Oracle application development. She even had me come in on weekends and help modify the original leads tracking system.

This book is a result of some of those first experiences I had at Oracle. Oracle Developer has evolved through many different versions, but the basic principles remain the same. It is easy to become bogged down in explaining all the new features and forget the basics. Hopefully, this book contains enough of both to satisfy your needs and interests.

Chapter 1, "Oracle Forms and Reports—Overview and Architecture," starts with a short history of the various development tools provided by Oracle Corporation. It also contains an introduction to each of the various components included with Oracle Developer.

Chapter 2, "Developer Basics," discusses installation. Although it would have been nice to include complete instructions for each platform, there simply was not enough space or time. Therefore, I condensed the important parts of the installation so that you know what pitfalls and problems to avoid.

Chapters 3, "Oracle Forms Developer," 4, "Oracle Reports Developer and Graphics," and 5, "Query Builder and Schema Builder," go into basics for the components included in Oracle Developer.

Chapters 6, "Procedure Builder and PL/SQL," and 7, "Using Java with Oracle Developer and the Oracle Database," expose the programming element of Oracle Developer.

Chapters 8, "Using Graphical Elements in Forms," 9, "More About Reports," and 10, "Oracle Graphics Builder Development," go into more detail with Forms, Reports, and Graphics Developer. They are based on the examples from previous chapters, but they explain in greater detail how to customize your application using more advanced features.

Chapter 11, "Developer Application Design," covers the basic design for a sample application. Big Jim is a fictitious individual who is looking for a simple database application. You will see the design and development of that application.

Chapter 12, "Making the Design a Reality," continues with Big Jim's sample application; you build Jim's application for client/server deployment.

ORACLE FORMS AND REPORTS—OVERVIEW AND ARCHITECTURE

ESSENTIALS

- Oracle Developer represents an evolution of database development tools dating back to the early 1980s.

- Oracle Developer enables you to develop client/server-based applications. These applications can then be deployed on the Web without any modifications.

- The two major development tools included with Oracle Developer 6i are Oracle Forms and Oracle Reports.

- Other tools included with Oracle Developer are Query Builder to build SQL SELECT statements, Schema Builder to create database objects, and Procedure Builder to create database stored procedures.

- Oracle Developer includes Project Builder to maintain the code for your application.

- PL/SQL and/or Java can to create your applications.

The current suite of development tools from Oracle Corporation represents significant product evolution. The first versions of the Oracle database relied on high-level programming languages (such as, COBOL, FORTRAN, C) to create interfaces. Although some developers still prefer using a high-level language , most are willing to give up a little flexibility in return for the rapid application development provided by tools like Oracle Developer.

History of Oracle's Development Tools

To understand the latest version of Oracle Developer, it helps to understand the history of its development products. Although you may want to skip over this section, it provides a lot of insight as to why the products and tools behave the way they do.

Before the Days of Graphical User Interfaces

The first forms development tool from Oracle Corporation to gain widespread acceptance was known as the Interactive Application Facility (IAF). It was made up of two basic components: Interactive Application Generator (IAG) and Interactive Application Processor (IAP). IAG would ask the developer a bunch of questions about how he or she wanted the application to look. It would then save the responses in a text file. IAP would interpret these responses from the saved file and display the forms interface to the user. The form could then be used to query, insert, update, or delete information from the database.

This basic architecture has remained with Oracle's forms development tools. Although the data file that controls the layout of the form is no longer stored in text as answers to questions, there is still an application generator and an application runtime.

EDITING TEXT FILES

One of my first jobs at Oracle Corporation was creating Oracle-based applications for the Telesales department. Oracle had just released version 4 of the database, and so I became quite familiar with IAF, IAG, and IAP.

Creating a form for the first time required a lot of work. I would lay out the design using graph paper to make sure that the screen geometry was correct. Then I would answer the questions posed by IAG. When the form was completed, I would run it to see how it turned out. It was not uncommon to have provided the wrong answers for some of the questions. Then the form would look nothing like the original design. My saving grace was that IAG stored the questions and answers in a text file that I could edit to correct problems.

I thought I had everything figured out, and was happily creating and modifying applications. Then the Oracle developers updated IAF and screwed up my whole system. For them to add new features, IAG asked more questions. That meant the old development files I had been using were no longer valid. To get around the problem, I had to re-create at least one form from scratch and pay close attention to the new questions. Then I had to go back to the text files and add the new questions and answers to my other forms.

Once again, I was happy. Once again, happiness was short-lived. Telesales would use nonnetworked PCs to enter new customers into a local database, and then upload the data to the central customer database at the end of the day. The central customer database ran on a Digital VAX and was too slow to handle real-time data entry. The DOS-based PCs were slow but did the job. IAF ran on both systems, so I had only one set of source to maintain—at least that's what I thought.

In the mid-1980s, Oracle's primary development platform was the Digital VAX. All code was originally developed there and ported to other platforms later. My problem occurred when they released a new version of IAF for the VAX, but not for the PC. I remember many nights sitting in front of the computer trying to get a form that was originally developed for the VAX to run on the PC.

I was extremely happy the day the PC version matched the VAX release. Of course, it was not long before the two versions were out of sync again, and I resorted to keeping two versions of each form.

Oracle's first widely used reporting tool worked very similarly to IAF. It was known as RPT/RPF and was made up of two components: Report Generator (RPT) and Report Formatter (RPF). First, you would write a report to pull information out of the database using a very simple reporting language. Second, you would run RPT against the program and it would pull out all the information with formatting commands and store it in a text file. Third, you would run RPF against the output text file and it would format the results.

RPT/RPF was such a popular reporting tool that it became difficult for Oracle to phase it out. With version 6 of the database, Oracle developed a more robust reporting tool called ReportWriter. However, there were so many reports developed with RPT and RPF, Oracle continued to support both tools through version 7. Even now, there are still production databases that continue to use this old reporting tool.

Oracle was one of the first to adopt the structured query language, or SQL (pronounced "se-quel"). Oracle decided to promote this through the naming of its products. IAF eventually became SQL*Forms. The reporting tools became SQL*Reports and SQL*ReportWriter.

One of the major selling features for Oracle in the mid-1980s was that it ran on every major computer platform. Back then, there were no widely used graphical user interfaces (or GUIs), so forms and reports had to run on text-based terminals. Although the displays did not look as nice as the GUIs we use today, they were functional and provided users with an effective way to get at information.

The limited interface afforded by text-based terminals required some additional products. With version 5 of the Oracle database, SQL*Menu was introduced. This enabled developers to create menus that ran, or invoked, forms and reports with a minimal amount of coding. When the GUI-based tools were released, SQL*Menu functionality was rolled into the forms building product.

As Microsoft Windows, the Apple Macintosh interface, and the X Window System gained popularity; Oracle evolved the developer products and included support for the more robust GUI environments. Oracle also retained support for text-based applications. Customers loved the flexibility of being able to update existing applications running on text-based terminals, and were also able to experiment with the newer GUI interfaces.

The jump from a text-based interface to the GUI came between versions 3 and 4 of Oracle Forms. To help with the transition, Oracle provided transition tools that help convert non-GUI forms. Oracle also continued support for outdated triggers—eliminating the need to re-code all your forms.

Eventually, the demand for text-based application development tools diminished and the GUI interface became the standard. This ushered in the era of client/server computing. Client/server computing enabled the database to reside on a centralized server while the application interface ran on a separate client. Clients were then connected to the server through networks.

Client/Server Computing

With client/server computing, new problems were introduced. When using the older text-based terminals, the central machine was responsible for maintaining connections and data integrity. If two users tried to update the same piece of information, the server would mediate the transactions and keep trouble to a minimum. With client/server network connections, the same mediation was required, but was slightly more difficult. Oracle created SQL*Net to seamlessly enable clients to have the same quality of data integrity that was provided with the earlier environment.

A by-product of client/server computing was that users could continue to use the Oracle database, but opt for different front-end application tools. This required other companies to create connection protocols that mimicked the behavior of SQL*Net. Most software vendors did not want to lock their front-end application tools with one database vendor, so protocols such as ODBC (Open Database Connectivity) were invented. The only problem was that applications could no longer leverage functionality provided for by the Oracle database, if it was not also provided for in other database vendors' products.

Another problem with alternative protocols to SQL*Net was how much data got passed down to the client from the server. Some protocols would send all the data returned from a query on the server to the client. This created a huge network bottleneck when a user mistakenly queried the entire database. The client machine would seem to freeze up until it ran out of memory or until the entire result set was returned.

As with all the development products from Oracle, SQL*Net's name no longer carries the SQL* prefix and has been combined with the version number. It is now known as Net8 and continues to be seamlessly integrated with Oracle Developer and the Oracle database server.

The Birth of Web-Based Applications

With the proliferation of the World Wide Web, additional shortcomings of client/server computing have become apparent. The most glaring problem is the expense of maintaining client software. Not only does this include the software necessary to run the client database applications, but also the code for the applications themselves.

When running Oracle Developer applications in client/server mode, you need to install runtimes for all the components you are using (for example, Forms and Reports). You also need to install Net8 to manage the connections to the server. Unfortunately, this cannot easily be done by a remote system administrator, and is generally done at the client computer's physical location.

The problem is further complicated by updates done to the actual application. As changes are made and bugs are fixed, someone generally has to make those updates to each individual client machine.

Although this might not seem too drastic for a small office with five or six client machines, it becomes so for large offices with thousands of clients. That is why many information technology (IT) organizations embraced the Web as quickly as they did.

Application distribution is greatly simplified with Web-based applications. The only application clients require is a browser meeting certain requirements. Most, if not all, computers now ship with highly functional browsers as part of the base system. One copy of the application is then placed on a central server for everyone to access. Should revisions need to be made to the application, they only have to be installed once. This architecture obviates the need to install runtime software as well as the potential for many updates of the application.

Advantages of Client/Server over Web-Based Applications

Although Web-based applications might solve some problems of client/server applications, there are also some shortcomings. The most notable is that transactions are difficult to maintain with Web-based applications. Web connections are maintained by Hypertext Transport Protocol (HTTP) and are stateless. Database transactions cannot be properly maintained using a stateless connection. This can be overcome by writing applications in Java and using Java Database Connectivity (JDBC) to connect to the database, but the same problems that existed in ODBC also are in JDBC. Although Oracle has developed SQLJ to solve the deficiencies of JDBC, it is still worth mentioning.

To help combat all the problems associated with Web-based application development, the Oracle Internet Developer Suite was created. In addition to being a full-fledged, Web-based application development environment, it also enables you to develop client/server and text-based applications simply by changing the method of deployment. This is done without requiring any coding changes.

Components of the Oracle Internet Developer Suite

The components of the Oracle Internet Developer Suite include the following products:

- Oracle Designer and Repository
- Oracle Forms Developer
- Oracle Reports Developer

- Oracle JDeveloper
- Oracle Discoverer
- Oracle Portal

Although this book focuses on Forms Developer and Reports Developer, it is important to understand what each of the products do. This will help you in the development of your database applications.

Oracle Designer and Repository

Oracle Designer is a visual modeling tool that enables developers to capture business requirements and rules. It supports a variety of modeling methods including ER diagram, information engineering, and object analysis and design. It is designed to aid in large projects and supports a team-working environment.

Oracle Designer is integrated with Oracle Repository in the 6i release. The repository is used to provide configuration management for Oracle database objects, Forms applications, Java classes, XML, and other kinds of files.

Anyone working on large development projects will want to invest some time in learning to use Oracle Designer and Repository. In addition to helping you and your team keep track of database table relationships, it can also be used to create tables (complete with integrity constraints) and to start some of the application forms and reports you need.

Oracle Forms Developer

Oracle Forms Developer is used to create efficient, scalable, and portable applications (or windows) in your database. These applications enable you to query, update, insert, and delete information in the database. You can create a single application and then deploy it using the Web, client/server model, or text-based terminals.

Because Oracle Forms Developer is one of the major focuses of this book, it is discussed thoroughly.

Oracle Reports Developer

Oracle Reports Developer enables you to create reports that can dynamically build and distribute reports based on database information. These reports can be distributed via the Web or printed out, depending on your requirements.

As with Oracle Forms Developer, Oracle Reports Developer is a major focus of this book and is discussed in much greater detail.

Oracle JDeveloper

Oracle JDeveloper is a full-featured, Java development environment for creating and deploying Java components and applications. As with most integrated development environments, it includes a comprehensive debugger to minimize errors and problems. There is also the usual syntax highlighting and coloring.

JDeveloper has complete support for JDK 1.1, 1.2, and 1.3, as well as the J2 Enterprise Edition programming model. This is important to those developers looking for a robust Java environment.

Oracle JDeveloper is integrated with Oracle Designer and Repository for use in team development projects.

Oracle Discoverer

Oracle Discoverer was created to help nontechnical users retrieve information from the database without having to learn the complexities of SQL. Generally, someone technical sets up predefined queries or windows to information. The nontechnical user is then able to easily modify search criteria and retrieve vital information.

Oracle Portal

Oracle Portal was previously known as WebDB and is used to help create enterprise Web portals. Unlike other Web development tools, there is no need to install anything on your computer. Simply point your browser at the machine running Web Portal, and you are ready to publish information.

With Oracle Portal, you can publish structured or unstructured data without the help of a Webmaster or application engineer. This enables employees to easily communicate and collaborate on projects without creating a lot of work for in-house IT staffs.

Oracle Forms Developer

Oracle Forms Developer is a very complex and robust product, and is made up of several components. The component that you spend most of your time in is the Forms Builder. Forms Builder is an IDE for creating windows in the database. These windows can then be used to query, update, insert, or delete information.

There are several built-in wizards that help you develop common forms quickly and effectively. These include

- Data Block Wizard   A data block corresponds to a selection of table data from the database. Although a data block can be mapped to only one table, a form may contain multiple data blocks.

Schema Builder

The Schema Builder is used to help create the tables that you use in your database application. If you are using Oracle Designer to help design your database application, you do not need to use the Schema Builder. However, if your application is small enough that you do not require all the features of Designer, the Schema Builder can be a great help.

The Schema Builder can be run as a separate application, or it can be called from either Oracle Forms Developer or Reports Developer.

Procedure Builder

The Procedure Builder is used to help create PL/SQL functions and procedures. One of the most helpful aspects of this tool is the PL/SQL debugger. It is similar to debuggers found with other development environments, and enables you to execute code line by line. The Procedure Builder is shown in Figure 1.3.

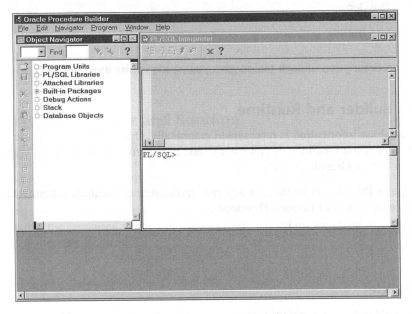

FIGURE 1.3
Procedure Builder enables you to create and debug PL/SQL functions and procedures.

PL/SQL is the language used to program the desired behavior in forms and reports. It is also used extensively by the database, and you will come to rely heavily on this tool.

The Procedure Builder can be run as a separate application, or it can be called from either Oracle Forms Developer or Reports Developer.

Project Builder

The Project Builder is used to manage the development process for your applications. It provides a level of security, so you can password-protect the development of your applications. It also provides check in and check out capabilities found in most source code control systems.

Although most developers might not see the need for project management functionality on small applications, using the Project Builder is a good habit to develop and highly recommended. You never know when you might have to go back to a previous version of the application in order to fix a critical bug or defect. Source code control also provides a backup copy of your work, which can be used in case of a machine crash or failure.

The Project Builder can be run as a separate application, or it can be called from either Oracle Forms Developer or Reports Developer.

Translation Builder

The Translation Builder is used to help make your application usable in more than one language. Most small applications do not require the use of the Translation Builder, however, it is one of those tools that you use extensively when your application requires it.

The Oracle Database Server's Role in Forms and Reports Development

When you start several of the development tools included in the Developer suite (Forms being one exception), you are asked to connect to a database. Without a database connection, you are not able to use the tool. This is because all the database development applications and tools make extensive use of the database. Not only are all normal database objects (for example, tables, indexes, triggers) stored in the database, but the engine that executes PL/SQL is integrated with the database as well. Starting with Oracle version 8i, the Java Virtual Machine (JVM) is also included in the database.

As you can guess, PL/SQL and Java can play an important part in the development of your applications. The Oracle database server also enables you to use objects in your application, creating a full-featured platform for your application development.

PL/SQL

When Oracle first touted the benefits of SQL, it promoted SQL as a non procedural language. It is interesting that in the evolution of the database, Oracle found it important to add procedural capabilities. The result is PL/SQL.

PL/SQL can be used extensively throughout your applications. Oracle Forms Developer uses PL/SQL as the programming language for event handling. Should the user click a button in your newly created application, it is PL/SQL that handles the event and determines what happens next.

Although the syntax might differ slightly from other procedural languages you might be familiar with, PL/SQL is not difficult to learn. Traditional language constructs such as IF-THEN-ELSE logic, looping structures, and exception handling are included in the language. There are also database-specific features, such as cursors. These all combine to enable you to create robust and complex applications.

Java

With Oracle version 8i and later, a JVM has been added to the database server. This enables developers to choose between PL/SQL and Java for creating stored procedures and packages. Because both languages are tightly coupled to the database and tuned for maximum performance, there is relatively little difference in speed of execution. Figure 1.4 shows the relationship of both PL/SQL and Java to the Oracle database server.

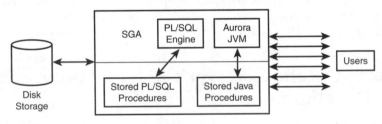

Oracle 8i Database Server

FIGURE 1.4
The PL/SQL engine and the Java Virtual Machine are both executed from within the Oracle database server.

Those developers who have been around Oracle products for a long time might want to continue using PL/SQL. Those developers who are new to Oracle, but already know Java, can use Java without the worry of performance degradation concerns.

Objects

One of the new features added to the Oracle8 database server was the capability to support objects as envisioned by object-oriented programmers. You can now create database objects using the CREATE TYPE SQL command.

Adding objects used to require that PL/SQL be augmented to handle object types within procedures and functions. With the inclusion of the JVM with the database, you have the ability to manipulate database objects using either PL/SQL or Java.

Deployment of Forms and Reports

When creating forms and reports for your application, you do not need to concern yourself with the method of deployment. You are able to test everything using either the client/server model or the Web-based model. After you are satisfied with all aspects of the application and have thoroughly tested it, you can then decide how you want to deploy it. If you choose, you have the option of deploying your forms or reports using text-based terminals (in addition to the client/server and Web-based models).

Deployment depends on several factors, one of which might be conforming to existing infrastructure. You might also plan to deploy using one method, only to discover that another method is preferred. Whichever method you choose, Oracle Developer does not require any changes to be made to the forms or reports.

The Three-Tiered Model

Often, you hear the Web-based deployment model referred to as the *Three-tiered* model. Figure 1.5 shows an example of this architecture.

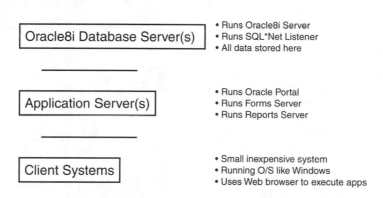

The Three-tiered model for deploying Developer Apps.

FIGURE 1.5
The Web-based deployment model is often referred to as the Three-tiered model.

The top tier is the Oracle database server and the middle tier is the application server. The client tier then, is the browser, Java applet viewer, or other presentation layer running on a user's computer. With applications developed using Oracle Forms Developer and Oracle Reports Developer, the application server is simply running the Oracle Forms Server and/or the Oracle Reports Server.

Summary

In this chapter you were given a brief history of Oracle's development tools and introduced to the Oracle Internet Development Suite. Although there are several products included in the Suite, the major focus of this book is Oracle Forms Developer 6i and Oracle Reports Developer 6i.

You were also given a short introduction to the Oracle database server and how it uses PL/SQL and Java to create database triggers, packages, procedures, and functions. Those who know PL/SQL can continue to use it, and those who prefer Java can do so knowing there is no penalty.

Finally, you were told about deployment options. You can code the application once, and then deploy it using any one of three different methods.

DEVELOPER BASICS

ESSENTIALS

- Make sure that your development computer meets the system requirements described in the installation manual specific to your platform.

- The Oracle Technology Network is an important resource that will help you with Oracle software installation as well as providing tips for completing your application.

- If you are installing Oracle Developer on the same machine as an Oracle database, do not use the same user accounts for both installations. Install the database in the oracle user account and install Oracle Developer in the oradev user account.

- The scott/tiger sample tables are used for examples in the book. If they are not already installed, ask your database administrator to help you install them.

- Forms Builder and Reports Builder use wizards to streamline application development. Use them to start your application development.

This chapter contains basic information about Oracle Developer to get you going. Guidelines are included to help with the installation of Oracle Developers and sample application tables. Also in this chapter, you will create simple applications using the Forms Builder, Reports Builder, and Graphics Builder. This chapter serves as a foundation for the later sections in the book, so if you are new to Oracle's development tools, be sure to read through the information very carefully.

Installation

It is beyond the scope of this book to cover every aspect of installation of the Oracle Developer products. The installation guide for Oracle Developer running on Linux is more than a hundred pages long, and trying to re-create it here would not leave much room for much else. However, some very important installation tips are given to help make sure that your install goes as smoothly as possible.

Operating System Requirements

Oracle Developer is supported on both Microsoft Windows and various Unix platforms. At the time of this writing, Version 6i Release 2 is available on the Oracle Technology Network (OTN) and freely downloadable for anyone willing to sit through the time it takes. Be fore-warned that the Linux version uses a 650MB TAR file that took more than two and a half hours to download using a fast DSL connection.

REGISTER WITH OTN

If you do not have an OTN login, you can sign up for one by going to Oracle's Web site at the following URL:

http://www.oracle.com

The OTN allows you to download the latest versions of Oracle's products. It also contains countless technical references and documentation. In addition to this book, the OTN is a great place to go to get help with any questions you might have.

Oracle is constantly updating the number of platforms that it supports for its various products. Developer 6i has been ported to the following platforms:

- Microsoft Windows 98, NT 4.0, 2000
- Compaq Tru64 Unix
- HP-UX version 11.0
- IBM AIX version 4.3

- Linux on Intel x86

- Sun Solaris for SPARC and Intel

At the time of this writing, Release 2 is available for only a subset of this list. Therefore, it is important that you check Oracle's Web site for an updated list of platforms.

Oracle Corporation treats the difference between 6.0 and 6i Release 2 as a series of patch releases. This means that additional functionality is fairly limited, with the majority of changes coming from bug fixes. Therefore, even if you are limited to running version 6.0, most of the examples and exercises should still work fine.

Hardware Requirements

Those experienced with Oracle's products know that when it comes to hardware, more is better. It is recommended that you use the fastest processor possible with the greatest amount of system memory and largest hard drive. The faster the computer you have, the happier you will be as you create your applications.

Specific system requirements depend on the platform you choose to develop for and whether the Oracle database is running on the same machine. It is generally assumed that the audience of this book is running some flavor of Windows with the database on a separate machine. If that is the case, Oracle recommends a Pentium III processor with 128MB of RAM to run Developer. Machines running the completed applications in client/server mode can get by with a 150MHz Pentium and 64MB of RAM.

For those of you who prefer to use Linux for your development environment (with a separate machine for the database), you can get by with a smaller system. Oracle's installation guide for Linux recommends a Pentium-class machine with only 64MB of memory. The tradeoff for less memory comes at the expense of a much more difficult software installation.

If you decide to run the Oracle database on the same machine as Oracle Developer, be prepared to use a faster machine with much more memory. Again, the system requirements differ depending on the platform. Be sure to consult recommendations from Oracle's Web site.

ADD MEMORY

With both Windows and Linux, adding more memory can solve speed problems. If your system barely meets the memory requirements and you find yourself coveting faster computers, try adding more memory. RAM is fairly cheap and you should notice an immediate improvement.

Database Server Requirements

Oracle Developer does not require that you use the Oracle database. There is ODBC support to access other databases. However, it is highly recommended that you use Oracle. The biggest reason is to eliminate the complexity of installation and setup for your development environment. Also, you will have a single point of contact for technical support.

Because you will most likely connect to an Oracle database when using Oracle Developer, the supported versions of the database are

- Oracle7—version 7.3.4
- Oracle8—version 8.0.5
- Oracle8i—all versions
- Oracle9i—all versions

TEST THE CONNECTION
The true test of whether you can use a database is if you can connect to it using Oracle's Net8 product. If so, Oracle Developer will work.

Installation Help for Microsoft Windows

At the time this book was written, Release 2 of Developer 6i was available only for Windows NT. If you want to develop applications on other versions of Windows such as 95, 98, or 2000, you might need to use a previous version of Oracle Developer.

One of the advantages of using the Windows version of Oracle Developer is that the installation is much easier. Be sure to read through the installation guide provided with the software before you attempt the installation. The installation guide tells you what service packs are required and anything else that might cause the installation to be difficult.

The installation is fairly straightforward. At a minimum, you must install Forms Developer and Reports Developer to complete the examples in this book. If you want to deploy your applications on the Web, be sure to install the Forms Server and the Reports Server.

If you run your database on a separate machine, you must install Net8. Net8 enables you to seamlessly access your database across the network. After Net8 is installed, modify the TNSNAMES.ORA file to include the connection information to your database machine. The installation program should perform the modification. However, if you change the machine that the database resides on, or you don't know the information at installation, you must use the Net8 Easy Config utility or go in and add TNSNAMES.ORA by hand. If you choose to edit TNSNAMES.ORA by hand, it is found in the admin subdirectory of the Net8 directory. The Net8 directory is located in the directory where you chose to install Oracle Developer. Instructions on how to modify an entry are detailed in the "Installation on Unix" section.

After you install Oracle Developer, proceed to the post-installation activities. This creates database tables that are required for certain features of Developer (such as saving forms and reports source code in the database).

Installation on Unix

Installing Oracle Developer on a Unix machine is much more complicated than on Windows. If you have downloaded Oracle Developer from the OTN site, the installation instructions might even be difficult to find. Therefore, it is important that you be familiar with your platform and have a good understanding of how Oracle organizes the software for Unix.

If your version of Oracle Developer came on a CD, the install should be a bit more straightforward. If you downloaded the TAR file from the OTN site, you must unpack the information onto a staging area on your hard drive. This requires you to have an additional 650MB of disk space in addition to what Oracle recommends.

The installation instructions for the Linux version of Developer are found in the unixdoc subdirectory. Most distributions of Developer for Unix should follow this organizational hierarchy. If you mounted your CD at /mnt/cdrom, the documentation can be found in /mnt/cdrom/unixdoc. If you are using a staging area, substitute the appropriate path.

Be sure to read through the installation instructions thoroughly before starting the installation. Pay close attention to account setup and all the environment variables that must be set before starting. The most important environment variable to worry about is ORACLE_HOME. Make sure that ORACLE_HOME is always set in your environment. If things don't seem to be going smoothly during the install, it is generally because an environment variable is not set appropriately.

CREATE SEPARATE LOGINS

If you decide to set up Oracle Developer on the same machine that is your database server, be sure to create separate logins for the owner of Developer and the owner of the database server. Oracle Developer uses libraries common to the database server. Using separate logins ensures that the correct versions of the libraries are available for both products.

The installation instructions say to run the Install program. Although that program might exist in the CD version, it does not exist in the download version. Instead, you must go to the orainst subdirectory and run the program orainst. The rest of the installation should be fairly straightforward.

LINUX WARNING

In the Linux version, the instructions lull you into a false sense of security by saying that Developer will run under a variety of windowing environments (that is, KDE, GNOME, WindowMaker, and so on). The installation process requires Forms Developer and Reports Developer to be relinked, and that requires you to have the Motif 2.1 libraries. If those libraries did not come with your Linux software, you will need to download them from the Net.

For systems that support RPM for package installation, you can simply go to www.rpmfind.net and search for "Motif." You can then download OpenMotif 2.1. Be sure to get the development libraries as well.

As the installation takes place, a log file is created. Should a problem occur, open another shell window and look at the contents of the log file. Often the problem is a minor thing, such as file permissions, and can be fixed without having to restart the installer.

After Oracle Developer is installed, you are asked to run the script root.sh as the root user. This is an important step and should not be forgotten.

As with the Windows installation, you might be required to modify your TNSNAMES.ORA file if your database resides on a separate machine. TNSNAMES.ORA resides in the $ORACLE_HOME/network/admin directory.

The TNSNAMES.ORA file is fairly easy and straightforward to modify providing there is an example that you can use as a template. Listing 2.1 gives a simple example of what the configuration file should look like.

Listing 2.1   A Sample TNSNAMES.ORA File

```
#Sample TNSNAMES.ORA configuration file
ALTA=
  (DESCRIPTION =
    (ADDRESS_LIST =
      (ADDRESS = (PROTOCOL = TCP)
                 (HOST = alta.mydomain.com)
                 (PORT = 1521)
      )
    )
    (CONNECT_DATA =
      (SERVICE_NAME = (SID = A))
    )
  )
```

The most important parts of the listing are the protocol used, the name of the system where the Oracle database resides, and the system identifier (or SID) of the database. In Listing 2.1, the protocol used is TCP/IP, as specified by TCP on line 5. The name of the machine on which the database resides is alta.mydomain.com. With TCP/IP, you want to be sure to use the name of the machine as it appears in the DNS entry. This means that on some networks, the machine name might be shortened to alta. Finally, the SID for the database we are using on alta is A.

When using TCP/IP as the protocol, you must specify a port number. The default port number is 1521. If the database administrator for the server has used a different port number, you must modify the TNSNAMES.ORA file accordingly.

SID TIP

Oracle allows multiple database instances to be installed on the same machine. This enables database administrators and developers to work on the same machine with different databases without worrying about crashing a production system.

SIDs can take many forms. Older versions of Oracle allowed only a single letter to be used (which is why the previous example uses an A for the SID), but this restriction has been lifted. Often, PROD refers to the production database, DEV refers to the development database, and TEST refers to a test database.

If you decide to install the Forms Server or Reports Server, you are asked to look at additional installation activities. It is easy to gloss over these installation instructions and not to execute them. The files forms6iconfig.txt and reports6iconfig.txt can be found in the same directory as root.sh. Be sure to read these instructions and do what they say—it involves setting up virtual directories with your Web server. Using the Apache server as an example, this can be accomplished using directory aliases in your httpd.conf file.

HOW TO GET THROUGH AN INSTALL ON UNIX

Installing Oracle software on Unix can seem like a daunting task to the an Oracle novice. Whether it is the Oracle database or Oracle Developer, there is a lot that can go wrong or be forgotten. Those of you who prefer to use the Microsoft Windows platforms have a high expectation of the installer and don't have as much to worry about. However, sometimes even a Windows installation can have some problems.

When I first started doing Oracle installs with version 5, the process was driven by shell scripts. Eventually, the shell scripts were replaced by the Oracle Installer program and were made much easier. Interestingly enough, however, the same problems that exist with an install using the shell scripts can haunt you with the Oracle Installer. Therefore, it is important that you develop a foolproof method to help install Oracle software.

Here are some steps that I use to help make sure that the installation goes as smoothly as possible:

- Locate the installation documentation and read it before you doing anything. This document could be anywhere between from 150 to 200 pages. Set aside a whole day if you need to, but make sure to read the documentation before you starting. If you only have the documentation in online format only, print it out. This will enable you to take notes and to provide comments in the margin. As you perform the installation, you will want to make additional notes just in case you find yourself doing another install in the future.

- Make sure that all of the requested environment variables are appropriately set. The number one cause of failure in Oracle installations is that one of the many different environment variables is not set correctly. As you read through the installation instructions, make notes as to the correct paths and values.

- Read the error messages—and don't just skip over them. If you encounter any error messages, read what they say. You can often bring up another shell and fix the problem and not have to exit the Installer. If the error message is not clear enough, don't hesitate to look at the log file created during the install.

- Pay attention to every message in the Installer. You will often get tired of going over every message printed out by the Installer, and not realize that you have just skipped an important message. This generally occurs when there are more installation steps, but the installer Installer cannot complete them until certain other steps have been taken. If you did do not pay attention to all of the Installer messages, you might think you are done with the installation and not realize that there is more to do.

- Allow plenty of time for the install. When you are rushed, you become frustrated and become more likely to make a mistake. Take your time and things will run more smoothly.

These tips will help you install your Oracle software on Unix. It is not uncommon for me to forget one or two of them. When that happens, I am stuck doing the installation over again, cursing my mistake, and pulling out my rapidly thinning hair.

Installing the Sample Tables

After you install Oracle Developer and have access to a database, you want to be sure that the sample tables are installed. Most database installations include the scott/tiger sample data. You want to be sure that they exist in your database. Check with the database administrator to see that the tables are installed.

SQL*PLUS TIP

What if you are the database administrator? If so, you can use the SQL*Plus utility to see whether the tables have been loaded. Simply use scott as the username and tiger as the password. If you are told that it is an invalid user/password combination, you need to consult your database documentation for getting those tables loaded. The script to do so is called demobld.sql, and is generally found in the $ORACLE_HOME/splplus/demo subdirectory. If you log in fine and are at the SQL> prompt, you want to make sure that the tables actually exist. Simply run the following command:

```
SELECT * FROM EMP;
```

You should see several screens of information scroll by. If you get an error saying that the table or view does not exist, you need to load the sample tables.

You will not create any large tables or add lots of data for the examples in this book. Therefore, the database should not require any additional modifications.

Using Forms Developer

After you install Oracle Developer 6i, you are ready to start creating simple forms, reports, and graphics. You will start by creating a simple form. If you are already familiar with the Form Builder, you might want to skip to the next section on using Reports Developer.

To start Form Builder for Windows, you can open the Start menu, navigate to the Oracle Developer menu entry, and click the Form Builder icon. On Unix, simply run f60desm. If you have any problems running f60desm on Unix, you might require your system administrator's help in setting up your development environment. Figure 2.1 shows the Welcome to Form Builder window for Windows, whereas Figure 2.2 shows it on Unix.

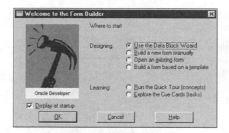

FIGURE 2.1
The Welcome to Form Builder window running in Windows.

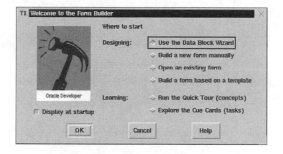

FIGURE 2.2
The Welcome to Form Builder window running in Unix.

You can see that the two environments are very similar. Of course, the Windows version uses check boxes and graphical elements familiar to Windows users, whereas the Unix version has a Motif look and feel. So as not to imply an endorsement of either environment, screenshots from both GUIs are used throughout the book.

Building Your First Form

As you become more familiar with the Forms Builder, you might want to build new forms manually. For the purpose of this exercise, you are using the Data Block Wizard. This is the default option, so simply press Enter or click on the OK button. Figure 2.3 shows the introduction page to the Data Block Wizard.

After clicking on the Next button or pressing Enter, you are asked whether the data block will be created using a table, view, or stored procedure. The default is Table or view. In this first example, you use a table. With Table or view selected, click on the Next button or press Enter.

You can now select the table or view on which to base the block. To get an idea of what tables are available, click on the Browse button. You are asked to log in to a database. You should be able to enter scott for the username and tiger for the password, unless your database administrator set up the demo tables in another account. Don't forget to enter the appropriate connect string.

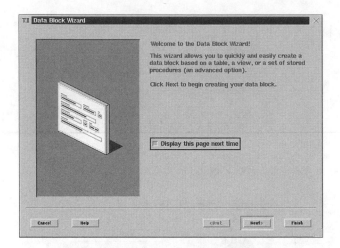

FIGURE 2.3
The introduction page to the Data Block Wizard describes some of the database objects you can use to create a form.

When you are logged in, you are given a list of tables to choose from as shown in Figure 2.4.

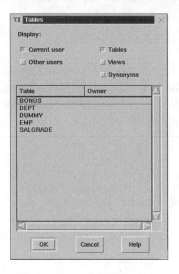

FIGURE 2.4
The table browser allows you to pick from a list of tables, views, and synonyms.

For this first example, select the EMP table. EMP is short for EMPLOYEE. The tables used in this demo have been around since before version 5 of the database. They represent an employee database complete with departments, salaries, and bonuses. After you select the EMP table, click on OK and you'll see that the values in the Data Block Wizard window are automatically filled in. Your window should look similar to Figure 2.5.

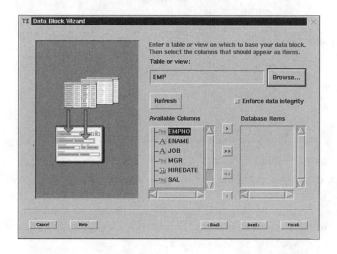

FIGURE 2.5
The main window of the Data Block Wizard allows you to specify the table and columns used in the block.

You want all the columns in the table to be displayed in the block and on the form. Use the single arrow button (>) to select one column at a time for display. Use the double arrow (>>) to select all columns for display.

You are now done with the Data Block Wizard and are presented with the choice of using the Layout Wizard. Because this is a beginning example, you want to use the Layout Wizard. Click on the Finish button, and you are shown the welcome screen for the Layout Wizard. Again, click Next and you see the canvas selection screen. Because this is a new form, there are not very many choices from which to choose. Therefore, click on the Next button, and you are given the option to show the fields that will appear on the form, as shown in Figure 2.6.

As you did with the Data Block Wizard, click on the >> button to move all the table columns from the left list box to the right. All the columns now appear as fields or entry areas on the form. Click on Next and you are given the chance to specify the width and height that each field will occupy on the completed form. Again, the defaults are acceptable, so click on Next.

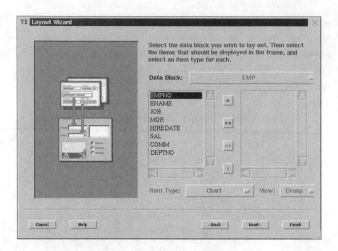

FIGURE 2.6
The Layout Wizard allows you to choose which table columns will appear as fields on the form.

There are two basic ways to display fields on a form. The first method is one row at a time. This corresponds to the Form option on the layout style page. The graphic on the left is meant to give you an idea of what this style looks like.

The second method of displaying rows from a table is in tabular format. This method is very handy if you want to display multiple rows at the same time. If you click on the Tabular option, the graphic on the left is updated to give you an idea of how this style looks.

For this example, use the Form layout style. After Form is selected, click the Next button. You are asked to name the block and specify the number of rows being displayed. Enter a block name, such as First Demo, and click the Next button. You are done. There is a final window congratulating you; the only action required is to click the Finish button. After you do so, you are rewarded with your first form as shown in Figure 2.7.

Running Your Form

Now that your form is designed, it is time to test it. You have the option of running the form using several different environments. The easiest to test with is client/server, but you might want to try the Web interface. You can choose either run option from the Run Form submenu found in the Program menu. Figure 2.8 shows the form running in client/server mode after querying the database.

As you can see, the client/server runtime environment provides a lot of default functionality that you didn't have to explicitly program into the application. One feature that is widely used when running forms is the ability to query the database. One way to query the database is to select the Execute menu option from the Query menu. You can also use the Execute Query button found on the toolbar.

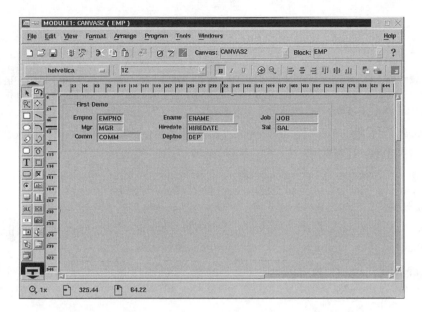

FIGURE 2.7
The completed form is now ready to be tested.

FIGURE 2.8
The completed form running in client/server mode can be used to query records in the database.

Take some time to familiarize yourself with the client/server runtime environment. Holding the cursor over the buttons on the toolbar will invoke tooltips and provide short descriptions of what each button does. The client/server runtime environment will be discussed in more detail in the next chapter. If you are interested in deploying forms applications in the Web environment, it is discussed in Chapter 13, "Deploying Developer Applications to the Web."

Building Complex Forms

The example you just completed was a very simple, single-table form. It is more common to build forms that are created from multiple tables, and that is covered in the next chapter. You also will want to leverage the full capabilities of the GUI environment and take advantage of pop-up lists, radio buttons, and check boxes. Here is a list of some features that Oracle Forms Developer supports:

- **Triggers**   A *trigger* is executed after a predefined event occurs. That event can be database specific, such as the insertion or deletion of a record. The event can also be GUI-based, such as a mouse click or a key press.

- **Alerts**   An *alert* is a pop-up window or dialog that provides some sort of user feedback. An alert is most often used for error messages or warnings.

- **Object Libraries**   An *object library* is a collection of form objects that can be used by multiple forms and applications. An object library can be stored in a file or in the database.

- **Lists of Values**   A *list of values*, often called LOV, can be used to provide a user with either a single column or a multicolumn selection list.

- **Property Classes**   A *property class* is a named object that contains a group of properties and associated settings. Objects based on a given property class inherit these common settings.

- **Record Groups**   A *record group* is a structure internal to forms that works like a database table local to a given application.

- **Visual Attributes**   A *visual attribute* is a characteristic of an object displayed on a form. There are many visual attributes including font, size, and color.

As you can see, Oracle Forms Developer is a robust database application development environment. As you start to build applications, it is helpful for you to think about how you can leverage some of them to make your job easier and quicker. Examples and helpful hints are provided throughout this book.

Using Reports Developer

As with Forms Developer, Oracle Reports Developer is a robust tool to help in the creation of database applications. Although there are generally a finite number of ways to enter information into the database, there are an infinite number of ways to retrieve it. Therefore, it is important to have a firm understanding of Reports Developer and how it can decrease the amount of time it takes to create reports.

To help you gain an understanding of how Reports Developer works, the following section shows how to create a simple report. If you have already created a report using Reports Developer and are familiar with the product, you might to skip to the next section on Oracle Graphics.

Creating Your First Report

Creating a report with Reports Developer is very similar to creating a form with Forms Developer. In this example, you leverage as many of the built-in wizards as possible to make the task easy. Start the Report Builder. On the Windows platform, this is done using the menu item from the Start menu. On Unix, this is done by running rwbld60. If you experience a problem running rwbld60 on your system, you might require your system administrator's help in setting up your development environment.

The welcome dialog for Report Builder (shown in Figure 2.9) should look somewhat familiar. As with Form Builder, you have the option of manually creating a report or using Report Wizard. Make sure that Use the Report Wizard is selected, and click OK or press Enter.

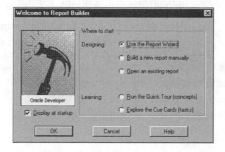

FIGURE 2.9
The Report Builder welcome dialog allows you to manually create a report or use the Report Wizard to help you.

Next, you should see the welcome screen to the Report Wizard. After reading through it, click on the Next button. You should now see the title and style definition page, as shown in Figure 2.10. Enter "Reports Demo" as the title for this example.

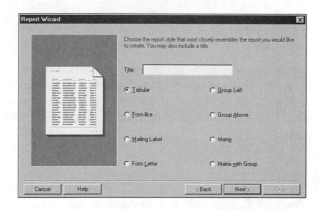

FIGURE 2.10
The Report Wizard allows you to define the title and style of your report.

Clicking on the various styles of reports should give you a thumbnail idea of what the completed report will look like. To help you understand the various types of reports, here are some definitions:

- **Tabular**   This is a common type of report that corresponds to displaying the rows in the database as rows on the report. It is a convenient way of displaying large amounts of information in a small amount of space.

- **Form-like**   This style of layout is best used to display lots of information for a single row in the database. Generally, you have only one row of information per page.

- **Mailing Label**   You will generally use this type of report to create mail labels. However, this style can be used to create any report in which you want data from different rows in the database to appear in a multicolumn format.

- **Form Letter**   This style of layout can be used to create form letters or any other report in which there is a large amount of static text combined with dynamic data.

- **Group Left**   This is a variation of the Tabular report in which rows from the table can be grouped together. For example, if you group all the employees by department number, the department number appears to the left of the first employee listed in each department. With the department number appearing only once, it is easy to see the groups of employees for each department.

- **Group Above**   This report layout is very similar to the Group Left layout, except that rather than having the grouping criteria listed to the left, it is listed above each group.

- **Matrix**   This report layout is used to cross tabulate two sets of data. An example is sales figures broken out by month and location.

- **Matrix with Group**   This report is a combination of the Matrix layout combined with a group report. For instance, in addition to cross tabulating a sales report by month and location, you can also group the information by years.

Hopefully, you now have a rough idea of how the various report layouts differ. Examples and more details are given in Chapter 4, "Oracle Reports Developer and Graphics."

Continuing with the sample report you're creating, you want to choose the tabular report. After entering Report Demo for the title and selecting the Tabular layout style, click the Next button. You are now asked to enter a SQL statement. If the report uses more than one table, it is best to use the Query Builder tool. Because your sample report uses only the EMP table, you manually enter the SQL query as

```
SELECT * FROM EMP
```

With the query entered, click on the Next button, and you are asked to log in to the database. Again, you use the scott/tiger account with scott as the username and tiger as the password. With the login complete, you are asked to define the columns displayed on the report, as shown in Figure 2.11. Click on the >> button to select all columns to be displayed. By selecting one column at a time and pressing the > button, you can control the order in which the columns appear in the report. In the Windows version, you can select the columns in the Displayed Fields list and arrange them in the desired order by using the mouse. Unfortunately, this trick does not yet work in the Unix version.

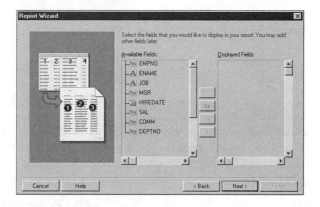

FIGURE 2.11
The Report Wizard allows you to specify the columns from the table that will be displayed in the report.

With the displayed columns defined, click Next and you are asked to calculate totals for any given column. Although *total* implies addition, you also have the options of averages, maximums, minimums, counts, and percentage totals. In the example, it would be nice to see the total salaries for everyone in the company, so click on SAL in the Available Fields list and move it to the Totals list using the Sum > button. Now click Next and you can specify labels and widths as shown in Figure 2.12.

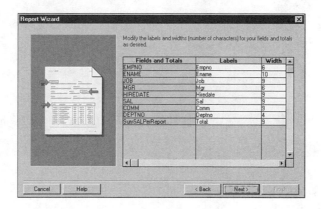

FIGURE 2.12
The Report Wizard allows you to specify labels on the report that are different than the database column names.

When the folks at Oracle created the scott/tiger demo tables a long time ago, they didn't feel like using very descriptive column names. They followed the Unix mentality and felt that shorter names meant less typing. Unfortunately, this does not make the report easy to read. Change some of the labels to be more descriptive as follows:

- Empno should be Emp #

- Ename should be Name

- Sal should be Salary

- Deptno should be Dept #

With the changes to the labels made, click on Next and you are ready to choose a report template. Several predefined templates are included in Report Builder, or you can create your own. Corporate 1 is the default template and includes a picture of the Emerald City (the nickname given to Oracle's headquarters campus because of the overwhelming matching green buildings). Because this report is not for Oracle Corporation, select Corporate 2, and then click on Next—your report is finished.

You should now see the congratulations page telling you that the Report Wizard is done asking you questions and is ready to generate your report. Click on Finish and the report is run and displayed to you as shown in Figure 2.13.

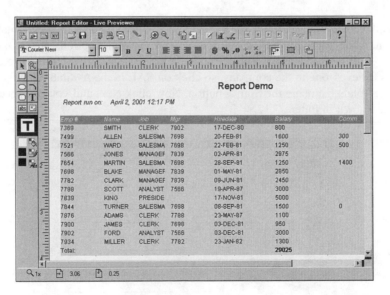

FIGURE 2.13
The Live Previewer window gives you an idea of what your report will look like.

Building Complex Reports

It is rare that the person creating the report is also the person responsible for printing and distributing the report. Therefore, Oracle has built-in some features to help make reports easy to produce.

As with Forms Developer, Reports Developer has a runtime component if you want to deploy a report using the client/server model. A common method of running reports in this environment is to have a form call the runtime report engine and execute your report. You also can have reports run from icons on your desktop. Reports Developer features that help with deployment include the following:

- **System Parameters**   Reports Developer includes a list of specific parameters that allow you to specify dynamic requests such as the number of report copies to make or the currency symbol to use.

- **User Parameters**   Reports can be defined so that user-defined parameters can be used to limit the results for a report as the report is being run. Perhaps you want only to run a report for orders made on a specific day. This can be accomplished with user parameters.

- **Parameter Form**   If you decide to run your report from an icon on the desktop, you have the ability to call a parameter form that enables the user to enter parameters into a GUI-based form. This greatly simplifies things for users not used to entering command-line parameters.

There are many features found in Oracle Reports Developer. Chapter 4 goes into more detail about how to leverage those features to create robust reports in a quick and efficient manner.

Using Oracle Graphics

With the proliferation of the various GUI environments, it is much easier to incorporate graphs and charts into forms, reports, and presentations. Unfortunately, most database developers have not had an easy way to create charts and graphs and, therefore, do not use them effectively. Users overcome the deficiency by importing the appropriate data into Excel spreadsheets and creating their own graphs and charts.

Oracle Graphics was developed to solve the graph and chart deficiency. Unfortunately, it is not utilized as often as it could be. As you design your database applications, pay close attention to how Graphics can help eliminate the unneeded step of manually creating charts and graphs.

Your First Graph

To create graphs and charts using Oracle Graphics, you must start the Graphics Builder program. On Windows, this is done from the Start menu. On Unix, it is done by running g60desm. If you experience any problems running g60desm, you might need to contact your system administrator for help in setting up your development environment properly. Figure 2.14 shows Graphics Builder after it is started.

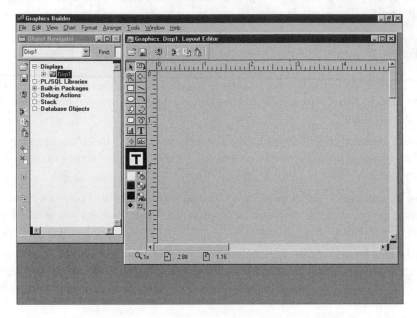

FIGURE 2.14
Graphics Builder is used to help create charts and graphs for your forms and reports.

The first thing you notice is that Graphics does not ask you to run a wizard to help create your graph. However, there is a Chart Genie that can be used to facilitate the process. Chart Genie is started using the Create Chart menu option found in the Chart menu. The Chart Genie appears and should look similar to the one in Figure 2.15.

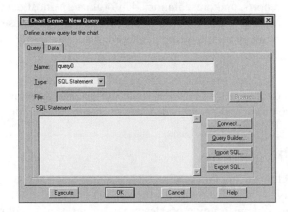

FIGURE 2.15
The Chart Genie allows you to enter the query information to be used by your chart or graph.

This is where you enter the query to display the information used by the chart or graph. In this example, you display all employees with a bar graph of their salaries. This is done by entering the following query:

```
SELECT ename, sal FROM emp
```

When you click OK, you are asked to log in to the database. Again, you use the scott/tiger account and enter scott as the username and tiger as the password. When you have logged on, you are asked to specify the chart properties using the screen in Figure 2.16.

For the name, enter Chart Demo; for the title, enter Employee Salaries. Click on OK. Next, you can preview the graph in the Layout Editor. If you want to see what the graph looks like when it is run, click on the green stoplight button on the toolbar. You are asked to save the file first; do so using the filename of your choice. Figure 2.17 shows the graph running on Windows, and Figure 2.18 shows it running under Unix.

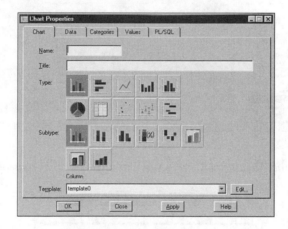

FIGURE 2.16
The Chart Genie allows you to specify properties and layout styles for your chart or graph.

Complex Charts and Graphs

When you specified the name and title for the graph, you probably noticed the large number of choices for different styles of charts and graphs. Oracle Graphics has support for the following types of charts:

- Bar charts (both horizontal and vertical)
- Line charts
- Combination line charts and bar charts
- Pie charts

- Table charts

- Scatter charts

- High-low charts

- Double-Y charts

- Gantt charts

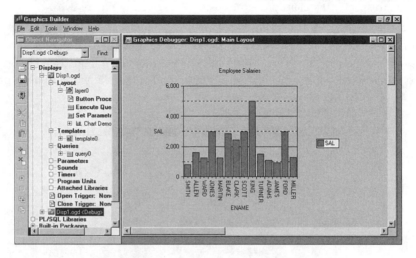

FIGURE 2.17
The chart running on the Windows platform is very similar to the chart running on Unix.

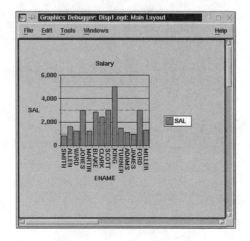

FIGURE 2.18
You can develop charts on Windows and then deploy them on Unix.

With all these supported charts and graphs, you have many options when creating your applications. Remember that a picture can be worth a thousand words: Graphs can be very useful in forms, reports, and presentations.

Summary

In this chapter, you were introduced to the major components of Oracle Developer 6i and created simple applications using the tools. This included Oracle Forms Designer, Oracle Reports Designer, and Oracle Graphics.

Oracle Forms Developer is used to create windows and forms into the database. These forms can be used to query, add, update, and delete rows from the database. Forms Developer includes several wizards to make form creation simple, but also allows for complex customizations.

Oracle Reports Developer is very similar to Oracle Forms Developer, except that it is used to create reports from information found in the database. It has wizards to help with the creation of reports. Reports Developer also includes several features that make running reports easier for end users.

Oracle Graphics is an underused product that can help add graphs and charts to your forms, reports, and presentations. The Chart Genie is used to help create graphs and reports that can then be used to help convey information about your data.

The information in this chapter is meant to give you only an idea of the capabilities found in Oracle Developer 6i. The rest of the book provides a deeper understanding of each product, and will help you to create feature-rich applications.

ORACLE FORMS DEVELOPER

ESSENTIALS

- Master-detail relationships are used to group the rows in one table with categories described in another table.

- Forms Builder makes use of an Object Navigator and Property Palette in building your application.

- The Data Block Wizard will automatically ask you to define a master-detail relationship when you add a second block to the form.

- Forms Builder provides alignment tools to ensure that objects on your form line up correctly. Simply Shift-click to select the multiple objects you want to align and click the proper tool on the toolbar.

- Your form can include many different visual objects provided by the tool palette. The objects include such items as check boxes, radio buttons, and pop-up lists, as well as drawing primitives such as rectangles, ovals, and lines.

This chapter concentrates on Oracle Forms Developer and how you can use it to create master-detail forms. You learn about the Object Navigator, the Property palette, and the Layout Editor. A good understanding of Chapter 2, "Developer Basics," is important because this chapter builds on Chapter 2's forms example. Don't hesitate to refer back if you run into trouble.

Creating a Master-Detail Form Using the Forms Builder

A review of master-detail relationships is important before creating a form that uses one. This review covers a few basic definitions and provides a quick example. This information is probably understood by most, but included nonetheless.

Master-Detail Relationships

One of the powers of a relational database, like Oracle, is the capability to create relationships between tables. A common example of this type of relationship is master-detail. In the sample tables included with the Oracle database, there is an example master-detail relationship between the DEPT and EMP tables. Table 3.1 shows the DEPT table and Table 3.2 shows an abbreviated version of the EMP table.

Table 3.1   The DEPT (or Department) Table

DEPTNO	DNAME	LOC
10	Accounting	New York
20	Research	Dallas
30	Sales	Chicago
40	Operations	Boston

Table 3.2   An Abbreviated EMP (or Employee) Table

EMPNO	ENAME	DEPTNO
7782	Clark	10
7839	King	10
7369	Smith	20
7499	Allen	30

As you can see, each row in the master department table contains a department number (DEPTNO). This corresponds to the DEPTNO column in the detail employee table. If you used these tables to create a list of all employees in the Accounting department, the list would contain Clark and King. If you used them to create a list of all the employees in the Operations department, nobody would be listed.

Note that both tables contain primary keys (or columns) uniquely identifying the rows. In the case of the DEPT table, the primary key is DEPTNO, whereas in the EMP table, it is EMPNO. DEPTNO in the EMP table is a foreign key (or column) that relates back to the primary key of the DEPT table.

Working with forms using master-detail relationships requires some programming to ensure data integrity. For instance, what happens if the Research department is deleted? Do all the corresponding rows in the EMP table also get deleted, or do they reference a department that no longer exists? One advantage of using Forms Builder, is that it automatically deals with this type of situation after the relationship has been defined. Using a general-purpose programming tool (such as Visual Basic or C/C++) requires that the application programmer write code to handle such a case.

Starting a Master-Detail Form

Armed with a basic idea of master-detail relationships, you are ready to create a form that uses one. To give you an example of how it looks, the completed form is shown running in Figure 3.1.

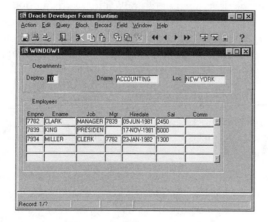

FIGURE 3.1
A completed master-detail form is the goal of your next example.

The first step is to create a form with Form Builder using the DEPT table. You can follow the same steps as in Chapter 2, substituting the DEPT table for the EMP table. When you are done it should look like Figure 3.2.

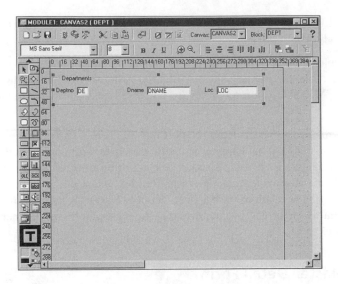

FIGURE 3.2
The Layout Editor showing the completed first step of our form.

As you complete steps in the development of applications, it is a good idea to save the form, and then run it to make sure that it behaves the way you intend. Save the form using the name ch3form. Execute a query and scroll through the department names in the DEPT table. When you are sure that the form behaves to your liking, move to the next step.

The Object Navigator and Property Palette

Understanding the role of the Object Navigator is important before moving onto the next step of our master-detail form. If you look at your Object Navigator, it should look similar to Figure 3.3.

The Object Navigator is generally used to help create forms. However, it also has the capability to show what you are currently working on. After creating the form with the DEPT table, you see that FRAME3 is highlighted. (A frame is a graphical element used to box in the elements of a block, and FRAME3 is the default name assigned to it.) It's highlighted because FRAME3 was the last thing the Layout wizard created or modified.

Both the Data Block and Layout wizard are re-entrant. Meaning that, if you go into the Data Block wizard while FRAME3 is still the active object, you will modify the current DEPT block instead of creating a new one. This can cause confusion if you are not careful.

Because you are creating a new block, not modifying the existing one, you want to select Data Blocks (or some other object not associated with the DEPT block) in the Object Navigator before continuing to the next step in our example.

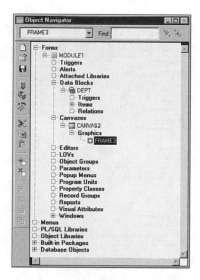

FIGURE 3.3
The Object Navigator after creating the DEPT block.

While you are looking at the Object Navigator, you might want to take a look at all the work you have done so far. As with most tree structures in GUI environments, you can expand branches by clicking the "+" and collapse them with the "–". So far, you have created the DEPT block and the CANVAS2 canvas. CANVAS2 is not a very descriptive name and should be changed. To do so involves using the Property palette.

Microsoft's Visual Basic was one of the first tools to leverage the concept of a Property palette in development environments. Since then, many development tools have adopted it in their environments, including Oracle Developer. To open the Property palette, right-click CANVAS2 and select Property palette from the pop-up menu. The Property palette appears and should look similar to Figure 3.4.

A more appropriate name for the canvas would be something like "MAINCANVAS". For now, the form is only using one canvas. Should there be a need to add more than one, "MAIN" serves as an identifier for the main drawing area of the form. The Name property serves as an identifier and can only be one word (hence "MAINCANVAS" was used, not "MAIN CAN-VAS"). To keep case sensitivity problems to a minimum, the Property palette automatically converts the Name property to uppercase even if you enter it using lowercase or mixed-case letters.

With the Object Navigator and Property palette displayed simultaneously, click various objects in the Object Navigator and watch as the Property palette changes. Notice that various objects have similar properties, but also a lot of differences.

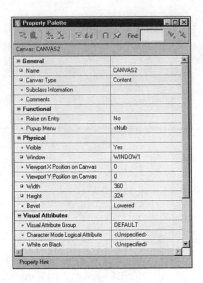

FIGURE 3.4
The Property palette showing the properties for CANVAS2.

One last change to make before continuing, is the name of FRAME3. FRAME3 is associated with the DEPT block (as shown by the Layout Data Block property), therefore, it is more descriptive to call it DEPTFRAME. Go ahead and make the change.

Remember that if you keep DEPTFRAME highlighted and try to start the Data Block Wizard, the Data Block Wizard tries to make changes to the DEPT block. Before continuing, click Data Blocks or some other object not associated with the DEPT block.

Adding the Detail Block

With the DEPTFRAME and MAINCANVAS renamed, you are ready to add the EMP table information to your form. To make things easy, you will again use the Data Block Wizard for this. Invoke the Data Block Wizard by selecting the Tools, Data Block Wizard menu option.

DATA BLOCK WARNING

If the Data Block Wizard seems to be filled out with column and table names already, you are going to modify an existing data block. Cancel out of the wizard, select Data Blocks in the Object Navigator, and then restart the Data Block Wizard.

You are using the EMP table with all its columns for this block. Because this is the second data block being added to the form, you see a new screen enabling you to specify a relationship for the two blocks. This is shown in Figure 3.5.

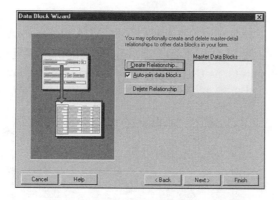

FIGURE 3.5
The Data Block Wizard asks you to specify the second block's relationship to the first block.

With a check mark in the Auto-join data blocks box, click the Create Relationship button, and then specify the relationship between the two blocks. When the EMP and DEPT tables were created, integrity constraints were included, so the Oracle database knows about the relationship between the two tables. Figure 3.6 shows the window that enables you to verify use of the existing relationship.

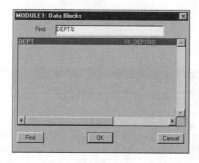

FIGURE 3.6
Forms Developer enables you to verify existing relationship definitions to be used in your form.

Click OK and the relationship values are automatically filled in. You see that the Master Data Block is DEPT with a join condition of EMP.DEPTNO = DEPT.DEPTNO. Click Next. You are done with the Data Block Wizard and ready to use the Layout Wizard.

Using the Layout Wizard to add the second block to the form is somewhat different from using the DEPT block. Because the master block (DEPT) shows the department number, there is no need to display it again. Another difference is using the Tabular layout instead of the Form layout. This enables you to see multiple rows displayed one record per row.

As you go through the Layout Wizard, pay close attention to the default values. For instance, you see that the canvas used for the new block is MAINCANVAS, as expected.

You want to display all the columns in the EMP table except the DEPTNO column. This is done adding all the columns to the Displayed Items list, and then removing DEPTNO as shown in Figure 3.7. You also have the option of selecting the columns one by one.

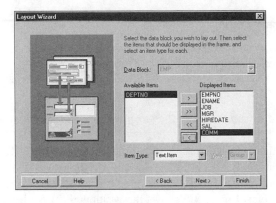

FIGURE 3.7
Display all the columns from EMP except for DEPTNO.

When you are asked to choose the layout style, be sure to choose tabular, as shown in Figure 3.8.

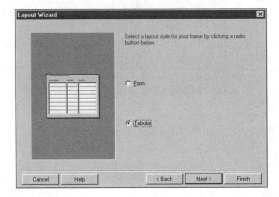

FIGURE 3.8
Choosing a tabular layout for the detail block enables you to see more rows.

The title for the frame of the detail block should be Employees. You want to specify five rows displayed and be sure to check the Display Scrollbar box, as shown in Figure 3.9. The scrollbar enables you to scroll through the records in the detail block if more than five employees are assigned to a particular department.

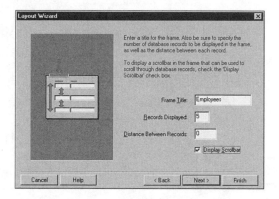

FIGURE 3.9
Specifying title, number of rows displayed, and a scrollbar for the detail block.

You are now finished and ready to run the form as it was shown in Figure 3.1. Notice that if you look at the employees in the Sales department, you can use the scrollbar in the EMP block to scroll through additional employees.

Using the Re-Entrant Layout Wizard

In the previous section you were told to select an object in the Object Navigator, not associated with the DEPT block, before trying to run the Data Block Wizard. This is because the Data Block Wizard is re-entrant, and can be used to modify the DEPT block even after the wizard is finished. This is true for the Layout Wizard as well and can be used to your advantage. If you need to, you can go back into the Layout Wizard and modify values previously entered. This eliminates the need to make the changes by hand.

Now that your master-detail form is running, you probably notice a few things you can clean up. For example, the column names in the DEPT block are not as descriptive as they could be. To fix this, select DEPTFRAME from the Object Navigator and run the Layout Wizard from the Tools menu. At the top of the wizard are some tabs; click the Items tab to display the screen shown in Figure 3.10.

FORMS BUILDER WARNING ───

Although Oracle does a good job of making their products look the same across all platforms, this is one area it missed. The Unix version of Forms Builder does not use tabs in the Layout Wizard, and you are forced to go through all the screens using the Next button.
──

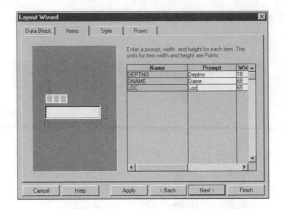

FIGURE 3.10
Using the Layout Wizard to help modify an existing block.

Make the following changes:

- Deptno to Dept #
- Dname to Name
- Loc to Location

While you are using the Layout Wizard, it's nice to add a scrollbar for the DEPT block (like the one on the EMP block). To do this, select the Rows tab and check the Display Scrollbar box.

After the changes are made, click the Finish button and the field descriptions change accordingly. Unfortunately, it has broken the information into two lines. You need to arrange the fields using the Layout Editor to get everything back on one line. Go ahead and correct the layout by selecting the fields and moving them to the desired position.

WAR STORY

While I was a project manager at Oracle Corporation, one of my major duties was to go out and train both Oracle customers as well as the Oracle sales force about the many different features of Oracle's development products. The first demo always included showing the users about how to create a form based on a single table. That generally took about five minutes. The next demo always was to show how to create a master-detail form.

Those users who were familiar with Oracle databases and development products enjoyed the demos but didn't really appreciate the significance of what was being shown. The developers who were new to Oracle or at least Oracle's development tools were amazed with the ease at which master-detail forms could be created. It was these developers that I enjoyed talking with after my presentations.

It was not uncommon to find developers who were great at writing elegant and sophisticated code, but lacked some good old fashion database theory. I remember talking with one developer who saw the department/employee master-detail relationship as a serious revelation. He had been creating tables for each department. The SALES_DEPARTMENT table contained all of the salespeople employees while the EXEC_DEPARTMENT table contained all of the company's executives. Once he saw the quick demo, he took a look at his database objects and changed them to more appropriate structures. Consequently, this had the effect of greatly simplifying application development.

I also remember a developer coming to me and showing me a layout where the DEPARTMENT table had a series of columns for each employee. The developer assumed that there would never be more than ten employees for each department and so the columns were labeled EMP1, EMP2, and so on to EMP10. This greatly complicated the application. Not only were columns being left blank, but eventually there was a department with more than ten employees and the database design had to be reworked.

Looking back on these two examples invokes a quick chuckle from myself and experienced database developers. However, the stories are true. If you are new to database applications, be sure to run your database table design by a seasoned or experienced developer. This will help ensure proper database object creation and could have the effect of helping make your application development easier.

Master-Detail Forms in the Runtime Environment

This is a good place to stop and test the form you have created so far. It gives you the chance to see how the form behaves in the runtime environment with multiple tables. Run the form and watch as the compilation process takes place. You should see a status bar, even if only for a moment.

Running a form causes it to be compiled and checked for errors. With a single table on a form there is not much complexity, so the compilation process is almost instantaneous. With multiple tables, there is a lot more checking that needs to be done. The Forms Builder automatically includes specific code for referential integrity. Chapter 8, "Forms Development," takes a look at this PL/SQL code and how you can modify it.

With the form running, execute a query. The first department should appear with the employees. Try deleting the Accounting department by using the Record, Remove menu option. You get an error saying:

```
Cannot delete master record when matching detail records exist.
```

The default behavior for master-detail relationships is to not permit deletion of a master record, until all the detail rows are deleted or are assigned to another master record. Because no employee records are associated with the Operations department, it can be deleted without a problem.

You have the ability to override this default behavior if you want. The options you have are

- Cascading Delete
- Isolated Delete
- Non Isolated Delete (Default)

Non Isolated Delete is the default. Cascading Delete causes the database to delete all employees in the Accounting department simply by deleting the department. Most of the time, this is too drastic and should only be used with caution. That is, of course, unless you are building an application for a dot-com.

Isolated Delete allows the department to be deleted and orphans the employee records. This reeks havoc with applications. If you have not provided for non-existent departments in your application code, the form becomes confused—and potentially, the user as well. Therefore, this option should also be used with caution.

Forms Developer does a good job of guessing which actions your users want. It provides some fairly sophisticated capabilities and keeps you out of trouble most of the time. Of course there are exceptions; Chapter 8 covers some of them in detail.

Using the Layout Editor

Certain things are made easier by the various wizards in Forms Builder. However, sometimes it is easier to use the Layout Editor. Most of the fine-tuning done to the user interface is done using the Layout Editor.

Moving Objects

The Layout Wizard left the example looking a little funny. You can use the Layout Editor to move things around a bit and give the application a more consistent look.

Click the field areas in the Layout Editor and handles appear. If you move the field, the description and Prompt text for the field move with it. Using the following steps, you are able to get your layout to look like Figure 3.11.

1. Drag the right frame handle so that the Departments frame is as wide as the Employees frame.

2. Click the DEPTNO field and move it slightly to the right. This enables you to enlarge the field description.

3. Right click the Dept # field description and select the Property palette.

4. Scroll down the Property list to the Prompt attribute (toward the bottom). Change "Dept|#" to "Dept #". The | character is used to signify a line break.

5. Click the DNAME field and move it to the left so that it is closer to DEPTNO.

6. Click the LOC field and move it to the same line as the other two fields.

7. Make any micro adjustments to the various fields by selecting the field and using the arrow keys. The arrow keys should move the fields one pixel at a time. There are alignment tools, which are discussed later in the chapter, to make the job easier. For now, try doing it the hard way.

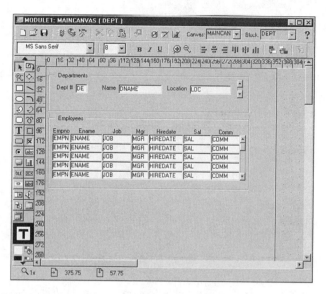

FIGURE 3.11
Modifying the form to have a more consistent look.

The Layout Editor Toolbars

The sample form is becoming quite powerful and useful. More importantly, it is becoming increasingly difficult to re-create should the power fail or the computer crash. Now would be a good time to save it. This is done by using the Save option from the File menu. For this example, feel free to use any filename that you can remember. As this is Chapter 3, a name like "ch3.fmb" can be used to cross-reference the example with the chapter in the book.

CREATE A DIRECTORY ————————————————————————

Creating a directory for all the example files in this book is strongly recommended. By doing so, you are able to retrieve them later if you have any questions about how to do something.

You can also use the Save icon, found on the toolbar, to save files. Figure 3.12 shows the top toolbar with descriptions of each button's use.

FIGURE 3.12
The top-level toolbar in the Layout Editor is used for the Layout Editor's most common functions.

New   Creates a new form.

Open   Opens an existing form.

Save   Saves the current form.

Run Form Client/Server   Runs the form using the client/server deployment method.

Run Form Web   Runs the form using the Web deployment method.

Run Form Debug   Runs the form in the debugger. The debugger is discussed in Chapter 8.

Cut   Cuts the currently selected object, or objects, and stores them on the clipboard.

Copy   Copies the currently selected object, or objects, onto the clipboard.

Paste   Pastes items from the clipboard onto the current form.

Updated Layout   Updates the layout display. As you make changes to fields on the form, Layout Editor performs some automatic updates. This can be annoying, so before you get surprised, it's important to see how the layout changes.

Data Block Wizard   Invokes the Data Block Wizard.

Layout Wizard   Invokes the Layout Wizard.

Chart Wizard   Invokes the Chart Wizard. It is discussed in Chapter 5, "Other Developer Components."

Canvas   Shows the current working canvas. If you want to change the canvas, you can do so by selecting a new one from the pop-up list.

Block   Shows the current working block. If you want to change the block, you can do so by selecting a new one from the pop-up list.

Help   Invokes the Oracle Developer help system. On Windows, the standard Help system is used. On Unix, it is HTML based.

The Layout Editor has a second-row toolbar with associated descriptions, as shown in Figure 3.13.

FIGURE 3.13
The second-row toolbar in the Layout Editor with short descriptions.

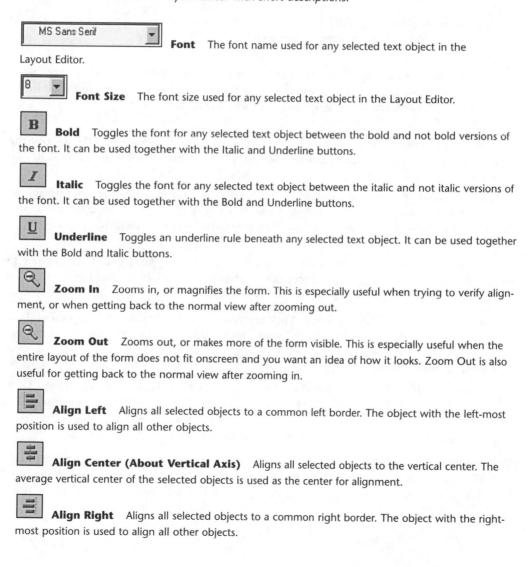

Font   The font name used for any selected text object in the Layout Editor.

Font Size   The font size used for any selected text object in the Layout Editor.

Bold   Toggles the font for any selected text object between the bold and not bold versions of the font. It can be used together with the Italic and Underline buttons.

Italic   Toggles the font for any selected text object between the italic and not italic versions of the font. It can be used together with the Bold and Underline buttons.

Underline   Toggles an underline rule beneath any selected text object. It can be used together with the Bold and Italic buttons.

Zoom In   Zooms in, or magnifies the form. This is especially useful when trying to verify alignment, or when getting back to the normal view after zooming out.

Zoom Out   Zooms out, or makes more of the form visible. This is especially useful when the entire layout of the form does not fit onscreen and you want an idea of how it looks. Zoom Out is also useful for getting back to the normal view after zooming in.

Align Left   Aligns all selected objects to a common left border. The object with the left-most position is used to align all other objects.

Align Center (About Vertical Axis)   Aligns all selected objects to the vertical center. The average vertical center of the selected objects is used as the center for alignment.

Align Right   Aligns all selected objects to a common right border. The object with the right-most position is used to align all other objects.

Align Top   Aligns all selected objects along a common upper border. The object with the top-most position is used to align all other objects.

Align Center (About Horizontal Axis)   Aligns all selected objects to the horizontal center. The average horizontal center of the selected objects is used as the center for alignment.

Align Bottom   Aligns all selected objects along a common lower border. The object with the bottom-most position is used to align all other objects.

Bring to Front   Brings objects placed behind other objects to the front. As you place objects on the canvas in the Layout Editor, they stack in the order they are placed. Use Bring to Front if you want earlier-placed objects in front and later-placed objects obscured.

Send to Back   Sends objects placed in front of other objects behind them. This is very useful if you have a large object obscuring a smaller one that you would like in front or moved out of the way.

Associate Prompt   Associates Text objects on the canvas with other objects (for example, Text Entry field) that have empty Prompt attributes. To use this button, select a text object and an object with an empty Prompt attribute (such as a newly created text entry field) and click Associate Prompt.

You can see that these toolbar items are very useful in laying out your form. When aligning the three fields in the DEPT block on the previous master-detail example, it would have been a lot easier to use the Align Top on the toolbar than to eyeball it.

The next couple of activities are aimed at helping you try out the toolbar and see its usefulness. These exercises should be done in front of your computer, so you can see what is happening.

Creating a New Form

If you have not already done so, save the sample application you have been working on. Then create a new form by clicking the New button on the toolbar. You should notice that the previous sample application you were working on is still in the Object Navigator. This is fine. To help you keep things straight, you might want to close the module name in the branch.

With the new form open, click the Data Block Wizard tool icon and create a single block table with all the items from the BONUS table. Use the Layout wizard to place all the columns on the form. When you are done with the wizards, your form should look similar to Figure 3.14.

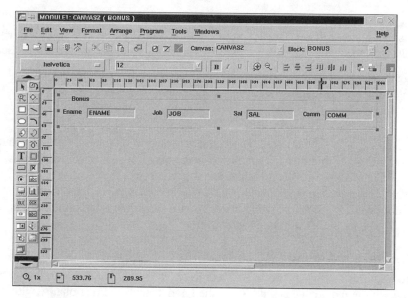

FIGURE 3.14
A new form created and ready to play with.

Aligning Objects

The goal of this exercise is to become familiar with using the alignment tools from the lower toolbar. First, you want to grab the lower handle of the block frame and drag it down, taking up as much of your screen as possible. When this is done, try the following activities:

1. Drag the JOB, SAL, and COMM fields so that they are on different horizontal lines from one another. Select all the fields by holding down the Shift key and clicking the Text-Field Entry section. Do this for all four fields, but be sure not to click the Prompt text. Now click Align Left. They should all line up under the ENAME field.

2. Drag the JOB, SAL, and COMM fields so that they are staggered progressively further away from the ENAME field on separate lines. Select all four fields using the Shift key as before. Click Align Center (About Vertical Axis). They should all line up under the ENAME field with the average of their vertical centers as the focal point.

3. Drag the JOB, SAL, and COMM fields so that they are all on separate lines but not aligned vertically in any way. Select all four fields again using the Shift key. Click Align Right, and they should all align with the right-most field.

4. Stagger each field so that no other field is directly above or below it (including prompt text). Select all four fields using the Shift key. Click Align Top, and they should all align with the top-most field. This should look the way it did when you started these exercises.

5. Stagger each field so that no other field is directly above or below it. Select all four fields using the Shift key. Click Align Center (About Horizontal Axis), and they should all align on the same line with the average of their horizontal centers as the focal point.

6. Stagger each field so that no other field is directly above or below it. Select all four fields using the Shift key. Click Align Bottom, and they should all align with the bottom-most field.

After this exercise, you should have a good understanding of alignment in the Layout Editor. Some important things to remember are not to select the Prompt text with the fields, and not to have any overlap of the objects you plan to align. If you select the Prompt text with form fields, the alignment tool tries to place the field over the Prompt text and causes an error. If you try to do a vertical alignment while there is some vertical overlap, fields end up on top of each other. The same is true with horizontal overlap.

Generally Playing Around

You are not required to save this form for future use. Knowing that, you should not hesitate to play around with it and get a general idea of the Layout Editor's functionality with respect to the toolbars. Here are some suggested activities:

1. Practice zooming in and zooming out. Try using the arrow keys to align the fields and see how close you can come with the help of Zoom In. Afterward, you should gain a huge appreciation for the automatic alignment tools.

2. Play around with the font styles and sizes. Select the Prompt text and change it to a different font style from the text field. Also play around with font sizes for text fields and try running the form.

3. Experiment with Bring to Front and Send to Back. They might not work the way you think they should, and now is a better time to find out than when you try putting together an application under a time crunch.

The Layout Editor Visual Tools

You have probably noticed the Tool palette on the left while working in the Layout Editor. This section describes what all the different tools are, how they are used, and how they help enhance your form. Chapter 8 will show how to implement and use these elements in your forms.

Figure 3.15 shows the Tool palette with short descriptions. The palette can be divided in two sections: Tool and Color palettes. The tools provide elements that can be added to the form. The Color palettes section is used to select colors for form objects (such as, text, lines, borders, fill, background). More complete descriptions for each of the graphics are provided below.

FIGURE 3.15
The Layout Editor Tool palette with short descriptions.

Select   This is the default tool. Use it to select the various objects on the form or canvas. You can then move, resize, and delete the object.

Rotate   Rotates selected drawing items. It cannot be used to rotate objects, such as database fields and text items. To use the tool, select the item you want to rotate, click one of the handles for the object, and drag it to the desired orientation.

Magnify   Similar to the Zoom In and Zoom Out buttons on the toolbar, except that you can specify the center of the zoom area. To zoom out, hold the Shift key and click the canvas.

Reshape   Reshapes drawn objects. The best way to see the effect of this tool is to draw some objects on your form (for example, lines, polygons, rectangles) and then attempt to reshape them.

Rectangle   Creates rectangles or squares on your form. You can use the rectangle to group database fields and provide a more aesthetically pleasing look. Holding down the Shift key creates a square.

Line   Creates lines on your form.

Ellipse   Creates ellipses and circles on your form. Holding down the Shift key creates a circle.

Arc   Creates arcs on your form.

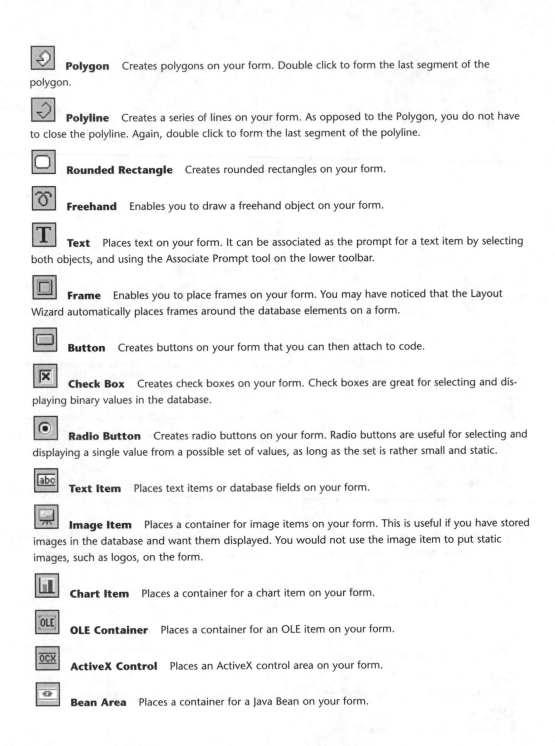

Polygon   Creates polygons on your form. Double click to form the last segment of the polygon.

Polyline   Creates a series of lines on your form. As opposed to the Polygon, you do not have to close the polyline. Again, double click to form the last segment of the polyline.

Rounded Rectangle   Creates rounded rectangles on your form.

Freehand   Enables you to draw a freehand object on your form.

Text   Places text on your form. It can be associated as the prompt for a text item by selecting both objects, and using the Associate Prompt tool on the lower toolbar.

Frame   Enables you to place frames on your form. You may have noticed that the Layout Wizard automatically places frames around the database elements on a form.

Button   Creates buttons on your form that you can then attach to code.

Check Box   Creates check boxes on your form. Check boxes are great for selecting and displaying binary values in the database.

Radio Button   Creates radio buttons on your form. Radio buttons are useful for selecting and displaying a single value from a possible set of values, as long as the set is rather small and static.

Text Item   Places text items or database fields on your form.

Image Item   Places a container for image items on your form. This is useful if you have stored images in the database and want them displayed. You would not use the image item to put static images, such as logos, on the form.

Chart Item   Places a container for a chart item on your form.

OLE Container   Places a container for an OLE item on your form.

ActiveX Control   Places an ActiveX control area on your form.

Bean Area   Places a container for a Java Bean on your form.

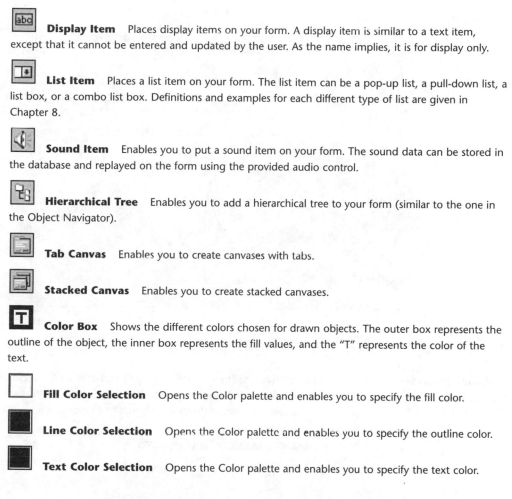

Display Item   Places display items on your form. A display item is similar to a text item, except that it cannot be entered and updated by the user. As the name implies, it is for display only.

List Item   Places a list item on your form. The list item can be a pop-up list, a pull-down list, a list box, or a combo list box. Definitions and examples for each different type of list are given in Chapter 8.

Sound Item   Enables you to put a sound item on your form. The sound data can be stored in the database and replayed on the form using the provided audio control.

Hierarchical Tree   Enables you to add a hierarchical tree to your form (similar to the one in the Object Navigator).

Tab Canvas   Enables you to create canvases with tabs.

Stacked Canvas   Enables you to create stacked canvases.

Color Box   Shows the different colors chosen for drawn objects. The outer box represents the outline of the object, the inner box represents the fill values, and the "T" represents the color of the text.

Fill Color Selection   Opens the Color palette and enables you to specify the fill color.

Line Color Selection   Opens the Color palette and enables you to specify the outline color.

Text Color Selection   Opens the Color palette and enables you to specify the text color.

As with the Layout Editor, it is best to learn about this tool by playing with it. Open a new form and experiment with placing the various objects on a canvas. Explanations for how to use database columns with the various display elements (for example, Check box, Radio button, List item) are given in Chapter 8.

The Layout Editor Ruler and Grid

The last items to cover in the Layout Editor are the Layout ruler and grid. The default unit of measure for the ruler and grid is pixels. Figure 3.16 shows the form you have been working on in the Layout Editor with the Layout ruler highlighted.

Horizontal ruler

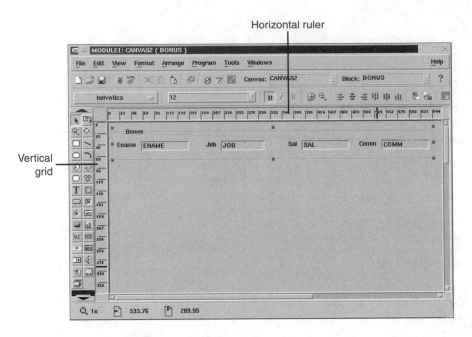

Vertical grid

FIGURE 3.16
The BONUS form has the rulers, using pixels as the default unit of measure.

Although pixels are the universal display element for screens, it is very difficult to differentiate a pixel found at 38, 123 and one found at 39, 124. If you go to the Format, Layout Options, Ruler menu, you find the options to change the ruler settings (as shown in Figure 3.17).

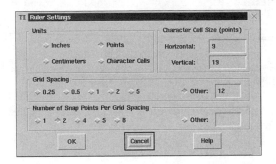

FIGURE 3.17
Options for the rulers in the Layout Editor.

You can change the unit of measure for the grid to something less tight, such as inches or centimeters. Developers who are used to working with units of length other than pixels might prefer this.

The ruler settings show the default character size in points. Use these settings when the Units option is set to character cell, and you want to change it. You also have the ability to view the grid settings and change them. Although the defaults work for most users, some developers have found a different grid system that works for them.

A More Detailed Look at the Object Navigator

You have used the Object Navigator for the examples throughout this book, but it has not been discussed in much detail. This section provides a brief overview, and hopefully answers any questions you have up to this point.

The Object Navigator is used as a road map to tell you about your application. When you have the Property palette open, you can find out what object you are working on by looking in the Object Navigator. If you want to change the object currently displayed in the Property palette, you would click it in the Object Navigator. The correct properties are then displayed.

In addition to being a road map, the Object Navigator provides some important functionality when creating applications. Figure 3.18 shows the Object Navigator after creating the Master-Detail form from earlier in the chapter.

The first nine items on the vertical toolbar correspond to items found on the Layout Editor toolbar. They are repeated in the Object Navigator because you do not always have the Layout Editor running, but might still want to perform similar functions. The repeated items are

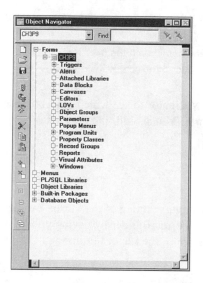

FIGURE 3.18
The Object Navigator after creating the master-detail form.

New   Creates a new form.

Open   Opens an existing form.

Save   Saves the current form.

Run Form Client/Server   Runs the form using the client/server deployment method.

Run Form Web   Runs the form using the Web deployment method.

Run Form Debug   Runs the form in the debugger. The debugger is discussed in Chapter 8.

Cut   Cuts the currently selected object, or objects, and stores them on the clipboard.

Copy   Copies the currently selected object, or objects, onto the clipboard.

Paste   Pastes items from the clipboard onto the current form.

The new toolbar items, which apply specifically to the Object Navigator, are

Create   Enables you to create new objects in the Object Navigator. The new object appears at the same level as the currently selected object. Therefore, if you want to add another field to the form, select one of the current fields and click Create. The new item is then added.

Delete   Enables you to delete existing objects in the Object Navigator. After creating a bunch of items, you can use this button to eliminate any that are unwanted. Delete is especially useful for eliminating all those unwanted modules from earlier in this chapter.

Expand   Expands the current item's branches.

Collapse   Collapses the current item's branches.

Expand All   Expands all the branches in the tree. Prepare to do a lot of scrolling on larger applications.

Collapse All   Collapses all the branches in the tree. This is especially useful after doing an Expand All and discovering that you have a lot of objects.

Play around with the Object Navigator to see which objects are automatically created by the Data Block and Layout Wizards. You should find all sorts of icons that help to describe the various objects.

Summary

You should now have a good understanding of the Forms Builder environment. This chapter covered the various aspects of Forms Builder by having you build a Master-Detail form. In doing so, you were able to use both the Layout Editor and Object Navigator much more extensively.

You were given an in-depth look at the Layout Editor, and shown how to use the various components to make application development easier. The toolbars and Tool palettes were summarized.

Finally, you were given an overview of the Object Navigator. The vertical toolbar and its necessity were explained. You had already been using the Object Navigator, so most of the explanation was simply to fill in the gaps of your knowledge.

All the skills and knowledge presented so far are built upon in following chapters. If you don't understand something, be sure to go over it again, or refer to this chapter as the need arises.

ORACLE REPORTS DEVELOPER AND GRAPHICS

ESSENTIALS ——————————

- Reports Builder leverages the Query Builder tool to create the queries used for the report.

- The Layout Wizard is re-entrant and allows you to see the results of your report. If you don't like it, you can reuse the Layout Wizard and change the appropriate values without responding to all the Layout Wizard's questions again.

- Reports Builder has three modes of operation: Live Previewer, Data Model, and Layout Model. Most of your work will be done using the Live Previewer. However, if you need to modify the report layout, use the Layout Model. Data Model view is used to look at the various tables and columns included in the report.

- To view the report as it will appear using the Web deployment model, toggle on the Web Preview button found on the toolbar. As changes are made to the report, they will be displayed in the Web preview window.

- Graphs can be added to reports by using the Chart Wizard.

This chapter focuses on building reports using Report Builder, a component of Oracle Reports Developer. In Chapter 3, "Oracle Forms Developer," you developed a master-detail form. In this chapter, you learn how to do the same thing for a report. You also learn how to use the Query Builder to create complex queries. Other products in the Oracle Developer suite can then use those complex queries. Finally, you learn how to add graphics to your reports.

Creating a Master-Detail Report Using Report Builder

Chapter 3 gave a brief, but useful, overview of master-detail relationships and described primary and foreign keys. The remaining majority of the chapter was spent helping you create a master-detail form. The report you create in this chapter looks very similar to that master-detail form.

Go ahead and start the Report Builder. Use the Report Wizard to help you create this report. The title for this report is Employees by Department. Chapter 2, "Developer Basics," gave a brief description of the different types of reports. For this report, use Group Left layout. You are now ready to specify the SQL query statement.

Using Query Builder to Create Database Queries

Most application developers who have spent much time writing SQL statements will feel comfortable entering the SQL query by hand. However, using the Query Builder reduces the possibility for mistakes. After the SQL statement has been created, you have the ability to fine-tune it.

When the Report Wizard dialog asks you to specify a query statement, click on Query Builder. Log in to the database. Again, use the scott/tiger account. After you log in, you will see the dialog asking to specify the tables for the query as shown in Figure 4.1.

FIGURE 4.1
The dialog to specify tables used in the query for the report.

You will be using the EMP and DEPT tables for this report. Select the DEPT table in the dialog and click the Include button. Do the same for the EMP table, and then click the Close button.

This should add the table definitions to the Query Builder tool as shown in Figure 4.2. You can see that the relationship between the DEPT and EMP tables is shown with a line from the DEPTNO column in the EMP table pointing back to the DEPTNO column in the DEPT table.

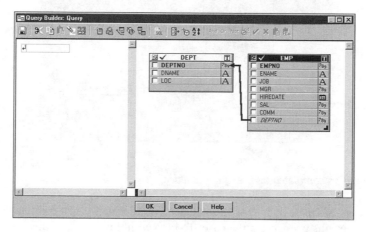

FIGURE 4.2
The DEPT and EMP table definitions in the Query Builder tool.

The Query Builder tool provides you some important visual information about the columns in the tables that you use for the report. Notice the primary keys DEPTNO and EMPNO are both highlighted with the bold font. Notice also that there is a data type symbol to the right of each of the column names. EMPNO is a number, as indicated by the ⬛ icon. ENAME is a character column, as represented by the Ⓐ icon; and HIREDATE is a date as shown by the ⬛ icon.

Now you have the ability to specify the columns that will appear in the report. Click the check box to the left of each of the column names to have the column appear on the report. The only column from the DEPT table to display is DNAME. All the columns except DEPTNO should be displayed from the EMP table. When you are done, click OK.

ORDER OF COLUMNS

The order in which you check the columns is the order in which they will be displayed on your report. So, if you want the ENAME column to appear before EMPNO, click ENAME first.

Don't worry if you don't get the order correct. The Report Wizard allows you to reorder them at a later time.

The Query Builder tool is complete and has filled in the SQL statement that will be used for the report. The SQL query in the Layout Wizard is shown in Figure 4.3.

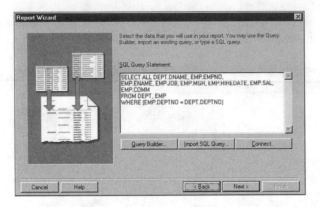

FIGURE 4.3
The SQL statement as completed by the Query Builder.

It is relatively easy to create queries with the Query Builder tool when the database is set up correctly. However, this is not often the case. To help with this problem, the next chapter goes into more detail about using the Query Builder tool.

After you read through and agree with the generated SQL statement, click Next. You now have the option to decide which column will differentiate the groups of employees. This report uses the Department name or the DNAME column. Select it and move it to the Group Fields list by using the > button. Now click Next.

Now you are asked to specify the columns that will be displayed as fields on the report. The report should display all the fields, so click on the >> button followed by Next.

You are now given the chance to add a predefined formula to your list. The report specifies salary totals for each of the various departments. Select SAL from the Available Fields list and then click Sum > to create a salary total in the Totals list, as shown in Figure 4.4.

Click on Next and you can modify some of the layout characteristics such as labels, heights, and widths. At this point, accept the defaults by clicking Next. As with the report in Chapter 2, use the Corporate 2 template and click on Next. Now you are finished with the Report Wizard. Using the Live Previewer view, the Report Editor should display the finished result shown in Figure 4.5.

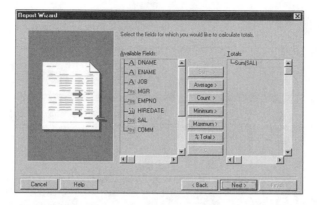

FIGURE 4.4
Adding salary totals for each of the departments for the report.

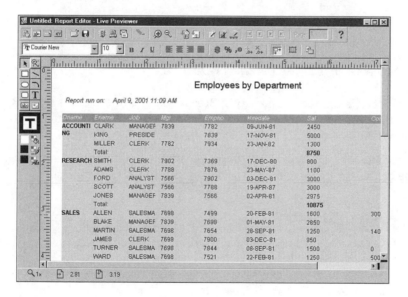

FIGURE 4.5
The Report Editor in Live Previewer view showing the completed report after running the Report Wizard.

Using the Re-entrant Layout Wizard

The report in Figure 4.5 looks a bit wide. There is probably a better layout format that could be used instead. Rather than trying to re-create everything, simply rerun the Report Wizard and choose a different layout. This can be done by selecting Tools, Report Wizard from the menu.

When you rerun the Report Wizard, you will notice a tab bar appears at the top of the wizard dialog. The different tabs give you access to the various screens you filled out when first running the wizard. Because all that needs to be changed is the layout, make sure that the Style tab is selected as shown in Figure 4.6.

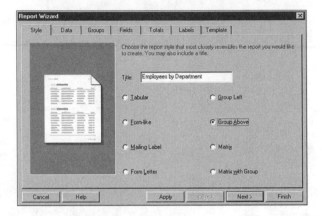

FIGURE 4.6
The Style attributes when rerunning the Report Wizard.

Now try using the Group Above report style. Because the rest of the values in the Report Wizard are already filled out, click on Finish and the new layout style is shown in the Report Editor as shown in Figure 4.7.

The report layout looks a bit less cluttered and more like the form created in Chapter 3. Now you can use the Report Editor to modify the report so that it is easier to read.

Using the Report Editor

The Report Editor can be used to clean up reports. In the current report, headings need to be more readable and the spacing between columns could be optimized. Although these functions can be taken care of with the Report Wizard, it is generally easier to use the Report Editor because you can see all of the changes interactively.

Changing Column Headings

The first change is to alter the column headings to be more descriptive. Although you know that Dname refers to the different department names, the manager reading the report might not know that. Therefore, you should change the column heading to Departments.

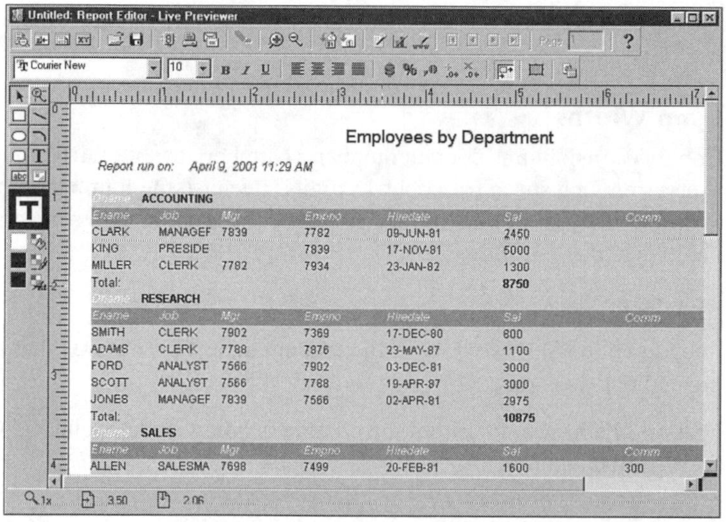

FIGURE 4.7
The report using the Group Above layout.

First, select Dname next to the Accounting department name. All three instances of Dname should be selected, as indicated by the outline handles. If you click on Dname again, you can change the heading to Departments. When you do so, the word *Departments* is wrapped because there is not enough space before the actual department names. Enlarging the viewing area for department names solves this problem.

To move the department names, click on Accounting and drag it to the right until there is enough room for the Departments heading. The three department headings should also appear farther to the right.

Next, you need to change the amount of viewable area that the Departments heading can use. Click on the viewable portion of Departments and then select the right-middle handle. Expand the area reserved for the heading. With the Departments heading appropriately sized, you can modify all the headings to be more descriptive.

Please make the following changes:

- Ename to Name
- Empno to Emp #
- Mgr to Manager
- Hiredate to Hire Date
- Sal to Salary
- Comm to Commission

With the column headings changed, you are now ready to adjust the widths of the columns to more appropriate widths.

Adjusting Column Widths

The Salary and Commission columns contain numbers. Numbers can be fairly wide, so the Report Wizard reserves enough space for about 15 digits. Because the numbers in this report are fairly narrow (only four or five digits), you can reduce the amount of reserved space. To narrow or widen columns, do the following:

1. Select the column heading.

2. While holding down the Shift key, select the column data. This ensures that both the column heading and data are selected.

3. Grab the right-middle handle for either the column heading or data, and reduce the reserved space for the column.

With the space reserved for the Salary and Commission headings reduced, you are now ready to widen some of the text columns that are truncated. However, first you must move some of the columns to the right to make room. If you fail to make room for the wider columns, the Report Editor continues to restrict column width. Moving or expanding columns too far to the right so that they run off the page will generate a warning message. To move columns, do the following:

1. Select the column heading.

2. While holding down the Shift key, select the column data. Both the column heading and data should be selected.

3. Grab the middle of the column heading or data by clicking down and dragging the column left or right. When you are done positioning the column, release the click.

Make sure that the Commission column is as far to the right as possible. Then move the Salary column close to the left edge of Commission.

The Hire Date column is also wide and can be narrowed. The Report Wizard makes sure to include room for long date formats. Because the nine-character default is fine, you can narrow and move the Hire Date column just to the left of the Salary column.

The Emp # and Manager columns also can be narrowed and moved. With all the number and date columns narrowed, it is time to widen the text columns. The Job column does not have enough room to show the entire job description and must be expanded.

Changing Column Order

In the example for this chapter, the Emp # column should appear before the Name column. To change the column order, go into the Report Wizard and select the Fields tab. You can then reorder the columns by dragging and dropping them. Grab the EMPNO column and drop it above the ENAME column, as shown in Figure 4.8. When you are done, click on Finish.

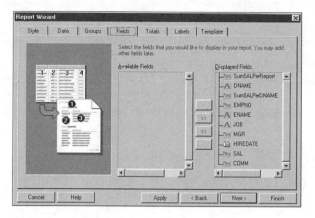

FIGURE 4.8
Reordering the columns using the Report Wizard.

The Report Editor Toolbar

Some useful tools to help you format the report are found on the toolbars. Figure 4.9 shows the upper toolbar with the name of each tool. Short descriptions of each tool follow the figure.

FIGURE 4.9
The upper toolbar.

Live Previewer The default mode for the Report Editor. It allows you to see how the report will look using live data from the tables.

Data Model Changes the mode of the Report Editor to show the data model. It is helpful to show the table relationships used in the report. This is discussed more in Chapter 9, "More About Reports."

Layout Model Changes the mode of the Report Editor to show an abbreviated model layout for your report. It can be helpful when there are different layouts for a report with lots of rows displayed. This is discussed more in Chapter 9.

Parameter Form   Brings up a parameter form editor to allow you to create a parameter form for the report.

Open   Opens an existing report.

Save   Saves the current report that you are working on.

Refresh Data   Refreshes the data in the Live Previewer.

Print   Prints the current report.

Mail   E-mails the current report.

Clear   Deletes the current selection without putting it on the clipboard.

Zoom In   Zooms in on or magnifies the report. This is especially useful when trying to verify alignment or coming back in after zooming out.

Zoom Out   Zooms out or makes more of the report visible. This is especially useful to get an idea of what the entire layout of the report looks like if it does not fit entirely on your screen. It is also helpful for getting back to the normal view after zooming in.

Insert Date and Time   Inserts a field on the report that displays the date and time the report was last run.

Insert Page Number   Inserts page numbers on the report.

Report Wizard   Invokes the Report Wizard.

Chart Wizard   Invokes the Chart Wizard.

Web Wizard   Invokes the Web Wizard.

First Page   Goes to the first page of the report.

Previous Page   Goes to the previous page of the report.

Next Page   Goes to the next page of the report.

Last Page   Goes to the last page of the report.

Page Number Description   Displays the current page in Live Previewer mode.

Help   Invokes the Oracle Developer help system. On Windows, the standard Help system is used. On Unix, the Help system is HTML based.

Figure 4.10 shows the lower toolbar with short descriptions. The descriptions are explained following the figure.

FIGURE 4.10
The lower toolbar.

Font   The font name used for any selected text object in the Report Editor.

Font Size   The font size used for any selected text object in the Report Editor.

Bold   Toggles the font for any selected text object between the bold and nonbold version of the font. It can be used together with the Italic and Underline buttons.

Italic   Toggles the font for any selected text object between the italic and nonitalic version of the font. It can be used together with the Bold and Underline buttons.

Underline   Toggles an underlining rule underneath any selected text object. It can be used together with the Bold and Italic buttons.

Start Justify   Lines up selected objects in the report to begin at the common left border.

Center Justify   Lines up selected objects in the report to the common middle.

End Justify   Lines up selected objects in the report to end at the common right border.

Flush Justify   Adds appropriate spacing so that selected objects in the report have common left and right borders.

Currency   Formats a data field to display as currency (using the currency symbol for the current local).

Percent   Formats a data field to display as a percentage including the percent symbol.

Commas   Formats a numeric data field to contain commas.

Add Decimal Places   Formats a numeric data field to display decimal places.

Remove Decimal Places   Removes decimal places from a numeric data fields.

Flex Mode   Toggles flex mode, in which the layout is resized to maintain existing relationships.

Select Parent Frame   Selects the parent frame of the currently selected object.

Web Preview   Toggles the Web preview mode, in which every change to the report is shown in your browser. This allows you to see how your report will be viewed using the Web deployment method.

Now that you have an idea of what each of the tools on the toolbar can do, you can finish formatting the report. Complete the following tasks:

- Add the currency symbol and commas to the department Salary totals

- Add commas to the Salary column

- Add commas to the Commission column

- End justify the Salary and Commission columns and headings

- Add commas and the currency symbol, and end justify the report salary total at the bottom

After completing these tasks, your finished report should be similar to Figure 4.11.

The Report Editor Tool Palette

The Report Editor also contains a Tool Palette similar to the one found in the Forms Editor. Because a report is static, or noninteractive, the Tool Palette does not contain as many objects. Figure 4.12 shows the Tool Palette found in the Live Previewer view mode.

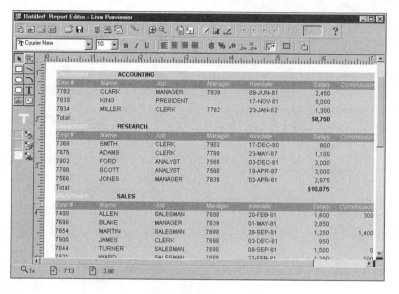

FIGURE 4.11
The sample report you are working on, completed to this point.

FIGURE 4.12
The Tool Palette.

Select   This is the default tool. Use it to select the various objects on the report. You can then move, resize, and delete the object.

Magnify   Similar to the Zoom In and Zoom Out buttons on the toolbar, except that you can specify the center of the zoom area. To zoom out, hold the Shift key and click on the canvas.

Rectangle   Creates a rectangle or square on your report. You can use the rectangle to group database fields and provide a more aesthetically pleasing look. Holding down the Shift key creates a square.

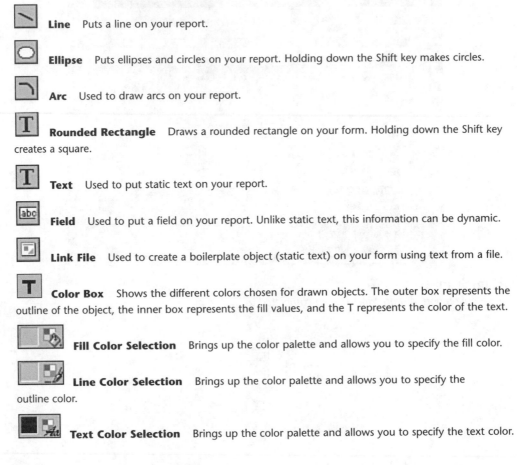

Line   Puts a line on your report.

Ellipse   Puts ellipses and circles on your report. Holding down the Shift key makes circles.

Arc   Used to draw arcs on your report.

Rounded Rectangle   Draws a rounded rectangle on your form. Holding down the Shift key creates a square.

Text   Used to put static text on your report.

Field   Used to put a field on your report. Unlike static text, this information can be dynamic.

Link File   Used to create a boilerplate object (static text) on your form using text from a file.

Color Box   Shows the different colors chosen for drawn objects. The outer box represents the outline of the object, the inner box represents the fill values, and the T represents the color of the text.

Fill Color Selection   Brings up the color palette and allows you to specify the fill color.

Line Color Selection   Brings up the color palette and allows you to specify the outline color.

Text Color Selection   Brings up the color palette and allows you to specify the text color.

The department totals are a little difficult to separate from the rest of the salaries in the column. To solve this problem, you can draw a line above each of the salary totals. Here is how:

1. Select the Layout Model tool from the upper toolbar. Live Previewer view mode does not allow you to add a line.

2. Select the Line tool from the Tool Palette.

3. Draw the line in the desired area by clicking down at the starting point and releasing at the ending point.

It is impossible to see the lines in the Layout Model view because of all the layout lines. To make sure that the lines are in the correct place, switch back to the Live Previewer view. Your report should look similar to the report in Figure 4.13.

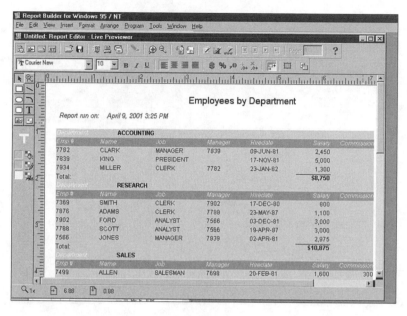

FIGURE 4.13
The report with lines above the department totals.

Using the Object Navigator

Oracle Report Builder includes the Object Navigator tool that is also found in Form Builder. The Object Navigator allows you to see what objects are currently being worked on and their relationships to other objects on the report. Figure 4.14 shows the Object Navigator for the report you have been working with.

You can see that there are a lot of objects created so far. However, none of them have descriptive names. There are a bunch of initials prefixing the column headings and data objects. Although this should not be a problem for simple reports, the names might be difficult to work with when creating longer and more complex reports. Name changes can be performed by clicking on the object name, waiting, and clicking again.

If you are not up to the task of changing all the report's object names, there are other tools in the Object Navigator to help you. The Find box can be used to help locate an object if you know the object's name. The Find tool looks for and displays the objects as you type. This is very helpful for locating various pieces of your report. Additional, the hierarchy box to the left can be used to see the genealogy of the object.

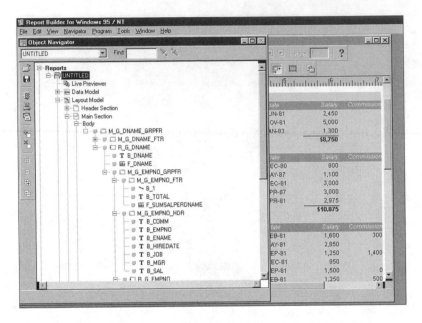

FIGURE 4.14
The Object Navigator found in Report Builder.

Play around with the Object Navigator to become familiar with it. Do a search for EMPNO and see how many levels down it is in the hierarchy tree.

For more information on the Object Navigator, refer to Chapter 3.

Integrating Graphics into Reports

The report you are working on is almost finished. The last thing to do is add a pie chart showing the breakdown of the various department salaries. This is done with the help of the Chart Wizard.

Invoke the Chart Wizard from the toolbar and you will see the welcome screen. Click on the Next button and you are asked to select the chart type as shown in Figure 4.15.

The title of the chart is Salaries by Department. Choose a pie chart. Start with the Plain subtype (you can always go back into the Chart Wizard and change it). Click on Next and you are asked to describe the category or X-axis. On a pie chart, there is no x-axis, strictly speaking. However, the column to be specified here is the Department name or DNAME. Select it, use the > button to add it to the list, and then click Next.

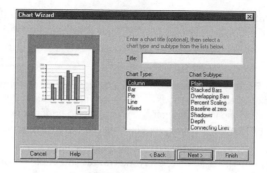

FIGURE 4.15
The Chart Wizard allows you to specify the chart type.

Now you are asked to specify the value or Y-axis. Again, pie charts don't have a Y-axis. The value to specify here is SumSALperDNAME, which is the report's way of describing the sum of all the salaries provided for each department. After selecting SumSALperDNAME using the > button, click on Next to specify where the graph will go. You can put it at the end of the report. Click Next.

Before the Chart Wizard can add the graph to the report, the graph must be saved. Accept the default filename and then click Finish. There is a bit of processing and then the graph is placed at the bottom of the report, as shown in Figure 4.16.

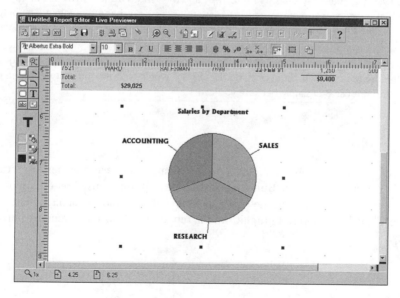

FIGURE 4.16
The chart showing the percentage of salaries for each department.

Save the report as ch4.rdf using the Save button on the toolbar. You are then able to use it with other examples later in the book.

KEEP IT SIMPLE

When I was taking my first Electrical Engineering course in college, the professor wrote the word "KISS" on the chalk board. He then explained that it stood for "Keep it Simple, Stupid." While he was not implying that anyone in the class was lacking in intelligence, he was trying to underscore the importance of keeping things as simple as possible and not try to over engineer our homework assignments.

It was about this time that everyone discovered the power of the what you see is what you get (WYSIWYG) word processors and laser printers. For a while, everyone was turning in papers using at least 25 different fonts. Why? because they could. It didn't take long for the college professors and other readers of papers to plead with us to find a font we liked and stick with it. Again, the KISS principle was driven home.

Eventually I graduated from college and was working at Oracle. My job was to manage a team of sample application developers. We were to create a bunch of easy to understand, yet complex sample applications showing the power of Oracle's development tools. As our division's flagship product was nearing alpha-release quality, we decided to take a couple of days and have an application development contest.

My boss took me aside and assigned me the task of recreating an Oracle utility that relied heavily on its graphical user interface. That made my life easy. All I had to do was copy an existing application. The only problem was our development product did not have the capability to create three-dimensional graphics elements. The product I was trying to copy relied heavily on 3-D graphs and GUI elements and I was stuck using 2-D.

After a couple of days, the applications were all finished and it came time to review everyone's applications. I first showed everyone the utility I was trying to copy and then showed them my version. To my surprise, everyone felt that my copy was more elegant and easy to understand than the original. The only difference was I didn't have the freedom to use 3-D graphical object.

This lesson underscored the importance of the KISS principle. From that point on, I have resolved to try and keep my applications as simple as possible. Oracle Graphics has the ability to create 3-D graphs and you may be tempted to use them for everything. However, I would recommend that you remember the KISS principle and not use 3-D simply because you can.

Summary

In this chapter, you learned how to create a master-detail report that matches the form created in Chapter 3. You used the Query Builder to create the SQL query used by the report. You then used the Report Editor to clean up the report and make it readable by management. Finally, you used the Chart Wizard to add graphics to the report and show the percentage of salaries by departments.

QUERY BUILDER AND SCHEMA BUILDER

ESSENTIALS ——————

- Query Builder is linked into Oracle Developer tools, but also can stand alone to help build complex SQL queries.

- Query Builder allows you to create simple or inner joins as well as outer joins. An outer join allows all rows for the specified table to be displayed regardless of whether there are corresponding rows in the lookup table.

- Query Builder allows you to save your query in three different formats. The first two formats are used to specify extra information used by Query Builder. The last method is to save a SQL SELECT statement that can is easily imported into other applications.

- Query Builder allows you to see the results of your query as you build it. Simply click the Execute Query button found on the toolbar. If too many rows are returned, you can qualify your query using conditional logic and rerun the query.

- Schema Builder is a tool used to create database objects such as tables, views, and indexes. It is geared toward small projects. Larger projects should utilize the enhanced features found in Oracle Designer.

- Specifying relationships between tables by using Schema Builder will help you create queries across tables later as you develop your application.

Oracle Developer 6i includes several other tools to help you create database applications. These tools include Query Builder, Schema Builder, Procedure Builder, and Project Builder. Procedure Builder is discussed in Chapter 6, "PL/SQL Workshop," and Project Builder is covered in Chapter 14, "Project Management and Source Code." This chapter covers the Query Builder running outside Report Builder and Schema Builder.

More About the Query Builder

Query Builder was used to help create the SQL query used for the report in Chapter 3, "Oracle Forms Developer." Although it can be used with Report Builder, it can also be used as a stand-alone application. Doing so allows you to create complex queries and save them for later use.

Query Builder can be used as a simple report-creation tool. If you get a one-time request for a complex but short report, it is often easier to create it using Query Builder than Report Builder. You can save the query, should the report be requested again.

In this section, you are shown how to use Query Builder to create short reports. Instead of creating the same master-detail request used in Chapter 4, "Oracle Reports Developer and Graphics," you create a lookup query. This requires you to use existing database table relationships as well as to create undefined ones.

Running Query Builder

Start Query Builder using the Start menu on Windows, or by running the obe60 program on Unix. If you have any problems running obe60, you may need to contact your system administrator to help correctly configure your environment. You are asked to log in to the database before you are allowed to do anything else. Use the scott/tiger account. If the Query Builder tables were not created in the database when it was installed, you get an informational message telling you such. Unfortunately, that informational message looks like an error message and might lead you to believe there is a problem. The message simply means that you can't store queries in the database and must store them in files. I suggest that you install the tables to take advantage of being able to create views from queries with the Schema Builder.

QUERY BUILDER TABLES

If you want to install the Query Builder tables, you can do so by rerunning the Oracle installer and selecting Create database objects. You can also create the tables by running the brwin60.sql script found in $HOME_ORACLE/browser60/admin/sql on Unix or $HOME_ORACLE\BROWSE60\SQL on Windows.

On login, Query Builder asks whether you want to create a new query, load one out of the database, or load one from the file system. If you have not installed the required tables in the database, the option to load a query from the database will be disabled. Create a new query by selecting Create New Query and clicking OK.

You are now asked to specify the tables to use for the query. Notice the icon on the left that indicates the database object is a table. A different icon is used to indicate views. For the first example, select the EMP table, click Include, and then click Close. The results in the Query window should look similar to Figure 5.1.

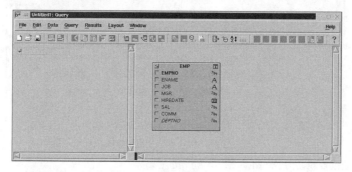

FIGURE 5.1
The Query window of Query Builder after selecting the EMP table to use for the query.

FIGURES MAY DIFFER

The Windows version of Query Builder uses a multiple document interface (MDI) to display both the Query and Results windows. On Unix, there will be two separate windows. This should not cause any problems. Just be aware that the toolbars in the figures might be slightly different than what is on your screen, depending on the platform you use.

You should be very familiar with all the values for the various columns in the EMP table by now. Therefore, select only the ENAME, DEPTNO, and MGR columns to display with this query. You select a column for display by checking the box next to the column name. As you select columns, they will appear in the results window. Execute the query using the Query, Execute menu item. The results are shown in Figure 5.2.

Creating Lookup Queries

The results from this query don't provide an easy way for the user to see department names and managers. This section shows how to replace cryptic values with easily readable ones by using lookup values.

The first value to change is DEPTNO. It should be replaced with DNAME from the DEPT table. The DEPT table is added to the Query screen by selecting the Data, Select Data Tables menu option. Again you are presented with the Select Data Tables dialog. Highlight the DEPT table, click on Include, and then click the Close button.

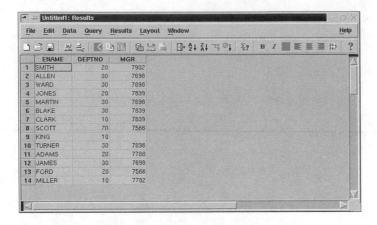

FIGURE 5.2
The Results window showing the rows from the query.

The Query window now contains both the EMP and DEPT tables, with the relationship between the two symbolized by a line. Deselect the DEPTNO column (so it is unchecked) and select the DNAME column instead. Execute the query and the DEPTNO column is replaced with the department names for each employee.

The MGR column in the report refers to the employee number of the manager for each employee. Notice that the employee named KING does not have a manager. Instead, KING's MGR column is left NULL or blank. It is important to make sure that KING appears in the final report, and that takes some modifications to the standard query lookup performed earlier.

Changing MGR from an employee number reference to the actual name of the manager requires adding the EMP table to the report for a second time. This is done in the same way the DEPT table was added. Notice that the second instance of the EMP table carries an A1 suffix in the table heading. Query Builder uses this accompanying suffix to differentiate between different instances of the same table. If you choose, you can change the assigned default name to something more descriptive.

Also notice that there is no relationship defined between the two EMP tables. Create one by choosing the Data, Set Table Relationship menu option. Doing so brings up the definition form shown in Figure 5.3.

The A-> prompt is used to create the relationship in the main EMP table. EMP.MGR is the value to type in . This refers to the manager's employee number in the table used to drive the query. Next, specify the join condition. As in most cases, the = (equal sign) is used. The B-> prompt is used to set up the lookup value and should be EMP_A1.ENAME. As you can see, the _A1 differentiates the second EMP table.

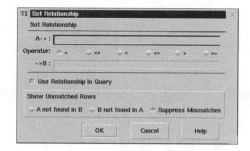

FIGURE 5.3
The dialog used to define table relationships.

Creating Table Relationships

The next value in the Set Relationship dialog is whether or not to use the relationship in the query. You can generally accept the default, which is to include the relationship. Should there be a reason not to include the relationship, you can exclude it at will.

Lastly, you have the option of including rows with no corresponding lookup values. Accepting the default of Suppress Mismatches would eliminate KING from the query results. Therefore, you should choose A not found in B to make sure that KING is included. This creates an outer join, as indicated by the + (plus sign) in the relationship line shown in Figure 5.4.

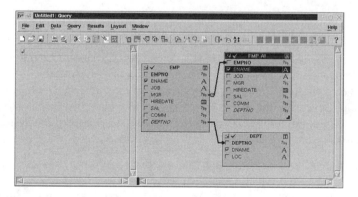

FIGURE 5.4
The two EMP tables shown joined together in the Query window.

Ordinary, or inner joins, discard all rows that don't have matching values in the other table being joined. An outer join makes sure that rows with no corresponding lookup values are included in the result. If the B not found in A option had been chosen, the plus sign, or outer join indicator, would appear next to the EMP_A1 table.

The query no longer needs to include the MGR column, but instead should include the ENAME column from the EMP_A1 table. Deselect MGR in EMP and select ENAME in EMP_A1, as is also shown in Figure 5.4. When that is done, execute the query; the results should be similar to those in Figure 5.5.

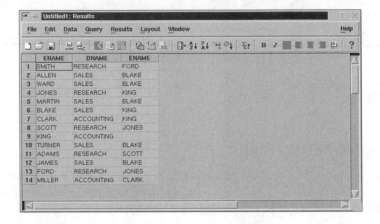

FIGURE 5.5
The results of the sample query with employee names replacing the employee number references for manager, and department names replacing the department numbers.

Saving the Query

Save the query so that it can be used for later exercises. Selecting the File, Save menu option calls the Save dialog, which asks for the format in which to save the query. If you installed the Query Builder tables in the database, you have the option of saving there as well as two different formats in the file system. The first file system saves the query in a data format, whereas the second option, QFX, stores it as text. The text save uses name-value pairs to describe the query. Try saving it in both formats using names such as ch5q1 for the file system save and ch5q2 for the QFX save.

You also have the option of saving the query in SQL. This is done by choosing the File, Save SQL menu choice. Although you can view the SQL in the Query window with the Query, Show SQL menu choice, saving the query as a SQL statement allows you to import it into other applications easily.

The Query Window Toolbar

The wide toolbar hints at a large amount of functionality available in the Query Builder. Some buttons invoke the tools used in the previous examples, whereas other help narrow down query results. If you use Query Builder on Windows, you will notice the toolbar changes depending on whether or not the Query or Results window is active. In Unix, there are two separate windows, each with its own toolbar. Figure 5.6 shows the toolbar for the Query window with short descriptions for each button.

FIGURE 5.6
The Query Window toolbar.

New   Creates a new query.

Open   Opens a saved query from a file or the database.

Save   Saves an existing query to a file or the database.

Print   Prints the results of the current query.

Page Setup   Allows you to set up parameters for what you are about to print. This includes layout style and margins.

Cut   Cuts the currently selected object or objects to the clipboard.

Copy   Copies the currently selected object or objects to the clipboard.

Paste   Pastes the object or objects from the clipboard into the current work area.

Clear   Deletes the currently selected object or objects without copying to the clipboard.

Select All   Selects all objects in the current work area.

Select Data Tables   Invokes the window to add tables to the query as demonstrated in the previous examples.

Select Related Tables   Shows tables related to the selected table in the Query window and allows you to add them to the query.

Rename Table   Allows you to rename a table for the query.

Get Info   Displays information about the selected table.

Set Table Relationship   Invokes the window to set up table relationships as shown in the previous examples.

Execute Query   Runs or executes the query and displays the rows retrieved in the Results window.

Count Rows   Displays a window showing the number of rows returned for the current query. This is very helpful when working with large tables that have the potential to return many rows.

Define Query Parameters   Allows you to create adjustable parameters used to run the report. For example, if you want to create one report that displays all the employees for a specific department, but you want to choose the department at runtime.

Show SQL   Brings up a window that displays a SQL SELECT statement for the query.

Column Sequence   Allows you to change the order of the columns returned for the query.

Define Column   Used to create a column for the report based on a calculation.

Sort   Provides an interface to choose the order in which rows are returned by the query.

Group by   Provides an interface to group rows with similar columns together.

AND   Specifies return criteria that must be the same for multiple column expressions.

OR   Specifies return criteria that must meet for at least one column expression.

NOT   Specifies return criteria that must not be met.

Ungroup Conditions   Provides a way to ungroup the AND/OR/NOT criteria for the report.

Accept   Accepts the limiting search criteria for the query. When clicked, it parses the SQL WHERE clause for correct syntax.

Cancel   Throws away the limiting search criteria just specified for the query.

Paste Column   Provides a list of columns for the query to include in the search criteria.

 Paste Function   Provides a list of SQL functions that can be included in the search criteria.

Help   Invokes the Oracle Developer help system. On Windows, the standard Help system is used. On Unix, it is HTML based.

More Examples

This next section contains more examples to show additional functionality of the Query Builder. The first set of examples shows how to restrict the number of rows returned by the query. The second shows how to add calculation columns to the query.

Restricting Rows Returned

The sample tables used for the exercises so far are not very large. Most real-world examples have some small lookup tables, but are mostly large main tables with many rows. Returning all those rows in a query can make reports large and unwieldy. Therefore, it is important to know how to limit the rows returned. This is accomplished with the WHERE clause in SQL.

The left pane of the Query window is used to specify the WHERE clause. Having a good understanding of SQL WHERE clauses is helpful when using Query Builder, but is not required. The key is to know which columns to limit and the functions available to do so. Some sample WHERE clauses are

- EMPNO = 7839
- EMPNO > 7800
- ENAME = 'SMITH'
- EMP.SAL < 1000

These clauses should be self-explanatory. To include them in the sample query, click on the rectangle in the left pane of the Query window and type them in. Because two tables contain an EMPNO column, the first two clauses generate an Ambiguous column error. This can be solved by prefixing EMPNO with the correct table name, as shown in the fourth sample clause you saw earlier. The same requirement is needed for the third clause.

TABLE NAMES IN QUERIES

If there were only one reference to the EMP table in the query, there would be no need to preface columns with the table name, and the first three clauses would be correct.

You will often see the database username included for even more explicit identification. Generally, it is not needed unless the referenced table is owned by another user.

Clauses can be combined using the AND, OR, and NOT operators found on the toolbar. For example, enter EMP.EMPNO > 7800 in the Query window. Click on the AND button in the toolbar and enter EMP.SAL < 1000. Now run the query. JAMES should be the only employee returned.

You can continue to narrow the search criteria until only the required information is returned. Before you run a query against large tables, always remember to check the number of rows returned.

ESTIMATE ROWS

A general rule is to estimate the number of rows expected when running any query. This is especially important with queries against tables with a high record count.

Adding Calculations

It is often necessary to perform calculations based on data in the database. In the sample tables being used, there is a Salary as well as a Commission column. To see an employee's total compensation, you need to add SAL and COMM. This eliminates the need to perform the calculation by hand.

To add the Compensation column, you should select the EMP table and click the Define Column button on the toolbar. You will see the Define Column dialog, as shown in Figure 5.7.

FIGURE 5.7
The Define Column dialog is used to create calculated columns.

The first thing to do is give the new column a name. Enter Compensation in the first or Defined columns text box. The list box below the column name is used to show all calculated columns. In Figure 5.7, there are no calculated columns yet, so it is blank. To complete the new column definition, you must provide a formula to calculate the column value in the Defined as text box. This formula can contain string, number, or date calculations. In this example, enter the formula EMP.SAL + EMP.COMM and then click OK.

The new column is added to the EMP table. It should be visible for the report, so make sure that it is selected. To verify that the equation is correct, you might also choose to view the SAL and COMM columns. Now execute the query. How come the formula works with only four rows and not all of them?

The Oracle database and development tools treat a NULL value differently than the number zero. A NULL value is undefined and cannot be used in a calculation (an undefined number plus anything is still undefined). Therefore, all NULL values must be converted to the number zero. This is done with the NVL() function.

Click on the Define Column button to bring up the Define Column dialog. Select the Compensation column and the previously defined formula appears. Use EMP.SAL + NVL(EMP.COMM,0) to replace the previously defined formula. This says to replace all NULL values in the EMP.COMM column with the number zero. Click OK and execute the query. If you remove the limits for the query, the results should closely match those found in Figure 5.8.

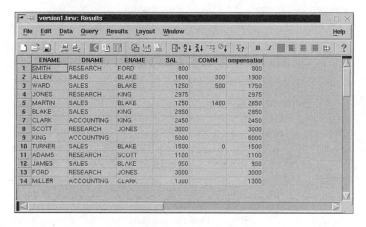

FIGURE 5.8
The results of the query using NVL() to help calculate total compensation.

The Results Window Toolbar

The Results window in Query Builder behaves similarly to a spreadsheet program such as Microsoft Excel. If you need to widen a column to see all the information, simply widen it in the same way you would widen a column in a spreadsheet. This is a very convenient way to display the results of queries.

The toolbar for the Results window is somewhat different than the one used in the Query window. It has tools that correlate with those required for a tabular report writing tool. The Results window toolbar is also somewhat dynamic, depending on whether you are using the format tools or the totals tools. Figure 5.9 shows the toolbar with format tools, whereas Figure 5.10 shows it with totals tools. Both figures are followed by short definitions as to what each tool is used for.

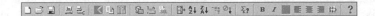

FIGURE 5.9
The Results window toolbar with format tools showing.

New   Creates a new query.

Open   Opens a saved query from a file or the database.

Save   Saves an existing query to a file or the database.

Print   Prints the results of the current query.

Page Setup   Allows you to set up parameters for what you are about to print. This includes layout style and margins.

Cut   Cuts the currently selected object or objects to the clipboard. This is generally disabled in the Results window.

Copy   Copies the currently selected object or objects to the clipboard.

Paste   Pastes the object or objects from the clipboard into the current work area. This is generally disabled in the Results window.

Execute Query   Runs or executes the query and displays the rows retrieved in the Results window.

Count Rows   Displays a window showing the number of rows returned for the current query. This is very helpful when working with large tables that have the potential to return many rows.

Show SQL   Brings up a window that displays a SQL SELECT statement for the query.

Column Sequence   Allows you to change the order of the columns returned for the query.

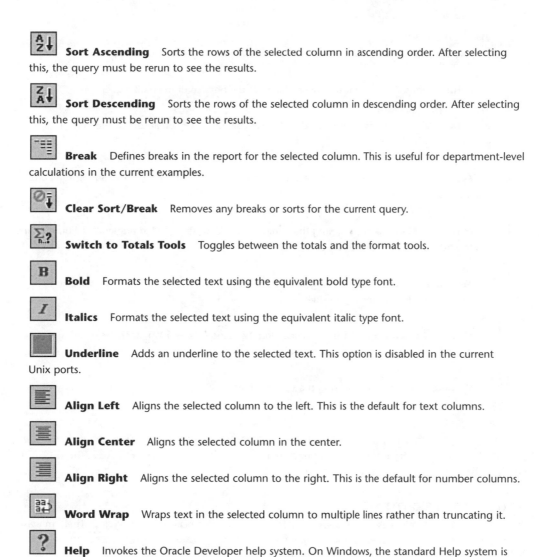

Sort Ascending   Sorts the rows of the selected column in ascending order. After selecting this, the query must be rerun to see the results.

Sort Descending   Sorts the rows of the selected column in descending order. After selecting this, the query must be rerun to see the results.

Break   Defines breaks in the report for the selected column. This is useful for department-level calculations in the current examples.

Clear Sort/Break   Removes any breaks or sorts for the current query.

Switch to Totals Tools   Toggles between the totals and the format tools.

Bold   Formats the selected text using the equivalent bold type font.

Italics   Formats the selected text using the equivalent italic type font.

Underline   Adds an underline to the selected text. This option is disabled in the current Unix ports.

Align Left   Aligns the selected column to the left. This is the default for text columns.

Align Center   Aligns the selected column in the center.

Align Right   Aligns the selected column to the right. This is the default for number columns.

Word Wrap   Wraps text in the selected column to multiple lines rather than truncating it.

Help   Invokes the Oracle Developer help system. On Windows, the standard Help system is used. On Unix, it is HTML based.

FIGURE 5.10
The Results window toolbar with totals tools showing.

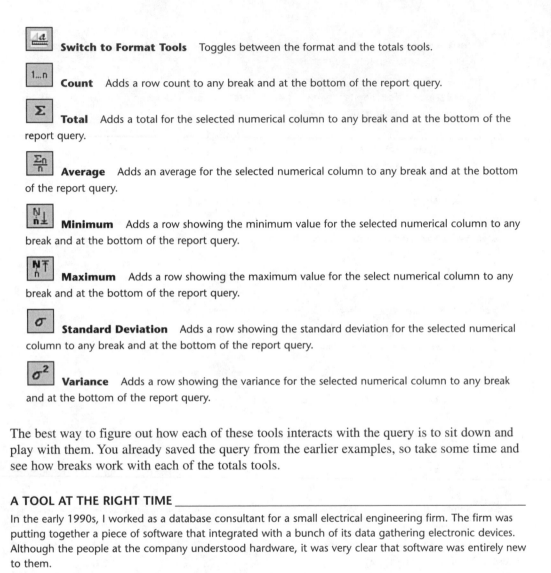

Switch to Format Tools   Toggles between the format and the totals tools.

Count   Adds a row count to any break and at the bottom of the report query.

Total   Adds a total for the selected numerical column to any break and at the bottom of the report query.

Average   Adds an average for the selected numerical column to any break and at the bottom of the report query.

Minimum   Adds a row showing the minimum value for the selected numerical column to any break and at the bottom of the report query.

Maximum   Adds a row showing the maximum value for the select numerical column to any break and at the bottom of the report query.

Standard Deviation   Adds a row showing the standard deviation for the selected numerical column to any break and at the bottom of the report query.

Variance   Adds a row showing the variance for the selected numerical column to any break and at the bottom of the report query.

The best way to figure out how each of these tools interacts with the query is to sit down and play with them. You already saved the query from the earlier examples, so take some time and see how breaks work with each of the totals tools.

A TOOL AT THE RIGHT TIME

In the early 1990s, I worked as a database consultant for a small electrical engineering firm. The firm was putting together a piece of software that integrated with a bunch of its data gathering electronic devices. Although the people at the company understood hardware, it was very clear that software was entirely new to them.

The company had sold a bunch of electronic devices used for gathering sound data to a large municipal government entity on the east coast. To seal the deal, the firm included custom software. The only problem was that the software hadn't been written. Therefore, the small company was trying to add the required features as fast as possible, but was very late and way over budget. I was called in to help at this point.

One of the software specifications stated that there needed to be an easy-to-use tool for ad hoc reports. As we went over the customer specifications, the other software engineers and I designed a tool that looked very similar to Oracle Query Builder. At the time, Query Builder didn't exist, but unbeknownst to us, it was about to be released.

I flew out to the San Francisco area to attend an Oracle Developer's conference and was shown Oracle Data Browser (the original name for Query Builder). I was amazed. It looked like Oracle had been listening in on our design meetings. Data Browser looked amazingly similar to what we designed back at this small engineering company.

It was nice having Oracle complete some of our development for us. We shipped this quick solution to the engineering firm, but quickly ran into problems. When the database was designed (before I came on to rescue the software project), cryptic table and column names were used. Therefore, it was difficult for the management people to understand what columns had to be included when creating a report.

The idea was thrown around to rename all the column and table names, but that would result in an incredible amount of application rework. Instead, we created a view and used the column alias features to provide more descriptive names. Using a sample table, the view creation statement looked like this:

```
CREATE TABLE DEPARTMENTS (dept_number, name, location) AS
(SELECT deptno, dname, loc
 FROM dept)
```

The customer appreciated the less cryptic names provided by the views. However, managers still had a problem figuring out all the relationships between the various lookup tables. We solved this problem by rolling the lookup tables into the view.

The customer was happy again. Although Oracle Query Builder might not be able to create all the reports you need, it can build many of them. Throw in its ease of use, and Query Builder becomes a powerful tool.

Query Builder Conclusion

Query Builder is a useful tool to create queries used by Report Builder. It can also be used to create simple tabular reports. If adequate table and column names have been used and integrity constraints defined, Query Builder can enable novice database users to create simple reports.

The Schema Builder

The Schema Builder is used to add or modify database schema. This includes tables, views, relationships, and indexes. For large database applications, it is advisable to use Oracle Designer and Repository to create the database schema. Schema Builder is more geared toward uncomplicated projects in which only a few small tables are used.

Examples of tables and relationships have been used extensively throughout the book. Indexes are used by the Oracle database to speed up queries at the expense of database space and a slight performance hit on inserts. Because they are not required for an application to run, many developers create indexes afterward in response to a performance problem relating to queries.

This section of the chapter shows how to use the Schema Builder to add a table to the database. The table then is related with an existing sample table, and an index on the new table is created. Finally, the toolbar is explained.

The Schema Builder can be run from the Start button on Windows or by using the obs60 executable on Unix. You are immediately asked to log in to a database before continuing. The examples in this chapter again use the scott/tiger sample account.

If you have not installed the tables for the Schema Builder, you might see an informative message saying that the database open/save option is disabled. Unfortunately, this looks like an error message, but it isn't. The message is there just to let you know that you cannot save the extra information used by the Schema Builder in the database. Schema Builder still works fine.

Creating a Table

The most common use of Schema Builder is to create new tables for your application. Perhaps it is up to your department to add some simple functionality to an existing system. For instance, the sample tables used so far might need to be augmented to help keep track of customers. This information will not be saved in the EMP table. Instead, a customer table named CUST must be created. To define the customer's sales representative, there will be a link from the new CUST table back to the EMP table. The new CUST table would look something like Table 5.1.

Table 5.1   The Sample CUST Table to Keep Track of Customers

Column	Data Type
CUSTNO	Number
CNAME	VARCHAR(25)
ADDR	VARCHAR(45)
CITY	VARCHAR(20)
STATE	VARCHAR(20)
ZIP	VARCHAR(10)
PHONE	VARCHAR(20)
FAX	VARCHAR(20)
SALESREP	Number

The CUSTNO column serves as the primary key for the table. The rest of the information is a subset of what you would normally keep track of for customers. You might want to include a Web address or contact name. In the interest of keeping this example short, those columns have been omitted.

To create the new table, click on the Schema, Create Table, Table menu choice. Nothing seems to happen on the canvas. However, if you click-and-drag in a diagonal (upper left to lower right) motion, you will see the outline of the table you are about to create. The new CUST table will have nine columns, so release the click when the number 9 appears by the new table outline. Default table and column names will be used as shown in Figure 5.11.

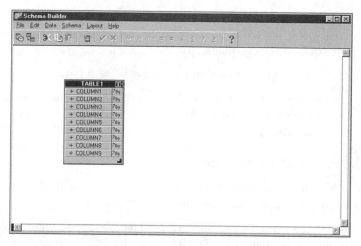

FIGURE 5.11
The Schema Builder window after creating the table.

The first thing to do is rename the table and columns to the correct names shown in Table 5.1. To change a name, click once on the table or column name, wait a bit, and then click on the name again. The first click selects the name and the pause between the second click only needs to be long enough to not be confused as a double-click. Change the names accordingly. Table and column names using lowercase letters are automatically converted to uppercase letters.

The next task is to change the default data types from numbers to text for all the text columns. Double-clicking on the CNAME column brings up the Define Column dialog shown in Figure 5.12.

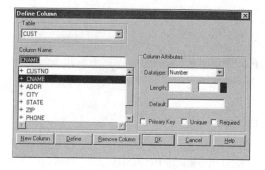

FIGURE 5.12
The Define Column dialog used to change the data type information.

The Column Attributes frame contains a pull-down list with all possible data types. Change the type from Number to Varchar, and set the length to 25 in the lower-right box. Notice that you also have the option to specify a default value, and whether the column is a primary key, unique, and required. When you are done changing the text columns, go back and check the Primary Key box for the CUSTNO column.

The following are possible data types for columns and what each type is used for:

- **Number**   Integer and decimal numbers. You can specify precision and scale. The lower-left field specifies precision and is the total number of digits. Values can range from 1 to 38. The lower-right field specifies the scale and is the number of digits to the right of the decimal point. Values can range from –84 to 127. Use a scale value of zero to specify fixed-point numbers of a given precision.

- **Varchar**   Variable-length character strings specified to a maximum length. You must specify a length and it can be no more than 2,000 characters.

- **Date**   Date and time including century, year, month, day, hour, minute, and second. Valid dates range from January 1, 4712 B.C. to December 31, 4712 A.D.

- **Long**   Variable-length character strings up to 2 gigabytes long. Longs are subject to a number of restrictions.

- **Float**   The ANSI floating-point data type. You must specify a binary precision ranging from 1 to 126.

- **Character**   Fixed-length character strings to a maximum size of 255 bytes and a default size of 1. This is equivalent to the CHAR data type in the database.

- **Raw**   Raw binary data. The maximum size is 255 bytes.

- **Long Raw**   Raw binary data up to 2 gigabytes. They are subject to the same restrictions as Long data type.

- **MLSLABEL**   Labels in binary format on secure operating systems. This is a Trusted Oracle data type.

You are ready to create the table in the database, which is done using the Schema, Commit Schema menu choice. You can now use this table in your application.

Creating Relationships

An important feature of the Oracle database is being able to define relationships. The CUST table just created must be related back to the EMP table. This could have been done before committing the schema, but is also possible with existing tables.

The first step is to include the EMP table in the Schema Builder window. This is done using the Data, Select Data Tables menu choice. It brings up the Select Data Tables dialog also used by the Query Builder. Select the EMP table, click Include, and then click Close. You now see the EMP table in the Schema Builder window.

Define the relationship between the EMP and CUST tables by clicking on the Schema, Define Relationship menu choice. It brings up the Define Relationship dialog shown in Figure 5.13.

FIGURE 5.13
The Define Relationship dialog.

The first text entry box is used to specify the foreign-key field or fields. For this example, the field is CUST.SALESREP. The second field is used to specify the primary key. For this example, the field is EMP.EMPNO. When you click OK, you should see the relationship between the two tables as shown in Figure 5.14.

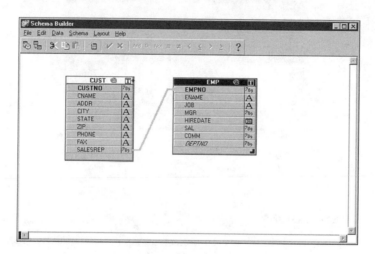

FIGURE 5.14
The relationship between the CUST and EMP tables.

Finally, you need to commit the schema or changes to have the relationship recorded in the database.

Creating Indexes

Another reason to use Schema Builder is to create indexes. It is not an intuitive process, so pay close attention to the example. In the sample tables, it will be common to search the CUST table based on the customer's name. Therefore, an index on CNAME would be useful and should be created.

Make sure that the CUST table is selected in the Schema Builder window. Click on the Schema, Define Index menu option to bring up the Define Index dialog. You should see the primary key index that was created with the CUST table. Select the CNAME column in the Use Columns: list and click on the New Index button. You now see a second name added to the list of indexes using an automatically generated name. Because it is a bit ambiguous, change the name to CUST_CNAME and click the Set Name button. The name change should now be in effect. Verify that the CUSTNO column is selected as shown in Figure 5.15.

Click OK to dismiss the dialog. Verify that the correct SQL statement is used to create the index using the Schema, Show SQL menu choice. This choice brings up a dialog that shows the SQL statement. Click Commit to create the index, and then click Close to dismiss the dialog. The index is created and active.

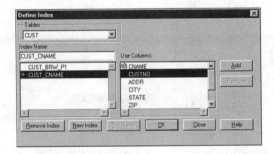

FIGURE 5.15
The index CUST_CNAME ready to be created.

Schema Builder Toolbar

The Schema Builder toolbar is much less complicated than the one used by Query Builder. It does, however, feature some of the same tools. The Schema Builder toolbar is shown in Figure 5.16.

FIGURE 5.16
The Schema Builder toolbar.

Commit Schema   Executes the SQL created by the Schema Builder.

Revert Table   Undoes the changes made to the current table.

Cut   Cuts the currently selected object or objects to the clipboard.

Copy   Copies the currently selected object or objects to the clipboard.

Paste   Pastes the object or objects from the clipboard into the current work area.

Select Data Tables   Invokes the dialog to add tables to the Schema Builder window as demonstrated in the previous examples.

Accept   Accepts the constraint information.

Cancel   Cancels constraint information.

AND   Defines AND conditions for constraint information.

OR   Defines OR conditions for constraint information.

NOT   Defines NOT conditions for constraint information.

Equal   Defines equal conditions for constraint information.

Not Equal   Defines not equal conditions for constraint information.

Less Than   Defines less than conditions for constraint information.

Less Than or Equal   Defines less than or equal to conditions for constraint information.

Greater Than   Defines greater than conditions for constraint information.

Greater Than or Equal   Defines greater than or equal to conditions for constraint information.

Help   Invokes the Oracle Developer Help system. On Windows, the standard Help system is used. On Unix, it is HTML based.

Creating Integrity Constraints

Most of the tools on the toolbar (those on the far right) deal with creating integrity constraints. Integrity constraints can be used to make sure that the data entered into a column meets predetermined criteria. For instance, if you are creating a column to denote the gender of an individual, you want the user to be able to enter only an M or an F for male or female, respectively.

Many developers leave it up to the application to ensure that correct data is entered. The problem with this is that not all applications enforce the same constraints. Placing integrity constraints at the database level ensures that all applications using the table are required to enter the data correctly.

Following an example is the best way to get experience with the integrity constraints. In this example, you create another table with several columns. Constraints for the various data types are then created.

Reconnect to the database using the File, Reconnect menu choice. This provides a blank work area to use to create the sample table. Now create a new table called CONTACT. It is described in Table 5.2.

Table 5.2   The New Contact Table to Help Illustrate Integrity Constraints

Column	Data Type	Description
CONTACTNO	Number	Primary key
CUSTNO	Number	Reference back to the customer
CNAME	VARCHAR(25)	Name of the contact person
GENDER	Character	Flag denoting male or female gender
LASTCONT	Date	Date of last contact

Creating CONTACTNO as the primary key defines all the necessary constraints. You may decide to enforce the primary key to be a positive number. This is done by selecting CONTACTNO in the Schema Builder, and then choosing Schema, Define Constraints from the menu. It brings up the Constraint Editor pane as shown in Figure 5.17.

Enter CONTACTNO > 0 in the Constraint Editor pane and click on the Accept button on the toolbar. Instead of typing, you also have the option of clicking on the CONTACTNO column in the table definition, clicking on the > button in the toolbar, and adding the 0 using the keyboard. CONTACTNO now has three dots to the right of it in the table definition.

There should be an additional blank constraint definition entry, which you can use to limit a gender entry to M or F. Click in the blank entry and type GENDER = 'M' or GENDER = 'F'. Clicking on the Accept button in the toolbar generates a formatted constraint similar to Figure 5.18.

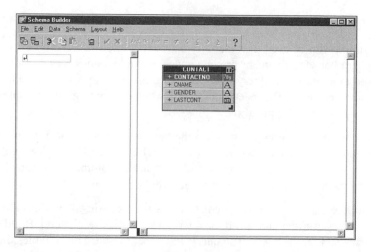

FIGURE 5.17
The Schema Builder with the Constraint Editor pane showing.

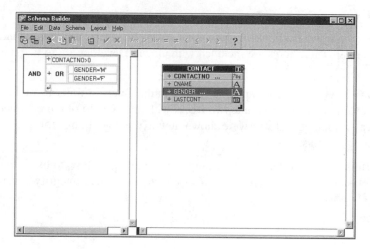

FIGURE 5.18
Constraints defined for the CONTACT table.

You can continue to add constraints for the other columns of the table if they are needed. Save the table and constraints by clicking on the Commit Schema button on the toolbar.

Creating Views

The Schema Builder can be used to create views of tables. Views can be used to simplify tables with a lengthy number of columns or provide understandable names for cryptic ones. Views can also be used to simplify the query interface for complex tables interrelated to each other with various join conditions. This is especially true when the same group of tables is used extensively throughout your application.

To create a view from an existing table, select the table and click on the Schema, Create Table, View menu option. The new view will appear in the Schema Builder window with a generated name. There you have the chance to rename the view and/or columns. You can also select a column, open the Define Column dialog, and remove the column.

The Schema Builder can also be used to create views from queries. If you installed the database tables for Query Builder and saved the query in the database, Schema Builder can be used to create a view based on the query. The query will appear in the Select Tables dialog as another data source.

Summary

In this chapter, you were given more information about the Query Builder and introduced to the Schema Builder. These tools are included with Oracle Developer 6i to help build database applications.

You were shown how to create complex queries with the Query Builder using lookup tables. There was an example of how to relate two tables without the help of a predefined relationship. The toolbar was explained and you were shown how to create columns for queries based on calculations and formulas.

The Schema Builder was explained and examples were given on how to use it to create tables, relationships, views and indexes. You were also shown how to add integrity constraints database tables.

PROCEDURE BUILDER AND PL/SQL

ESSENTIALS —————————————————————————————

- PL/SQL procedures and functions can be written for the database as well as for application code. Common code that will be used by multiple forms or reports should be included at the database level.

- Procedure Builder is built into Forms and Reports Builder. It can also be used as a standalone product to build database code. It is a complete integrated development environment (IDE) and includes a debugger.

- Procedure Builder includes a syntax palette that can be used to ensure that you are using program statements correctly. It is invoked using the Program, Syntax Palette menu option.

- PL/SQL data types are similar to Oracle's SQL data types. However, there are some differences among the lengths of data types. These differences should be carefully noted.

- INSERT, UPDATE, and DELETE SQL statements can be embedded in PL/SQL code without any modification.

- Multi-row selects can be done in PL/SQL using cursors.

In the early versions of SQL*Forms (the precursor to Oracle Forms Developer), there was limited programming functionality. This hindered developers from creating complex applications. Oracle solved the problem by creating *user-exits*, which allowed forms to execute programs written in a higher-level language such as C or COBOL. Unfortunately, user-exits were complicated to use, and the source had to be compiled on all the different platforms on which the application was expected to run.

SQL*Forms version 3 included support for Oracle's newly developed procedural language called PL/SQL. This allowed developers to use a common language that could interact with the database, and still use familiar programming constructs such as IF-THEN-ELSE conditional statements and WHILE or FOR loops. Although this meant that some developers had to learn a new language, it eliminated the need to create user-exits for the majority of Oracle database applications.

Oracle Developer 6i continues to leverage PL/SQL as the programming language for application development. There also continues to be support for user-exits, even though the majority of application programmers will ignore it. The success of the Java programming language has spurred Oracle to add support for it in the database. Starting with the release of Oracle 8i, the database allows for stored procedures and triggers to be written in either Java or PL/SQL. This support is trickling into the development products as well, starting with Oracle Developer 6i.

This chapter concentrates on using PL/SQL in Oracle Developer to help add functionality to forms and reports. Oracle has created the Procedure Builder to help create database procedures, functions, and packages. Procedure Builder has also been integrated into the Forms and Reports Builder tools when programming logic is required.

It is not the intent of this chapter to be a comprehensive guide to PL/SQL. You are encouraged to use the reference guides included with the online documentation to help answer questions.

Role of PL/SQL in Developer

PL/SQL is used at both the application level and at the database level. The Oracle database allows you to create procedures, functions, triggers, and packages to help facilitate building applications. If a business rule states that an action must be taken every time you add a new employee, a trigger will be created using PL/SQL to carry out the action. The trigger can be made up of other PL/SQL blocks or modules such as procedures, functions, and packages.

Forms Developer is where PL/SQL will be used most often in creating applications. Although the database supports triggers for database actions, Forms also uses triggers. These triggers can execute based on a GUI event such as a button being pressed or the mouse being moved over a specified area. Triggers can also be used with form events such as a form being closed or the cursor moving from one field to the next.

Some developers who are new to PL/SQL find themselves apprehensive about using it. There is no reason to be concerned. Oracle has included many different predefined procedures and packages. This eliminates the need to do a lot of programming because all you need to do is call a single function or procedure. Therefore, all the examples in this chapter are similarly short and easy to understand.

Procedure Builder

Procedure Builder is a PL/SQL integrated development environment (IDE). It can be used from within the Forms Builder and Reports Builder as well as run in a standalone environment. To run Procedure Builder, use the Start menu in Windows or run de60desm in Unix. When Procedure Builder opens, it should look similar to Figure 6.1. If you have problems starting Procedure Builder, you might need to contact your system administrator to make sure that your environment is correctly configured.

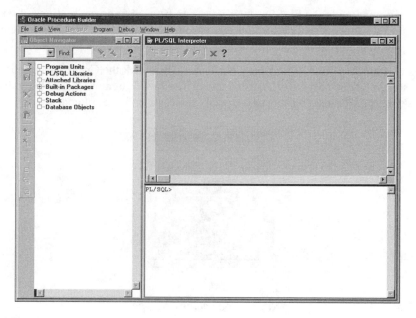

FIGURE 6.1
Procedure Builder just after starting.

Three main windows are used with Procedure Builder. As with the other Oracle Developer tools, the Object Navigator helps to manipulate PL/SQL objects. The other two windows are combined in the PL/SQL Interpreter. The top window is used to display code segments, and the lower window is used to execute both SQL and PL/SQL commands.

Running through some examples is the best way to become familiar with Procedure Builder. Log in to the database by using the File, Connect menu choice. You will be presented with the familiar Login dialog. As with the earlier examples, you will use the scott/tiger account.

You should notice that there are now database objects to browse in the Object Navigator. You also have the ability to query the database using the PL/SQL Interpreter. Click in the window with the PL/SQL> prompt, type the following command, and press the Enter key:

```
SELECT dname FROM dept;
```

If you forget to include the semicolon at the end, you will see a +> prompt. Simply add the semicolon to this line and press Enter. You should see the four department names listed as well as a message saying "4 rows selected."

The Program Unit Editor

The command window of the PL/SQL Interpreter can be used to create sections of code. However, most developers will prefer to use the Program Unit Editor. The following example introduces you to the Program Unit Editor as you create a very simple procedure.

First, click on Program Units in the Object Navigator. Then click the Create tool on the vertical toolbar (it should be one of the few available tools). The New Program Unit dialog will appear as shown in Figure 6.2. This dialog is used to specify the name and type of code you're creating.

FIGURE 6.2
The New Program Unit dialog to specify the code name and type.

Use the name PBTEST, specify Procedure as the type, and then click OK. The Program Unit Editor window will appear, with some boilerplate information already filled out, as shown in Figure 6.3.

Included with the Program Unit Editor is a horizontal row of buttons to help create code. Underneath the buttons is a pull-down list that enables you to edit other code objects you have created. Here is a list of those buttons with a short description of their functions:

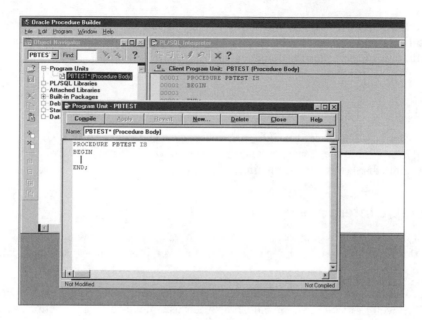

FIGURE 6.3
The Program Unit Editor window ready to write code.

Compile—Compiles the code and checks for errors. If errors are found, they are displayed underneath the editor in an error pane.

Apply—Applies changes without recompiling.

Revert—Discards any edits since the last time changes were applied.

New—Creates a new program unit.

Delete—Deletes the current program unit.

Close—Closes the Program Unit Editor.

Help—Invokes the Help system.

Add the following line in the Program Unit Editor between the BEGIN and END statements:

```
TEXT_IO.PUT_LINE("This is a test.");
```

When you click on the Compile button, you will see an error generated in the error pane. The error reports that the identifier 'This is a test.' must be declared. In reality, single quotes should be used instead of double quotes. Change the line to

```
TEXT_IO.PUT_LINE('This is a test.');
```

Notice how the color coding scheme changes when the single quotation marks are used. This is an indication that things are as they should be. Now click Compile again, and the error pane should go away.

With valid PL/SQL code in the editor, it is time to run it and test it out. Close the Program Unit Editor. The edited text should appear in the upper pane of the PL/SQL Interpreter. Run the procedure using the following command at the PL/SQL prompt:

```
PBTEST;
```

You should see the message, "This is a test."

It is rare that you will ever use the PUT_LINE statement in production PL/SQL code. PL/SQL is generally run behind the scenes in the database server or in a form. However, it makes a simple example that is easy to see running.

The PL/SQL Interpreter

The PL/SQL Interpreter is composed of two windowpanes. The upper window is for display only and does not allow you to change the code. However, it is useful for setting break points used to debug code.

The lower window is a command-line interface to the interpreter. Here you can execute standard SQL as well as PL/SQL commands. It also acts as a message area for actions performed in the code display pane.

The primary use of the PL/SQL Interpreter is to help debug code. In the next example, you will add several more PUT_LINE statements and then use the debugger. Use the Program, Program Unit Editor menu option to open the editor. Next, add the necessary lines so that the program looks like Listing 6.1.

Listing 6.1   Sample PL/SQL Script

```
PROCEDURE PBTEST IS
BEGIN
    TEXT_IO.PUT_LINE('This is a test.');
    TEXT_IO.PUT_LINE('Line 2.');
    TEXT_IO.PUT_LINE('Line 3.');
    TEXT_IO.PUT_LINE('Line 4.');
    TEXT_IO.PUT_LINE('Line 5.');
    TEXT_IO.PUT_LINE('Line 6.');
    TEXT_IO.PUT_LINE('Line 7.');
END;
```

Compile and run the procedure to make sure that it works as you expected. The first line should contain the original message, and the following lines should be numbered accordingly. With a short program, you are now ready to test the debugging capabilities of the PL/SQL Interpreter.

Select the second PUT_LINE statement in the code display pane. Set a breakpoint using the Debug, Break menu option. This brings up the PL/SQL Breakpoint dialog shown in Figure 6.4.

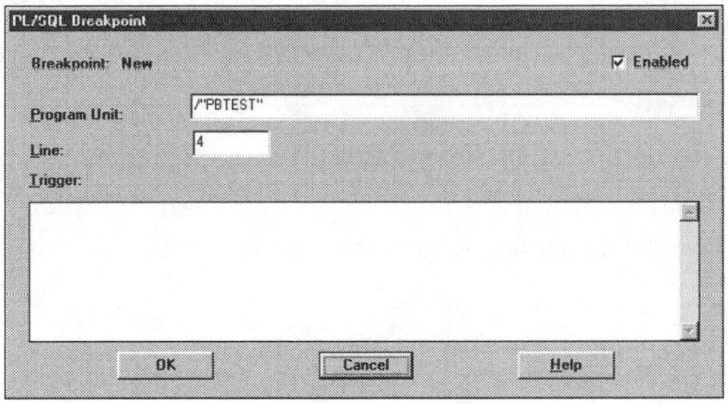

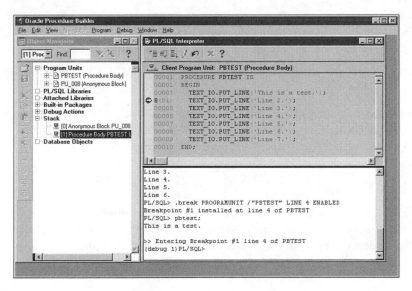

FIGURE 6.4
The PL/SQL Breakpoint dialog is used to help with debugging.

The breakpoint is new and should be enabled as indicated on the first line of the dialog. The Program Unit text field indicates the program unit to which the breakpoint is to be applied. This field should be automatically filled in with /"PBTEST". If you are working with multiple PL/SQL program units, you will want to verify this value. The Line field indicates the line for the breakpoint to be set. If you selected the wrong line in the PL/SQL Interpreter, the Line field is where you can to correct your mistake. Finally, you have the option of providing a trigger. Ignore this option for now.

Because everything is filled out correctly, click OK and you will see a breakpoint icon in the code display pane. In the interactive pane below, run the procedure with the PBTEST; command. You will see the first line print, followed by a message about the first breakpoint as shown in Figure 6.5.

FIGURE 6.5
The PL/SQL Interpreter running in debug mode.

The PL/SQL Interpreter toolbar has several tools to help with the debug process. They are as follows:

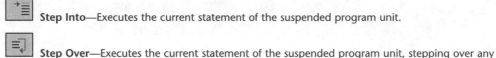 **Step Into**—Executes the current statement of the suspended program unit.

Step Over—Executes the current statement of the suspended program unit, stepping over any calls to nested subprograms.

Step Out—Resumes execution of a nested subprogram, suspending execution at the next executable statement in the calling program unit.

Go—Continues execution of the current program unit to the end of the program or the next breakpoint.

Reset—Exits the current debug level.

Close—Closes the PL/SQL Interpreter window. This is disabled during the debug process.

Help—Invokes the Help system.

Step to the next line in the program using the Step Into button. You will see "Line 2." displayed with a message that the debugger is now at line 5 of the program. In the code display pane, there is an arrow indicating the next line to be executed.

Step to the next line in the program using the Step Over button. You can see that, in this instance, the Step Over button has the same effect as the Step Into button. Now try Step Out. Clicking the Step Out button executes the rest of the program, as would clicking the Go button.

Run the program one more time. This time, click the Reset button. Notice how program execution terminates and the given message states "Resetting to debug level 0...".

After your brief introduction to the debugger, you are now ready to eliminate the breakpoint. This is done by double-clicking on the breakpoint icon in the code display pane. You can now run the program to completion without stopping at the breakpoint.

The Object Navigator

The Object Navigator is included with several of the different programs bundled with Oracle Developer. It is also included with Procedure Builder to help the developer visualize the various PL/SQL objects used in application creation. As you worked through the previous examples in this chapter, you probably noticed all sorts of objects being highlighted and selected.

All the objects created with Procedure Builder are local to the client machine. This is handy when testing and debugging procedures, functions, and packages. However, that PL/SQL code remains on the client and is not used in the database. After you test a procedure or function and verify that it does what it was created to do, you might want to add it to the database. This is done with the aid of the Object Navigator.

To add the sample procedure you have been working on to the database, you need to make sure that you are logged in to the scott/tiger account. Next, expand the Database Objects section in the Object Navigator. You should see a bunch of database users. Expand the SCOTT user's objects. Select PBTEST in the Program Units section of the Object Navigator, and drag it down to the Stored Program Units for the SCOTT user. PBTEST is now stored in the database and can be used outside the Procedure Builder.

Unfortunately, the example you have been working on contains PUT_LINE statements that don't execute very well in the database. To remove the procedure from the database, simply select it in the Object Navigator and click on the Delete button found on the Object Navigator's vertical toolbar. Notice that even though the procedure is deleted from the database, it is still available in the client Procedure Builder.

The Syntax Palette

There is one more tool in the Procedure Builder that is helpful for building PL/SQL code. That helpful tool is the Syntax Palette and it is shown in Figure 6.6. Use the Program, Syntax Palette menu option to invoke it.

FIGURE 6.6
The Syntax Palette included with Procedure Builder.

The Syntax Palette is there to help when you have forgotten the syntax for one of the statements you want to use in your code. Across the top is the tab bar, which allows you to choose between PL/SQL commands and built-in procedures or functions.

Invoking the Syntax Palette from the Program Unit Editor allows you to insert code segments directly from the palette into the editor. This template text can then be modified as needed by your application code.

There are many different statements, procedures, and functions that can be added to your code. The pull-down list below the tabs is meant to reduce the amount of information overload associated with all the statements, procedures, and functions available in PL/SQL. The initial value is set to Blocks. Looking at the pull-down list reveals many different topics under which statements are listed. Selecting the Control Flow topic allows you to see examples of IF-THEN and IF-THEN-ELSE statements.

The built-in help provided by the Syntax Palette dramatically reduces the need to memorize all the various commands. It also facilitates looking up the different statements and syntax notation. If you find yourself wondering about a certain language feature, the Syntax Palette should be the first place to go for help.

The PL/SQL Language

With a good understanding of the Procedure Builder, you are now ready to dive into PL/SQL and work with some more examples. This section is meant to introduce PL/SQL to application developers with little to no exposure experience. If you are already a seasoned pro, feel free to skip to the next chapter.

Declaring and Using Variables

Being able to declare and use variables is an important part of any programming language. The code in Listing 6.2 provides a good example of how to include variables in your PL/SQL program units.

Listing 6.2   Sample PL/SQL Script That Declares and Uses Variables

```
PROCEDURE vartest IS
  num1 NUMBER;
  txt2 VARCHAR(25);
BEGIN
  num1 := 10;
  txt2 := 'My Company';
  TEXT_IO.PUT_LINE('The customer # is: ' || num1);
  TEXT_IO.PUT_LINE('The company name is: ' || txt2);
END;
```

Two variables are declared between the procedure declaration and the BEGIN statement that denotes the beginning of the procedure body. In this example, num1 is declared as a number and txt2 is declared as variable-length text type, not to exceed 25 characters. Table 6.1 lists possible data types.

Table 6.1   PL/SQL Data Types and Descriptions

Data Type	Description
BINARY_INTEGER	Used to store signed integers. Values are represented as signed binary numbers (unlike NUMBER values), and can be used in calculations without conversion. This can boost performance.
BOOLEAN	Used to store the values of TRUE and FALSE.
CHAR	Used to store fixed-length character data.
CHARACTER	Just another name for CHAR.
DATE	Used to store fixed-length date values.
DEC	NUMBER subtype included for compatibility with ANS/ISO, IBM SQL/DS, and IBM DB2. Also used as an identifier more descriptive than NUMBER.
DECIMAL	NUMBER subtype included for compatibility with ANS/ISO, IBM SQL/DS, and IBM DB2. Also used as an identifier more descriptive than NUMBER.
DOUBLE PRECISION	NUMBER subtype included for compatibility with ANS/ISO, IBM SQL/DS, and IBM DB2. Also used as an identifier more descriptive than NUMBER.
FLOAT	NUMBER subtype included for compatibility with ANS/ISO, IBM SQL/DS, and IBM DB2. Also used as an identifier more descriptive than NUMBER.
INT	NUMBER subtype included for compatibility with ANS/ISO, IBM SQL/DS, and IBM DB2. Also used as an identifier more descriptive than NUMBER.
INTEGER	NUMBER subtype included for compatibility with ANS/ISO, IBM SQL/DS, and IBM DB2. Also used as an identifier more descriptive than NUMBER.
LONG	Used to store variable-length character strings of up to 32760 bytes. You can insert any LONG value into a LONG database, but not vice versa. LONG columns in the database can be up to 2147483647 bytes.
LONG RAW	Used to store binary data up to 32760 bytes. The restriction on LONG database columns also exists for LONG RAW columns.
NATURAL	A subtype of BINARY_INTEGER used to define integers from 0 to 2147483647.
NUMBER	Used to store fixed or floating-point numbers of virtually any size.
NUMERIC	NUMBER subtype included for compatibility with ANS/ISO, IBM SQL/DS, and IBM DB2. Also used as an identifier more descriptive than NUMBER.
POSITIVE	A subtype of BINARY_INTEGER used to define integers from 1 to 2147483647.
RAW	Used to store binary data of up to 32767 bytes in length.
REAL	NUMBER subtype included for compatibility with ANS/ISO, IBM SQL/DS, and IBM DB2. Also used as an identifier more descriptive than NUMBER.
ROWID	Used to store the unique address of rows in a table. This is the fastest way to access a record in the database.
SMALLINT	NUMBER subtype included for compatibility with ANS/ISO, IBM SQL/DS, and IBM DB2. Also used as an identifier more descriptive than NUMBER.

Table 6.1 Continued

Data Type	Description
STRING	Just another name for CHAR.
VARCHAR	Just another name for VARCHAR2.
VARCHAR2	Used to store variable-length character data with a maximum length up to 32767 bytes.

As in the Pascal programming language, := is the assignment operator in PL/SQL. The values 10 and "My Company" are assigned to the variables num1 and txt2, respectively.

The last two lines before the END statement print out static text with the variables. Notice how the Oracle SQL concatenation operator, ||, is used to join them.

Integrating with SQL

The true power of PL/SQL is the ability to interact with the Oracle database using SQL. This section provides three different types of examples. The first example uses non-retrieval statements such as INSERT, UPDATE, and DELETE. The next example uses a single-row SELECT, and the third uses a multi-row SELECT.

All the examples assume that you have a good understanding of the SQL language. If this is not the case, you might want to read over the examples, and supplement your learning with a good SQL tutorial or book.

In Chapter 5, "Query Builder and Schema Builder," you created the CUST table to store customer information. This table will be used for the examples in this section. If you have not created the CUST table, you might want to go back to Chapter 5 and do so now.

Inserts, Updates, and Deletes

The first example involves modifying the previous PL/SQL code in Listing 6.2 to insert a row into the CUST table. This is done by deleting the two PUT_LINE statements and replacing them with the INSERT command as shown in Listing 6.3.

Listing 6.3 Sample PL/SQL Script That Inserts a Row into the CUST Table

```
PROCEDURE instest IS
  num1 NUMBER;
  txt2 VARCHAR(25);
BEGIN
  num1 := 10;
  txt2 := 'My Company';
  INSERT INTO cust(custno, cname) VALUES(num1, txt2);
END;
```

The values for the variables num1 and txt2 are substituted appropriately. Running the program inserts a row into the table. You can verify the INSERT by using the following from within the PL/SQL Interpreter command window:

```
SELECT * FROM cust;
```

To update the row in the CUST table and add an address line, change the INSERT statement to the following UPDATE statement:

```
UPDATE cust SET addr = 'My Address'
WHERE custno = num1;
```

Running the SELECT statement after the procedure has been executed shows the ADDR column has been updated. To delete the newly added row, simply change the UPDATE to the following DELETE statement:

```
DELETE FROM cust WHERE custno = num1;
```

Run the procedure to delete the row from the table.

Single-Row Selects

Querying the database with PL/SQL requires that the returned data be put into variables using the INTO clause. The simplest example of this is a query that returns a single row. Listing 6.4 shows such an example.

Listing 6.4 Sample PL/SQL Script That Queries a Single Row

```
PROCEDURE sstest IS
  num1 NUMBER;
  txt2 VARCHAR(25);
BEGIN
  num1 := 10;
  SELECT dname INTO txt2
    FROM dept WHERE deptno = num1;
  TEXT_IO.PUT_LINE('The Dept name is: ' || txt2);
END;
```

The WHERE clause limits the rows returned because an exact value of the primary key is specified. If more than one row is returned, an error is generated. Therefore, you want to either eliminate all chances of multiple rows being returned or change how the SELECT is done. The next section will show how to do multi-row queries.

Multi-Row Selects

There will be plenty of occasions when you want to select multiple rows from a table. This is accomplished using cursors and a looping construct. PL/SQL requires that multi-row selects declare a cursor that acts as a pointer to the current row being retrieved from the database. You then have a loop that fetches rows out of the database until no more rows are selected.

A cursor is declared in the same place as variables. The following line declares a cursor to retrieve the department number and name from the DEPT table:

```
CURSOR cur1 IS
  SELECT deptno, dname FROM dept;
```

Notice that is no need to define the INTO variables in which to put the values retrieved by the SELECT statement. This is done later in the program.

To use the cursor, open it using the OPEN statement as in the following line:

```
OPEN cur1;
```

When you are finished with the cursor, close it using the following line:

```
CLOSE cur1;
```

PL/SQL uses the LOOP and END LOOP statements to create an infinite loop. The EXIT WHEN <condition> clause is then used to break out of the loop when proper conditions are met. In the case of fetching rows from a table, the condition is met when no more rows are available in the table. The loop structure should look like this:

```
LOOP
  ...
  EXIT WHEN cur1%NOTFOUND;
  ...
END LOOP;
```

With the cursor declared and opened, you can fetch rows into declared variables by using the FETCH command. It is placed inside the loop. The SELECT statement (declared previously) returns two values and they must be assigned to declared variables as shown in the following statement:

```
FETCH cur1 INTO num1, txt2;
```

Putting it all together gives the procedure found in Listing 6.5.

Listing 6.5   Sample PL/SQL Script That Retrieves Multiple Rows from a Table

```
PROCEDURE mstest IS
  num1 NUMBER;
  txt2 VARCHAR(25);
  CURSOR cur1 IS
    SELECT deptno, dname FROM dept;
BEGIN
  OPEN cur1;
  LOOP
    FETCH cur1 INTO num1, txt2;
    EXIT WHEN cur1%NOTFOUND;
    TEXT_IO.PUT_LINE('Deptno = ' || num1);
    TEXT_IO.PUT_LINE('Dname = ' || txt2);
  END LOOP;
  CLOSE cur1;
END;
```

Running the procedure lists the department numbers and names from the DEPT table.

PL/SQL is an extension to the SQL database language and allows you to use data definition commands such as CREATE TABLE and DROP TABLE. This is helpful for creating temporary tables needed for calculations and lookups, but should be used only when necessary.

Common Language Constructs

PL/SQL is a powerful language that can be used to perform many different tasks. This next section provides an overview of some of the more common statements such as IF-THEN-ELSE and FOR-LOOP. As I've mentioned, this is only an introduction to the various language elements.

IF-THEN-ELSE

One of the most common elements found in any programming language is conditional logic or the IF-THEN-ELSE statement. Sometimes the ELSE is omitted, as in the following PL/SQL example:

```
IF department = 'SALES' THEN
  compensation = salary + commission;
END IF;
```

This looks very similar to IF-THEN statements found in other languages. A condition is checked and if it is found to be true, a series of statements is evaluated. If the condition is false, program execution begins following the END IF clause.

Adding an ELSE to the previous example produces the following example:

```
IF department = 'SALES' THEN
  compensation = salary + commission;
ELSE
  compensation = salary;
END IF;
```

Notice how the IF-THEN and ELSE lines are not terminated with a semicolon. Also note that even though the example uses a single statement for the true and false cases, any number of statements could have been used. However, remember to follow good programming style and limit the number of lines to keep the program readable. This can be accomplished with the help of procedures and functions described later in this chapter.

EXIT

The EXIT statement was used previously in the multi-row SELECT example. The simplest form of the EXIT statement is used without a WHEN clause and jumps to the line of code following the next END statement.

EXIT can also be used with conditional statements as in the following example:

```
EXIT WHEN count > 100;
```

This would cause the loop to terminate when the count exceeded 100. In the multi-row SELECT example, the EXIT was used when the cursor returned no more rows.

GOTO

The GOTO command is used with labels that are defined using double less-than (<) and greater-than (>) symbols, as shown in this example:

```
...
GOTO delete_row;
...
<<delete_row>>
...
```

GOTO can be used to jump to labels defined throughout your code. Notice that the label does not require a semicolon terminator.

WHILE-LOOP

The WHILE loop evaluates a condition. If the condition is true, a block of statements is executed before the condition is evaluated again. The block of statements is enclosed with the WHILE clause at the beginning and the END LOOP statement at the end, as in the following example:

```
WHILE total < 5000 LOOP
  total = total + 250;
END LOOP;
```

When the total exceeds 5000, the loop terminates. If total was 5000 before reaching the WHILE loop, none of the statements inside would be executed.

FOR-LOOP

The FOR loop is used to execute a known number of iterations of code. Here is an example:

```
FOR i IN 1..10 LOOP
  TEXT_IO.PUT_LINE('This is time ' || i);
END LOOP
```

The first line uses a counter, "i", that can be used in the loop. Unlike some languages in which the number of iterations can be changed from within the loop, PL/SQL determines the total number of times that the loop will be executed when it is first entered.

NULL

The NULL statement is used to explicitly do nothing. This can be useful for defining stubs of procedures or functions. You can test the function declarations and parameter passing without having to actually include code. NULL is used without any parameters as shown here:

```
NULL;
```

Functions

Functions are like procedures except that functions return values and procedures do not. If you wanted to define a function to calculate the average of two numbers, it would look like Listing 6.6.

Listing 6.6   PL/SQL Script Creating a Function

```
FUNCTION average (num1 NUMBER, num2 NUMBER) RETURN NUMBER IS
  result NUMBER;
BEGIN
  result := (num1 + num2)/2;
  RETURN (result);
END;
```

The function is passed two numbers as described in the first line. The result of this function will be another number. The body performs the calculation and then returns the result as shown in line 5.

This sample function can be called from a procedure as shown in Listing 6.7.

Listing 6.7   PL/SQL Script Calling a Function That Was Created Earlier

```
PROCEDURE functest IS
  num1 NUMBER;
BEGIN
  num1 := average (5, 7);
  TEXT_IO.PUT_LINE('The average of 5 and 7 is ' || num1);
END;
```

Calls to procedures and functions can both take parameters, if necessary. They can also be called from anywhere except from within a SQL statement. Therefore, if you are trying to insert values calculated by a function into a table, be sure to store the calculated value in a variable. Then use the variable in the INSERT statement.

Packages

Packages are a way of storing related PL/SQL program units, objects, and subprograms in the database. For instance, you might have a bunch of procedures used to take care of human resource actions such as hiring and releasing employees. These actions could be encapsulated within a package.

Packages are defined in a two-step process: The first step is to specify what the procedure will contain, and the second is to create the actual code, or body, to do the work. Listing 6.8 creates a package to add and delete employees.

Listing 6.8   PL/SQL Script Creating a Package Header

```
PACKAGE employee IS
  PROCEDURE add_emp(ename VARCHAR2,
                    job   VARCHAR2,
                    sal   NUMBER);
  PROCEDURE del_emp(empid NUMBER);
END;
```

The two procedures add_emp and del_emp are used to add and delete employees from the database, respectively. After the package is defined, the body must be created. Creating a package header and body in two steps allows the user to modify the body, while keeping the header information constant. This enables you to fix bugs or problems with the actual procedures without modifying any of the code that uses the package. Listing 6.9 shows the body of the employee package.

Listing 6.9   PL/SQL Script Creating a Package Body

```
PACKAGE BODY employee IS
  PROCEDURE add_emp(ename VARCHAR2,
                    job   VARCHAR2,
                    sal   NUMBER);
       new_empno NUMBER;
  BEGIN
    SELECT empno_seq.NEXTVAL INTO new_empno FROM dual;
    INSERT INTO emp (empno, ename, job, sal, hiredate)
         VALUES (new_empno, ename, job, sal, SYSDATE);
  END add_emp;

  PROCEDURE del_emp(empid NUMBER);
  BEGIN
    DELETE FROM emp WHERE empno = empid;
  END del_emp;
END employee;
```

The procedures are fairly self-explanatory. Those familiar with the Oracle database will recognize the use of SYSDATE to retrieve the current date in the add_emp procedure.

Database Triggers

Database triggers are PL/SQL program units used by the database to perform actions based on defined database actions. If a new record is added to a table, a corresponding action will be performed.

Unfortunately Procedure Builder does not allow you to create database triggers.

Handling Exceptions

PL/SQL allows you to use exception handling to deal with errors and warnings. There are built-in exceptions such as divide by zero and out of memory errors, but PL/SQL also gives you the ability to create your own exceptions.

Without exception handling, you would be forced to check for errors after every SQL command. With exceptions, you can provide a common set of handlers for a group of SQL commands found within the PL/SQL block.

To use the built-in exceptions, simply add the appropriate handlers at the end of the PL/SQL block as shown in Listing 6.10.

Listing 6.10   PL/SQL Script with Exception Handling

```
PROCEDURE etest (deptid NUMBER) IS
  department VARCHAR2(25);
  err_num number;
BEGIN
  SELECT dname INTO department FROM dept WHERE deptno = deptid;
  TEXT_IO.PUT_LINE('Department name is: ' || department);
EXCEPTION
  WHEN NO_DATA_FOUND THEN
    TEXT_IO.PUT_LINE('There is no department with that number.');
  WHEN OTHERS THEN
    err_num := SQLCODE;
    TEXT_IO.PUT_LINE('Error: ' || err_num);
END;
```

When you run the procedure, it will list the department name for a given department number. If an invalid department number is given, the NO_DATA_FOUND exception is raised. It is also good practice to include an error handler for any other errors that might occur. Displaying the error number will help you figure out the problem. Table 6.2 lists some common built-in exceptions.

Table 6.2   PL/SQL Built-in Exceptions

Exception	Description
CURSOR_ALREADY_OPEN	You are trying to open an already open cursor. You must close a cursor before reopening it.
DUP_VAL_ON_INDEX	You are trying to store duplicate values in a column with a unique index (for example, primary key).
INVALID_CURSOR	You are trying an illegal cursor operation such as closing an unopened cursor.
INVALID_NUMBER	A SQL statement contains an invalid number conversion.
LOGIN_DENIED	You are trying to log in to the Oracle database with an invalid user-name or password.
NO_DATA_FOUND	A SELECT returns no data.
NOT_LOGGED_ON	You are not logged in to the Oracle database.
PROGRAM_ERROR	PL/SQL has an internal problem.
STORAGE_ERROR	PL/SQL has run out of memory or memory is corrupted.
TIMEOUT_ON_RESOURCE	A timeout occurred while waiting for an Oracle database resource.
TOO_MANY_ROWS	A SELECT INTO returns more than one row.
TRANSACTION_BACKED_OUT	The remote part of a transaction has been rolled back.
VALUE_ERROR	An arithmetic, conversion, truncation, or constraint error has occurred.
ZERO_DIVIDE	You are trying to divide a number by zero.

The predefined exceptions can be helpful in PL/SQL programs. However, you will want to be able to create your own exceptions. You can create your own exceptions with the following steps:

1. Declare the exception

2. Raise the exception

3. Handle the exception

Listing 6.11 gives an example of a user-defined exception.

Listing 6.11   PL/SQL Script with User-Defined Exceptions

```
PROCEDURE uetest (deptid NUMBER) IS
  department VARCHAR2(25);
  unused_dep EXCEPTION;
BEGIN
  SELECT dname INTO department FROM dept WHERE deptno = deptid;
  IF department = 'OPERATIONS' THEN
    RAISE unused_dep;
  END IF;
  TEXT_IO.PUT_LINE('Department name is: ' || department);
EXCEPTION
  WHEN NO_DATA_FOUND THEN
    TEXT_IO.PUT_LINE('There is no department with that number.');
  WHEN unused_dep THEN
    TEXT_IO.PUT_LINE('Unused department OPERATIONS.');
END;
```

The exception unused_dep is declared before the beginning of the procedure body. Then an IF-THEN statement tests whether the exception should be raised. Finally, there is the exception handler at the end of the procedure body.

Those developers who are used to exception handling will enjoy this capability in PL/SQL. Those developers who have not had much experience using exceptions will find them easy to use and helpful with the projects they are working on.

PL/SQL in Developer

PL/SQL is used extensively in Oracle Developer 6i. I've mentioned that PL/SQL can be used in the database for stored procedures, functions, packages, and triggers. This is helpful for centralizing common business rules that will be enforced independently of the application code.

Forms and Reports will also use PL/SQL to handle all user interaction. If you have a button on a form, PL/SQL will be used to program the desired actions when the button is clicked. It will also be used to validate text field entries and provide complex calculations for reports.

There are many different predefined functions and procedures built into Developer to help you create applications. Although a good understanding of PL/SQL definitely will be helpful, it is not required for building most applications. The majority of application PL/SQL code will be only one or two lines.

LEARNING PL/SQL

My first experience with PL/SQL was when Oracle moved from version 2.3 of SQL*Forms to version 3.0. I was so used to massaging the archaic trigger syntax that I was reluctant to use PL/SQL. Forms 3.0 supported Forms 2.3 trigger syntax so that you could migrate existing forms to the new version. However, once the forms were migrated, the triggers could not be modified or even seen. This made it necessary to learn PL/SQL.

One thing that helped me learn PL/SQL was that I was the Oracle expert working for a financial consulting firm in Seattle. Not only was I supposed to design and create Oracle applications, but I was also responsible for teaching the other consultants how to become Oracle experts. When you are learning for yourself, you have the luxury of being able to gloss over some of the details. When you are responsible for teaching others, you have to know the material.

Tuesdays and Thursdays after lunch I would spend an hour teaching my coworkers about Oracle and PL/SQL. Most of the material I could put together without much thought. When it came time to teach PL/SQL, I was concerned. I spent the weekend coming in and running examples on the system so I would know the answers to all of the questions. I also worked through lunch preparing the hour long lessons. When it came time to teach the PL/SQL lessons, everyone thought I had been using it for years.

The moral of the story is that if you want to really learn something, learn it so that you can teach it to someone else. If you are having trouble with a particular topic in this book, go through the examples and then try to teach the skill to someone else. It doesn't matter if your coworker knows the material already. The act of trying to explain it to someone else will help you learn the material more completely.

Summary

In this chapter, you were given a brief overview of Procedure Builder and the PL/SQL database programming language. You should be able to use Procedure Builder to help create PL/SQL procedures and functions. You were also introduced to packages and how to create them. This information will help you create your applications by allowing you to encapsulate business rules into the database as well as how to create your forms and reports.

USING JAVA WITH ORACLE DEVELOPER AND THE ORACLE DATABASE

ESSENTIALS —————————————

- The Oracle database allows you to use Java for creating store procedures and database triggers. Oracle Developer allows you to include Java Beans in your Forms applications.

- Creating a stored procedure using Java involves creating the Java class, loading the class, and publishing the class. You can then call the stored procedure as you would with PL/SQL.

- Oracle provides the loadjava utility to load the compiled Java class into the database.

- Publishing the Java class involves using alternative syntax for the CREATE FUNCTION or CREATE PROCEDURE command in SQL.

- Use JDBC to perform database operations in Java based stored procedures and database triggers.

Oracle has recognized the value and popularity of the Java programming language. Some of the benefits of the Java language include

- **Automatic storage management**—Java does not require programmers to allocate or free memory. This is a welcome feature to those constantly battling the memory leaks that sometimes happen with C and C++.

- **Exception handling**—The advantages of exception handling were discussed in the previous chapter. Exceptions are a convenient way to handle error conditions without being required to check the result of every statement.

- **No pointers**—Java passes all parameters (except primitive types) by reference as opposed to by value. This eliminates the requirement for pointers and also eliminates the possibility of memory corruption and leaks.

- **Portability**—Java was designed to run on any platform that supports a JVM (Java virtual machine). That means if you create a program in Windows, it will run without modification on any other platform that has a JVM.

- **Security**—The byte-code created by compiling a Java program has built-in mechanisms to ensure that it has not been tampered with. This eliminates the possibility for viruses.

- **Strong typing** —The type of a variable must be explicitly declared before using it to store an object. This eliminates the possibility of writing data to invalid memory locations.

This chapter gives you an overview of how to use the Java programming language with the Oracle database and Oracle Developer. It is not meant to be a tutorial on Java, so none of the language elements are discussed. All the examples are simple so that even a novice Java developer will be able to understand.

Mixing Java and Oracle

Oracle 8i was the first version of the Oracle database to integrate a Java virtual machine (JVM). It offered the ability to create stored procedures in Java as well as in PL/SQL. This gave application developers who were familiar with Java but new to PL/SQL an easier way to create stored procedures and triggers. Both PL/SQL and Java continue to be natively supported by the database, eliminating any performance concerns.

Oracle Developer 6i provides a way to include Java code in both forms and reports. You will most likely use Java objects in forms and reports deployed on the Web. This enables you to use a Java Bean in place of another standard form object. A Java Bean is a reusable object written in Java that can be manipulated visually. If you didn't like the look and behavior of a standard push button, you could create a new one using a Java Bean.

SHOULD I REALLY USE JAVA WITH ORACLE?

Java has evolved a lot since that early version, but I still hear experienced developers asking if they really should use Java for developing Oracle applications. Some are concerned about execution speed for Java. However, most are concerned about giving up PL/SQL in favor of this new language the developer has yet to learn.

It would be nice to come up with a single answer that would fit for all situations. Unfortunately, that is not possible. I am a firm believer in the saying "When your only tool is a hammer, you tend to treat all your problems as nails." Java is one tool in your arsenal of development tools that has specific uses. PL/SQL is another tool that has some similar uses to Java, but also some that are different.

I was working on a project in which a mix of both Java and PL/SQL stored procedures was the right solution. The application used the database to store large amounts of numerical data. This data was then run through complex mathematical computations that were originally written using publicly available libraries. It was much easier to create stored procedures and functions using Java than it was to use PL/SQL.

In the same application, it was necessary to perform a lot of database operations. For these stored procedures, it was easier to use PL/SQL.

By combining the two languages, we were able to create a complex application. Trying to stick to one language or the other would have complicated things too much and put us behind schedule.

Which language should you use? I would have to say that it depends on your application, timeframe, and experience with PL/SQL or Java. Only you can decide which is best for your environment and application.

This chapter provides some examples for creating stored procedures using Java. It also provides some guidelines for building objects to be used in forms and reports.

Creating Stored Procedures with Java

The greatest advantage of using Java to create stored procedures and database triggers is that it is a language you might already know. If you are familiar with Java but new to PL/SQL, I recommend that you use Java for stored procedures and database triggers. Oracle claims that performance between a Java stored procedure and a PL/SQL stored procedure should be almost identical.

Developers familiar with Oracle's PL/SQL will probably want to continue using it for stored procedures and functions. There is talk from Oracle, however, about replacing PL/SQL with Java. Therefore, it is in your best interest to go through this chapter, even if you are a PL/SQL expert.

A Simple Stored Procedure

The first example shows you the basics of creating a stored procedure using Java. There are four steps to follow:

1. Create the Java class
2. Load the Java class

3. Publish the Java class

4. Call the stored procedure

Create the Java Class

Procedure Builder cannot be used to create stored procedures written in Java. However, you can use your favorite Java interactive development environment (IDE), such as Oracle's JDeveloper or Borland's JBuilder. The example in this section is only six lines, so you can use your favorite editor.

This is not a Java tutorial, so the example is brief. Listing 7.1 shows a public Java class that returns a simple statement.

Listing 7.1 *Public Java Class That Returns a Simple Statement*

```
public class Emplist {
  public static String topemp() {
    return "KING is the top employee.";
  }
}
```

The class contains a method that returns a string informing the user that "KING is the top employee." With the class typed in, save it as Emplist.java and compile it to Java bytecode using javac or the equivalent for your environment.

A JAVA DEVELOPMENT ENVIRONMENT

If you do not have a Java development environment on your system, you can download one from Sun's Web site at java.sun.com.

You should now have two files in your directory: Emplist.java and Emplist.class.

Load the Java Class

With the class file created, you are ready to load it into the database. Make sure that the database you are using is Oracle 8i and that the Java option is installed.

A simple way to verify that the Java option has been properly installed is to log in to the database using SQL*Plus. At login, you should get a message telling you the version of JServer in use. This is your indication that things are working properly.

The Oracle database includes a command-line tool called loadjava. It does not come with Oracle Developer 6i. If you will be creating stored procedures using Java, you will want to install the database tools on your client machine. Otherwise, you will have to transfer the Java class file to the database machine (or other machine with the proper database tools) and load it from there.

The loadjava program uses the following syntax:

```
loadjava -user <username>/<password> <class_name>.class
```

The scott username and tiger password will work fine for this sample application. The class name is Emplist.class.

Running the loadjava program should not produce any output. When the program has loaded the Java class into the database, the command prompt will return and this step is completed.

Publish the Java Class

Those developers familiar with Java will recognize that the sample program contains the method topemp. To allow this method to be called from SQL or PL/SQL, a call specification must be created. Call specs can be generated automatically from Oracle's JDeveloper, or you can create them yourself.

To create a call spec, log in to the Oracle database using SQL*Plus. Make sure that you are connected to the scott/tiger account. Because the sample Java class returns a value, the call spec will specify a stored function rather than a stored procedure. To create the call spec, run the following SQL statement:

```
CREATE FUNCTION emplist_topemp RETURN VARCHAR2
AS LANGUAGE JAVA
NAME 'Emplist.topemp() return java.lang.String';
```

WORKING WITH THE SQL*PLUS EDITOR

When you type this statement into the SQL*Plus editor, you might get a 4> prompt after the third line. Press Ctrl+C to get the SQL prompt. Press the L key followed by the Enter key to list the CREATE FUNC-TION command and make sure that you have typed it in correctly (including the ending semicolon). Then press the R key followed by the Enter key to run the command.

Running the CREATE FUNCTION command create the call spec and publishes the class so that it is available for use by SQL and PL/SQL statements and code.

Notice how similar the first line is to the average function you saw in Chapter 6, "Procedure Builder and PL/SQL." The second line specifies that the function uses Java instead of PL/SQL. The third line gives the name of the class and the method to use. There is also a conversion that must take place from the Java string that is returned to the VARCHAR2 string that SQL and PL/SQL expects.

Call the Stored Procedure or Function

You are now ready to run the stored procedure. Because this example returns a text string, it is necessary to create a variable to hold the result. From within SQL*Plus, create the variable using the following command:

```
VARIABLE theTextOutput VARCHAR2(50);
```

You are ready to run the stored procedure. This is done with the following:

```
CALL emplist_topemp() INTO :theTextOutput;
```

The Java stored procedure runs and the output is placed into the variable theTextOutput. If you do not use the INTO keyword to store the result, you will get an error message saying, "Not a valid function or procedure name."

This example is meant to give you an overview of the steps to create a stored procedure written in Java. It is probably too simple, and you might have questions about how to interact with the database. That is shown in the next example.

Using SQL with Java Stored Procedures

The next example uses JDBC to insert a row into the customer table. There was a similar example in Chapter 6 using PL/SQL, but this time the stored procedure takes two parameters: the customer number and name. These values are then inserted into the CUST table as shown in Listing 7.2.

Listing 7.2   Java Code Using JDBC to Insert a Row into the Customer Table

```
import java.sql.*;
import java.io.*;
import oracle.jdbc.driver.*;

public class CustProc {
  public static void custins (int c_num, String c_name) throws SQLException {
    Connection  conn =
      DriverManager.getConnection("jdbc:default:connection:");
    String sql = "INSERT INTO cust(custno, cname)
                ➡VALUES (" + c_num + ",'" + c_name + "')";
    try {
      Statement stmt = conn.createStatement();
      stmt.executeUpdate(sql);
      stmt.close();
    } catch (SQLException e) {System.err.println(e.getMessage());}
  }
}
```

Those familiar with JDBC will recognize the commands to connect to the database and to create the SQL statement. Compile the program in Listing 7.3 and load it into the Oracle database with the loadjava command.

If you get an error saying "oracle.jdbc.driver cannot be found," make sure that you are using the proper CLASSPATH to the classes111.zip file provided with Oracle.

Next, log in to the database with SQL*Plus and create the call specification. This is done using the following statement:

```
CREATE PROCEDURE custins (
   c_num NUMBER,
   c_name VARCHAR2)
AS LANGUAGE JAVA
NAME 'CustProc.custins(int, java.lang.String)';
```

Notice how the stored procedure can use the same name as the method in the class. Also notice that the String data type must be prefaced with "java.lang." whereas the int data type does not.

You can run the procedure with the following command:

```
call custins(33, 'My New Customer');
```

Querying the database will reveal the new row added to the CUST table.

This chapter is meant to introduce you to creating stored procedures using Java. Oracle provides the document "Java Stored Procedures Developer Guide" to help you if you have more questions. You may also want to pick up a copy of *Oracle Java Development* by Bulusu Lakshman (ISBN 0-672-321-173).

Dropping a Stored Procedure Written in Java

The original stored function example at the beginning of the chapter does not really need to be kept in the database. Because it is no longer needed, it would be nice to delete it. This is as a two-step process:

1. Drop the procedure or function
2. Unload the Java class

To drop the procedure, use the following command:

```
DROP FUNCTION emplist_topemp;
```

As is generally the case with Oracle database objects, dropping or deleting them is much simpler than creating them.

To unload the Java class from the database, you use the dropjava command-line tool. Type the following:

```
dropjava -user scott/tiger Emplist.class
```

The database no longer contains the Java code. As you develop Java stored procedures, you might discover that Java code compiles correctly, but does not run perfectly. You might be required to drop the call spec as well as the class bytecode in order to fix the problem.

Using Java with Oracle Developer

Oracle Developer enables you to use Java Beans in your forms and reports. A *Java Bean* is a reusable software component that can be manipulated visually. In the simplest form, it can be a Java 1.1 AWT individual component (for example, a button to click on with the mouse). Java Beans can be much more complex, and include objects such as embeddable spreadsheets and word processors. The example that Oracle includes with Developer is a juggling clown.

Developers using the client/server deployment method generally choose to use the native visual components provided by Oracle Developer. Java Beans most likely will be employed with applications using the Web deployment method. Chapter 13, "Deploying Developer Applications to the Web," discusses Web deployment in detail. Therefore, this section of the book will highlight considerations that must be taken into account when creating beans.

In the Web deployment method, users interact with a Java applet called WebForms. The WebForms applet communicates with interface elements (for instance, a radio button group) using a handler class. The handler class then communicates with the visual representation of the interface element using a second view class.

The WebForms applet dynamically loads the implementation classes as it needs them. Therefore, the classes must be available on the Web server in a JAR file.

The following steps should be followed when creating a custom interface element:

1. Write the custom interface element using a view class that implements the FView interface

2. Put the program files in a JAR file on the server relative to the code base directory

3. Set the Implementation Class property in the item's property sheet to the name of the view class

Listing 7.4 shows the definition of the FView interface that must be used for the custom interface element.

Listing 7.4   The Definition of the FView Interface Used for the Custom Interface Element

```
public interface FView {
  public void init (FHandler handler);
  public void destroy();
  public Object getProperty (ID id);
  public boolean setProperty (ID id, Object value);
  public void addListener (Class type, EventListener listener);
  public void removeListener (Class type, EventListener listener);
  public void paint (Graphics g);
  public void repaint (Rectangle r);
}
```

The WebForms applet expects the FView constructor to take no arguments. Following is a list of the methods and a brief description for each.

```
public void init (FHandler handler)
```

This is the handler called after the WebForms applet constructs the object. The handler is passed by reference to the view object and given the opportunity to perform initialization.

```
public void destroy ()
```

Destroys or eliminates the object and releases any system resources.

```
public Object getProperty (ID id)
```

Returns the value of the requested property.

```
public boolean setProperty (ID id, Object value)
```

Sets the value of the named property. If the object supports the named property, the method returns TRUE. Otherwise, it returns FALSE.

```
public void addListener (class type, EventListener listener)
```

Adds the listener of the named type to the view object.

```
public void removeListener (Class type, EventListener listener)
```

Removes the listener of the named type from the view object.

```
public void paint (Graphics g)
```

Paints the view object using the specified AWT Graphics object.

```
public void repaint (Rectangle r)
```

Repaints the specified rectangle. If the rectangle is NULL, it repaints the entire object.

Those developers familiar with Java Beans and custom interface objects should now have a rough understanding of what to add them to Web-deployed applications. Chapter 8, "Using Graphical Elements in Forms," further exposes the properties and methods used by forms. Chapter 13 discusses the deployment of Web-based applications.

Summary

This chapter showed you how to use Java to create stored procedures. You were given a simple example that was easy to follow and that didn't use any SQL database object manipulations. A second example used JDBC to connect to the database and insert a row into the CUST table.

At the end of the chapter, you were introduced to using Java for custom form objects in Web-based applications. You were shown the FView class definition that must be implemented for the WebForms applet to communicate with your custom interface object.

If you are doing extensive work with Oracle and Java, you might want to pick up a copy of Bulusu Lakshman's book called *Oracle and Java Development*. It is also published by Sams Publishing and its ISBN is 0-672-321-173.

USING GRAPHICAL
ELEMENTS IN FORMS

ESSENTIALS ————————————————————

- The Forms Builder runtime environment automatically builds in many of the features your application will need to ensure data integrity and complete database functionality.

- The runtime environment allows you to perform queries using all the conditional operators (that is, <, >, <=, >=, !=, and so on).

- It is possible to create a form manually. However, if you plan to access database information with the form, it is much easier to use the wizards and then modify the nearly completed form to meet your specifications.

- Calculation fields can be included on your form by adding the formula in the Property Palette. You will also want to make sure that you change the database property so that the form does not try to perform database operations on the calculated field.

- Various graphical elements can be added to your form. These can include static images, push buttons, list items, check boxes, and radio buttons.

- Running the form in the debugger can help find and eliminate problems with any PL/SQL used in your form.

- A list of values (LOV) can be used to look up possible values for a specific field. An advantage that an LOV has over list values is that it can be more complex and descriptive.

- Dialog boxes can be added to your form to help communicate information to the user.

In Chapter 2, "Developer Basics," you were introduced to Form Builder and used it to create a simple form. Chapter 3, "Oracle Forms Developer," gave you an even broader understanding by having you create a master-detail form. This chapter goes into much more detail about Forms Developer and how to use it to create forms using the different graphical elements available.

This chapter starts out with an in-depth overview of the client/server runtime environment and all the functionality built into a default form. Next, the discussion covers more detail about what the various wizards do and how to incorporate the many different GUI elements. This will require some of the PL/SQL that was discussed in Chapter 6, "Procedure Builder and PL/SQL." The text also introduces you to the Forms Debugger and shows you how to use it.

At this point, you should have a good understanding of Form Builder and how to create fairly complex forms. You should be able to use the Data Block and Layout Wizards. If not, you might want to review the examples in Chapter 2 and 3.

The Forms Runtime Environment

The examples up to this point have talked about the client/server runtime environment, but have not gone into much detail. Even if you plan to use the Web deployment method, the information in this section will help you understand the complexity that goes into building a database application.

Build a quick form using the CUST table to use as an example. Remember to use the Data Block Wizard and include all the columns from the table. After the form is built, it should look very similar to Figure 8.1.

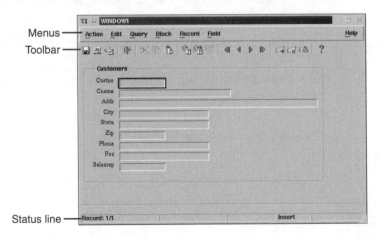

FIGURE 8.1
A quick default form for the CUST table.

Closely look at all the visual elements automatically added to the form. Also included are unseen features that are crucial to data integrity and proper behavior of the form. After discussing the visual environment, I will explain these hidden features.

The Visual Runtime Environment

Some important things to notice about the visual environment are the menus, the toolbar, and the status and message lines at the bottom. All these elements are bundled into the form without any work by the application developer.

The Status and Message Lines

Two lines are reserved at the bottom of the client/server runtime environment form. The top line is used for error and informational messages. For example, if you enter a query, instructions on how to complete the query are displayed in the message line. Also note that if there is a database error, it is displayed in the same message area.

The status line is the bottom line of the form and contains important information. With a simple form, this line tracks rows inserted, rows queried, and whether typing replaces or inserts text. Forms with complex features such as a list of values (LOV) use the status line to indicate that the feature is available (LOVs are covered later in this chapter).

The Toolbar

The client/server runtime environment toolbar is optimized for database transactions. It is shown in Figure 8.2 with short descriptions of each tool.

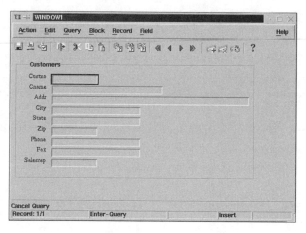

FIGURE 8.2
The client/server runtime environment default toolbar.

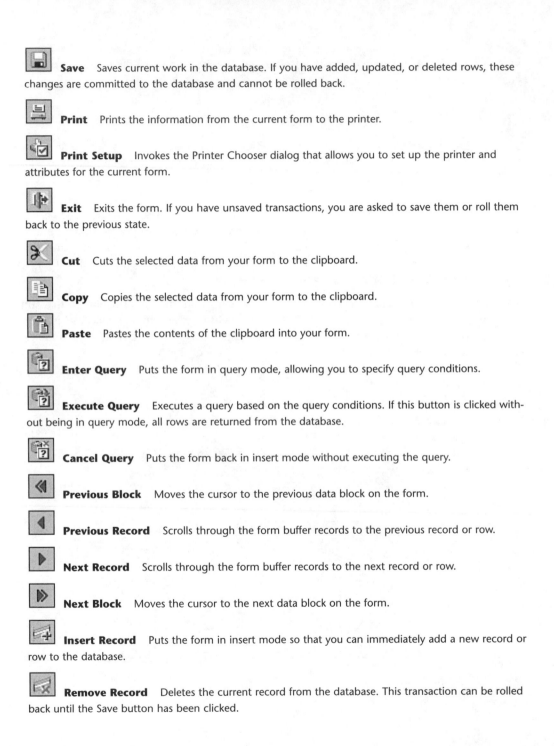

Save   Saves current work in the database. If you have added, updated, or deleted rows, these changes are committed to the database and cannot be rolled back.

Print   Prints the information from the current form to the printer.

Print Setup   Invokes the Printer Chooser dialog that allows you to set up the printer and attributes for the current form.

Exit   Exits the form. If you have unsaved transactions, you are asked to save them or roll them back to the previous state.

Cut   Cuts the selected data from your form to the clipboard.

Copy   Copies the selected data from your form to the clipboard.

Paste   Pastes the contents of the clipboard into your form.

Enter Query   Puts the form in query mode, allowing you to specify query conditions.

Execute Query   Executes a query based on the query conditions. If this button is clicked without being in query mode, all rows are returned from the database.

Cancel Query   Puts the form back in insert mode without executing the query.

Previous Block   Moves the cursor to the previous data block on the form.

Previous Record   Scrolls through the form buffer records to the previous record or row.

Next Record   Scrolls through the form buffer records to the next record or row.

Next Block   Moves the cursor to the next data block on the form.

Insert Record   Puts the form in insert mode so that you can immediately add a new record or row to the database.

Remove Record   Deletes the current record from the database. This transaction can be rolled back until the Save button has been clicked.

Lock Record Locks the current record in the database so that it can't be updated by another user until the Save button has been clicked.

? **Help** Displays information about the current field or block that might be useful to the user.

Take some time to go through this simple application and play with the different tools on the toolbar. Notice how the Previous Block and Next Block tools don't provide any additional functionality because the example is only a single-block form. You might try running one of the previous multiblock examples created in Chapter 3.

The Menus

The toolbar provides access to those tasks that are commonly required by the application user. However, those developers familiar with database forms will realize that some additional functionality that must be accessed. This is done through the menu system.

Most of the menu choices are easily accessible through the toolbar or GUI interaction. There are one or two, however, that require some explanation.

One of the most important functions in any software environment is the ability to undo a mistake. In database terms, this is known as a *rollback*. The user has the ability to undo any non-saved or uncommitted transactions using the Action, Clear All menu choice. When the user clicks on the tool, he or she is presented with the option of saving changes or rolling them back. This confirmation dialog prevents the user from accidentally performing a rollback.

An area in which problems might occur is in doing queries. The most easily discovered problem is the retrieval of too many rows from the database. Use the Query, Count Hits menu choice to see how many rows will be returned for the given criteria. If you intentionally use a query that generates a significant number of rows, the forms buffer will fill to capacity. This will require you to use the Query, Fetch Next Set menu choice to continue retrieving records from the database.

Another query feature that is often helpful is the ability to use the previous conditions for a new search. This is done by clicking on the Enter Query button and using the Query, Last Criteria menu choice. The previous search conditions will be included in the form.

The Help menu included in the runtime environment might be confusing to some, so it merits some explanation. Forms Developer has been around for many different versions and runs on a variety of platforms. Oracle discovered early on that not all keyboards look the same, so it was impossible to describe key combinations for all the different computer systems. Therefore, all the documentation referring to keyboards uses generic labels. For instance, the COMMIT key on a VT 220 keyboard has always been the Do key. The Do key does not exist on a PC keyboard, so it was mapped to another key sequence. The GUI environment eliminated the reliance on so many key sequences, but is not good enough to eliminate them entirely. The Help, Keys menu choice brings up a dialog to show the various key shortcuts for your computing environment.

Finally, there is a chance that a user will encounter an error message from the database when running an application. A short message appears, letting the user know that something is wrong. Sometimes this short message is of little help in letting you, the application developer, know what the real problem is. In that case, you can use the Help, Display Error menu choice to see the true Oracle error message. It will be cryptic to the untrained user, but extremely helpful to an Oracle application developer like you.

The WHEN OTHERS exception handler is a great place to print out Oracle error codes for unexpected errors encountered during runtime. This eliminates the need to use the Display Error menu choice.

Take some time and play with the sample form in the runtime environment to get a better understanding of some of the menu choices.

Hidden Features of the Runtime Environment

Certain built-in features of the client/server runtime environment do not appear visually. The first feature has to do with row locking to ensure data integrity, whereas the second feature involves complex queries. The next two sections provide some insight into these features, complete with some examples for you to try.

Locking and Data Integrity

One of the reasons that application developers stopped working with flat files and moved to database environments is the ability to ensure data integrity. What happens when two people try to edit the same record? Should the first user be able to modify it and not the second? Or vice versa? The answer to these questions is provided by database locks. When one user locks a row, that row is not updateable by another user. Here is an example to try using the sample form on the CUST table:

1. Enter information for a fictitious customer using the sample form. Use a CUSTNO of 10.

2. Save the row in the table using the Save button on the toolbar.

3. Click the Execute Query button on the toolbar. You should see the previously entered company in the form.

4. Click the Lock Record button on the toolbar.

5. Log in to the database using SQL*Plus from another window on your screen. Execute the following SQL command:

```
UPDATE cust SET cname = 'New Name' WHERE custno = 10;
```

SQL*Plus should wait patiently trying to update the record. However, it will wait until you click the Save button in the runtime window's toolbar. The record you are trying to update is locked by the form and can't be changed until the row is unlocked (which happens on a commit or save). After the commit takes place (and a warning message says that no changes were made), the update in SQL*Plus should execute fine. Saving a record, even though no changes were made, releases the lock on the table.

Without doing anything else in SQL*Plus, try to add something to the ADDR column. You will get an error dialog that says, "Could not reserve record ..." This error occurs because the UPDATE command run in SQL*Plus has not been committed. To do so, run the following command in SQL*Plus:

```
COMMIT;
```

Now all the locks are released. To see the change made by SQL*Plus, you must execute another query in the form.

In the steps listed previously, you locked a row in the CUST table using the Lock Record button on the toolbar. However, you are not required to use the Lock Record button to lock a row in a table. The default form that you created automatically locks the current record whenever you try to make a change to it. Use the following steps to verify this:

1. Enter information for a fictitious customer using the sample form. Use a CUSTNO of 20.

2. Save the row in the table using the Save button on the toolbar.

3. Click the Execute Query button on the toolbar. Use the down-arrow and up-arrow keys to scroll to the customer with a CUSTNO of 20.

4. Update one field for the new customer.

5. Log in to the database using SQL*Plus from another window on your screen. Execute the following SQL command:

```
UPDATE cust SET cname = 'New Name' WHERE custno = 20;
```

Again, the UPDATE command in SQL*Plus cannot execute until the commit frees the lock. Go ahead and free up all the locks as you did with the previous example.

The client/server runtime environment provides locking to maintain data integrity. It is well thought-out and should not be taken for granted when developing your own applications.

Complicated Queries

Most of the time, a user will be able to query information from the database using an exact match. A salesperson can query her customers by providing the exact customer names or numbers. Sometimes, however, this is not what the application user is looking for. Perhaps she wants to see all the customers who have generated more than $2 million in sales and she doesn't have time to wait for a report to be written.

The query form understands greater-than and less-than symbols to help execute these kinds of queries. In the sample form, click on the Enter Query button. Then enter >15 as shown in Figure 8.3.

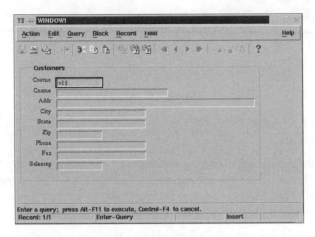

FIGURE 8.3
Entering a query using conditional operators other than the equal sign (=) is possible in the runtime environment.

Executing the query should produce the customer with a CUSTNO of 20. You can also use the other numerical conditional operators in your queries (such as <=, >=, !=, and so on).

There is also the case in which you do not remember the exact customer name, but you remember some substring of it. For this, you can use the % wildcard character. If you have a customer whose name appears in the database as "My Company, Inc.", you can do a search for the customer name using "%Company%" in the query field.

Although this discussion doesn't list all the functionality available for doing queries, it does give you an idea of some of the more common features. The client/server runtime environment is fairly robust and provides a lot of default functionality with little to no additional programming.

A Final Word About the Runtime Environment

This concludes the examples using the runtime environment. Feel free to close all forms and exit from the Form Builder program. You don't need to save any of the forms; they will not be used again.

You should be very familiar with Forms Developer's client/server default runtime environment. The automatically generated toolbar contains tools to help with most of the functionality that your users will require. There are some additional menu choices to help users recover from mistakes and to help them do their work. Also built into the environment are locking (to maintain data integrity) and a powerful query engine (to help display database information).

Now you are ready to dive into Forms Developer and really learn how to create spectacular applications.

Creating a Form Manually

Up to this point, you have relied on the various wizards to help build your forms and reports. Now it is time to build a simple form using one of the sample tables. This accomplishes two goals: First, it shows you what the wizard is doing to generate your form. Second, it helps to instill an appreciation for doing a large amount of work in a short amount of time.

The result of this section will be to create a form that displays the employees in the EMP table with their salaries, commissions, and total compensation as shown in Figure 8.4.

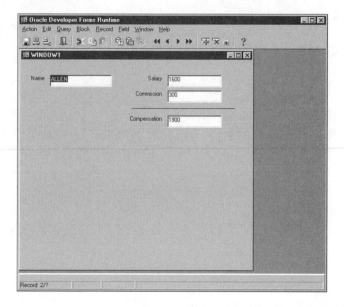

FIGURE 8.4
The employee form built without any help from wizards.

Start Form Builder and you are immediately given several options. In earlier examples, you used the Data Block Wizard to help create the form. This time, select Build a New Form Manually and click OK. This time, Form Builder is started without showing any tools or windows except the Object Navigator.

The first thing to do is log in to the database. This is done using the File, Connect menu option. Again, you will use the scott/tiger account. Next, click on the Tools, Layout Editor menu item to bring up the Layout Editor. This is what you will use to lay out your form.

Now is when the real work begins. The Data Block Wizard was used to create data blocks on your forms in the previous examples. Following the wizard's example, create a data block by selecting Data Blocks in the Object Navigator and clicking on the Create tool found in the vertical toolbar. You will be asked whether you want to use the Data Block Wizard or to do it manually. Choose the manual option and click OK.

You will use the Property Palette to connect this data block to the database and corresponding table. Right-click on the newly added name under Data Blocks in the Object Navigator. Then click the Property Palette option in the resulting pop-up menu. The Property Palette should appear as in Figure 8.5.

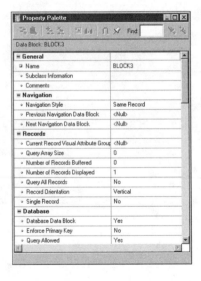

FIGURE 8.5
The Property Palette for the newly created data block.

You will now connect the data block to the proper table and columns in the database. This is done by filling in the correct values in the Property Palette. Use the following steps to help you:

1. Change the Name value from the automatically created BLOCK3 (or some other number) to EMP.

2. Set Query Data Source Name to EMP.

3. Click on Query Data Source Columns. There should be a More... value that you can click on to bring up the Query Data Source Columns dialog. Specify the ENAME, SAL, and COMM columns as shown in Figure 8.6. Be sure to specify the proper data types. ENAME is a VARCHAR2 of length 10. SAL and COMM are both NUMBER columns with a precision of 7 and a scale of 2. When you are done, click OK.

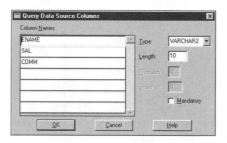

FIGURE 8.6
The Query Data Source Columns dialog is used to specify columns to appear in the data block.

You are now ready to define the fields. Go into the Layout Editor and add four text items. To add a text item to your form, select the text item tool from the palette. Then click and drag the mouse to put a text item on the form. Don't worry about making it the correct size. This will all be adjusted from the Property Palette.

Select the first text item and then click on the Property Palette. If it was closed, you can open it again with the Tools, Property Palette menu choice. Now change the properties to the following corresponding values in Table 8.1.

Table 8.1   Properties to Be Changed for the Manually Created Form

Property	Value
Name	ENAME
Maximum Length	10
Column Name	ENAME
Width	95
Height	19
Prompt	Name
Prompt Attachment Offset	9

You might want to experiment with these values depending on the platform you are using. Comparing between the Unix and Windows versions, these values are the larger of the two and should work fine on both systems.

Table 8.2 lists the properties and values for the next two text items that will correspond to the SAL and COMM columns.

Table 8.2   Properties to Be Changed for the SAL and COMM Columns

Property	Value for SAL	Value for COMM
Name	SAL	COMM
Datatype	Number	Number
Maximum Length	9	9
Column Name	SAL	COMM
Width	86	86
Height	19	19
Prompt	Salary	Commission
Prompt Attachment Offset	9	9

It would be nice to test the form now to see whether it works. However, a fourth text item was added. Running the form now would cause an error because the fourth text item is assigned to a database column that doesn't exist but will be used later. To fix this, change the Database Item property from Yes to No.

Now run the form to make sure that it works. Executing a query with no limitations allows you to scroll through all the employees in the EMP table.

Calculation Fields

The fourth text item was added to the form to allow you to display a calculated field. In this example, it will be used to calculate the total compensation or sum of the salary and commission columns. First, set up the properties for the text item using Table 8.3 as a guide.

Table 8.3   Properties to Be Changed for the Calculated Field

Property	Value
Name	comp
Datatype	Number
Maximum Length	9
Width	86
Height	19
Prompt	Compensation
Prompt Attachment Offset	9

You are now ready to assign a calculated value to this text item. To do so, change the Calculation Mode property to Formula. Then add the following PL/SQL to the Formula property:

```
:emp.sal + NVL(:emp.comm, 0)
```

Remember that the NVL function converts NULL values to the second argument in the function; in this example, the second argument is the number zero. If there is a chance that the SAL column will contain a NULL value, you will want to use the NVL function with it as well.

There is one last problem with the Compensation field. It is a display-only field, meaning that the user should not be able to have the cursor enter it. The field should be a display item instead of a text item. Rather than deleting it and creating a display item using the tool palette, simply change the Item Type property from Text Item to Display Item.

Run the form to see how it works. The form starts in insert mode to allow you to enter new employees into the database. Notice that there is no calculated compensation. This is because the salary is currently NULL, so compensation must also be NULL. After you enter a value in the salary field, the compensation will show up.

Execute a query in your new form to make sure that the compensation field is working correctly. As you scroll through the records, the correct values for salary, commission, and compensation are displayed for each employee. Try to alter the compensation value—it is not possible to do so while running the form.

Wizards Make Life Easier

The form you created from scratch is now complete. It was a good experience to help you understand what the Data Block and Layout Wizards do. You should now also have a healthy appreciation for them when creating forms that access database tables and columns.

As you become more familiar with Form Builder, you will discover that there are some instances when you will not want to use the wizards. A good example of when not to use a wizard is when you create forms that act as menus and call other forms or reports. However, a good rule to follow is this: If your form will tie into one or more database table, use the wizards.

Various Visual Elements

The form you built without the help of wizards introduced you to display items. Up to this point, all interaction with the database has been through text items. GUI environments offer several more graphical elements and it would be a shame not to incorporate them into applications. This next section gives examples on how to use the different elements effectively in your forms.

Static Images

One of the easiest ways to impress application users with the quality of your form is to add a company logo. Although this has little functional value, the perceived value is high (providing it does not make your form look cluttered).

To add a company logo to your form, use the File, Import, Image menu choice. It brings up the Import Image dialog as shown in Figure 8.7.

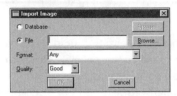

FIGURE 8.7
The Import Image dialog used to add static graphics to your forms.

You have the option of using an image from the database or an image from the file system. Because most company logos are stored in files, this example uses a file called my_company.bmp. You can use your own logo or download this one from the Web site for the book.

After the graphics file is selected, either through the Browse button or by explicitly typing in the name, click OK. The graphics file is now in the Layout Editor. To properly place the company logo graphic, you might be required to move some of the other objects around. Remember to use the alignment tools from Chapter 3 to help ensure that the fields line up correctly. When you are done, the form should look similar to Figure 8.8.

Graphics such as logos are not complicated to add to forms, but they help to provide a finished look. It is important to remember to use them appropriately and not cover your form with needless images that can detract from the application. Images also add to the size of the executable and can impact system resources.

Push Buttons

A push button is another element you can put on a form that provides a finished look but is not complicated to add. A button can be used to call another form, commit the current addition or changes, or exit the current form. The trick to making a button behave correctly is making sure that the PL/SQL is correct.

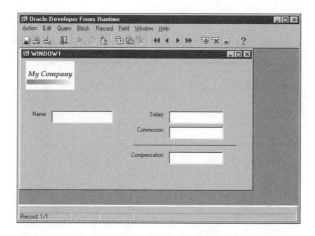

FIGURE 8.8
The employee compensation form, complete with company logo.

To create a button to exit the current form, do the following:

1. Select the push button on the toolbar.

2. Click and drag to make a rectangle of the desired size on the form in the Layout Editor.

3. Change the Name property to EXIT_BUTTON and the Label property to Exit.

4. Right-click on EXIT_BUTTON in the Object Navigator and select PL/SQL Editor from the pop-up menu. This brings up the Triggers dialog shown in Figure 8.9.

FIGURE 8.9
The Triggers dialog used to select the type of trigger to write PL/SQL code for.

5. Select WHEN-BUTTON-PRESSED from the Triggers dialog and click OK. This brings up the PL/SQL Editor shown in Figure 8.10.

FIGURE 8.10
The PL/SQL Editor used inside of Forms Developer to create PL/SQL code.

6. Notice that the object in the PL/SQL Editor is EMP.EXIT_BUTTON (as shown by combining the two pull-down lists). This is an important indicator that you are creating the trigger on the correct form object. Enter the following code in the PL/SQL Editor:

```
exit_form();
```

7. Click the Compile button to make sure that there are no errors. Then close the PL/SQL Editor.

You can see that adding the code for this button was very simple. Just one line of PL/SQL is all it took. There was no need to enter the BEGIN and END keywords as shown in Chapter 6. Most of the PL/SQL in application forms will be this simple.

Now run the form and verify that the new button works. You have the option of exiting by using the Exit button found on the toolbar, in the runtime menu, or by clicking on the newly created button.

You can add another button to your form to commit changes to the database. To do so, follow the previous steps and be sure to change the Name property to COMMIT_BUTTON and the Label property to Commit. You can also change the Default Button property from No to Yes. This will provide a highlight (depending on platform) to indicate that it is the default button.

For the WHEN-BUTTON-PRESSED trigger, enter the following code:

```
commit;
```

Figure 8.11 shows the form running in the Windows environment. Notice how the Commit button has darker shading around it to indicate that it is the default button.

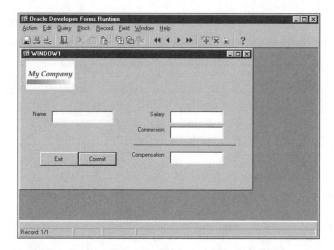

FIGURE 8.11
The employee compensation form with Exit and Commit buttons added.

Many more PL/SQL functions and procedures, such as exit_form(), are included with Form Builder. Also included with the software distribution are reference manuals in PDF format that explain all these functions and procedures. There are lots of explanations as well as examples to help you add them to your applications. If you run into problems or have a question about what is possible, don't hesitate to refer to these reference documents. They can be found in $ORACLE_HOME/doc60/admin/manuals/US/ref60 directory on Unix and in $ORACLE_HOME \TOOLS\DOC60\US\GUIDE60 on Windows. If you have problems accessing the system documentation, contact your system administrator for help.

List Items

List items, or list boxes, are another graphical element that you might want to add to your form. There are three variations of the List item in Forms Developer: the combo list, the pop-up list, and the traditional list. They are different from each other in their own subtle ways.

- **Combo list** —The combo list is similar to the Popup list except that in addition to being able to choose from the list, you also have the ability to create your own value.

- **Pop-up list** —Sometimes also referred to as a *pull-down list*. Use this graphical element when you have a static list of values to choose from and the form or canvas does not have a lot of extra space.

- **Traditional list**—This graphical element allows you to see more than one choice at a time. It is useful when you are not constrained by a crowded form and want to be able to see several choices at the same time.

To help you get an idea of how to use each type of list, the following sections provide at least one example for each type.

The Combo List Item

The combo list is probably the easiest to use because the user has the ability to enter his or her own values. Therefore, the values that populate the combo list are only suggestions and can be fairly static. When you start using pop-up lists with dynamic values that are maintained in a database table, there is a bit more programming.

In the sample form that you have been working on in this chapter, you have added a calculated field to show the total compensation. To get an idea of why the employee has the salary that is assigned, it would be helpful to see what the person's job is. The database column in the EMP table is a VARCHAR2 data type and allows any text entry. This column is a prime candidate for a combo list item.

The first thing to do is add the JOB column to the data block. This is done by selecting the EMP data block in the Object Navigator and modifying the Query Data Source Columns property. Click on the More button in the Property Palette next to the Query Data Source Columns property, and the dialog to specify columns will appear. Add the JOB column and specify a data type of VARCHAR2 with a length of 9. Close the dialog by clicking OK.

Add a list item from the vertical tool palette on the left of the Layout Editor. Remember to select the item, and then create it on the canvas by clicking and dragging the outline rectangle to the desired size. Now change the default List Style property from Poplist to Combo Box. Modify some of the other properties to correspond to those found in Table 8.4.

Table 8.4   Properties to Change to Make the Combo List Item Work Properly ———

Property	Value
Name	JOB
Maximum Length	9
Column Name	JOB
Prompt	Job
Prompt Attachment	9

Now the only thing left to do is fill in the values. This is done by clicking the More button next to the Elements in List property. A List Elements dialog similar to Figure 8.12 will appear.

The values listed in the top half of the List Elements dialog are displayed when the user clicks on the pull-down button. The List Item Value text entry area is used to specify the value to be stored in the row. This is helpful when the value stored in the table is different from the value displayed in the form. However, for this combo box, the values will be the same. Enter the following values: ANALYST, CLERK, MANAGER, PRESIDENT, and SALESMAN. Be sure to use the same values in both the List Elements and List Item Value entry areas.

FIGURE 8.12
The List Elements dialog used to specify a list of values to use in a list item.

Your combo box is added to the form. Go ahead and run it. Notice that you can add new employees, and either choose a job title from the list or type in a different job title, such as Developer or Mail Boy. You can query the EMP table and have the jobs already assigned in that table appear as well.

Perhaps you want the database to generate the values used in the combo box. You could select all the unique jobs from the employee table to create your list. You will be shown how to do that using the pop-up list and the same principles would apply here.

The Pop-up List

Management likes the work you are doing on this form so far. However, now they want you to show the department name for each employee in the database. Department names are fairly static and should be easy to add by using a pop-up list.

Here are the steps to follow to add a department name pop-up:

1. Add the DEPTNO column to the data block Query Source Data Columns property. Make sure that it is a number data type, and uses a precision of 2 and a scale of 0.

2. Set the usual properties to make it look nice on the form. Set the Name property to DEPTNO because it will be used later.

3. Set the Elements in List property to the values in Table 8.5.

Table 8.5   List Elements and List Item Values for the Pop-up List

List Element	List Item Value
ACCOUNTING	10
SALES	20
RESEARCH	30
OPERATIONS	40

Run the form and query the employees from the database. As you scroll through the records, the correct department names should appear. The list works, but it is not an elegant solution. If your company adds a new department, you will be required to modify your application code. A better solution would be to create the pop-up list values from the database.

To populate the pop-up list values from the database requires a bit of PL/SQL code. These steps should help you accomplish that. First, remove all the values for the Elements in List property. Then add a PRE-FORM trigger to initialize the values for the elements in the pop-up list.

Right-click on the module name in the Object Navigator and select the Smart Triggers, PRE-FORM menu option from the pop-up menu. This brings up the PL/SQL Editor. Add the following code found in Listing 8.1.

Listing 8.1   PL/SQL Code to Populate a Pop-up List

```
DECLARE
  rg_name VARCHAR2(40) := 'Dept_RG';
  rg_id   RecordGroup;
  errcode NUMBER;
BEGIN
  rg_id := CREATE_GROUP_FROM_QUERY(rg_name,
             'SELECT dname, to_char(deptno) FROM dept');
  errcode := POPULATE_GROUP(rg_id);
  POPULATE_LIST('EMP.DEPTNO', rg_id);
END;
```

Run the form and it will behave as expected. However, this time it fills the values for the pop-up list from the database.

A PRE-FORM trigger executes on startup and is where you would put all the initialization information for your form. The only drawback is that if someone were to add a department to the DEPT table, you would need to exit the form and restart it to be able to see the new department.

The PL/SQL code declares a record group to hold the results of a database query. The record group holds two columns for every row. The first column is the text that is displayed in the pop-up list, and the second value is the list value that is used by the field in the form. Both values are expected to be VARCHAR2 data types, so it is necessary to convert the DEPTNO column from a number to a character string. The procedure POPULATE_LIST then takes the record group and inserts it into the pop-up list.

POPULATING THE LIST

The first time I tried to populate a pop-up list using database values, I went bald trying to figure it out. I was working as a consultant for a very important client that I was trying to impress. Luckily, I was working overtime at home during the evening so the customer was not a witness to my colorful language.

I started out by putting the trigger PL/SQL in the PRE-FORM trigger as in the previous example. I did not have any of the printed documentation and there was no online documentation that I could find to show me how to populate the list. However, there were some indications in the online help that using the ADD_LIST_ELEMENT and POPULATE_LIST functions in PL/SQL would do the trick.

My first stop was the Forms Reference Manual, which comes in PDF format with the software. It includes help for all the built-in functions and procedures for Forms. I hoped that there would be an example to use and I would be done. Nope. There were some fabricated examples that showed me Oracle's documentation writer didn't have the faintest clue about how to build a reasonable example for either ADD_LIST_ELEMENT or POPULATE_LIST. So, I went to the table of contents hoping I could find a clue on where to go next.

The documentation for POPULATE_LIST mentioned that it worked with record groups and I just happened to find a reference to CREATE_GROUP_FROM_QUERY. There was even a relatively good example to follow. So, I slapped the code together and tested it. It still didn't work.

To make things easier on myself, I moved the trigger code from the PRE-FORM trigger to fire from a button. That way, I would see any error messages as they happened. Doing so showed me that the pop-up list was not being seen by the POPULATE_LIST procedure. After playing around with the code for a while, I discovered that the list item name needed to be enclosed in single quotes and not the way I was expecting it. Then the PL/SQL started working correctly.

I went in the next morning and added the code. Everyone was pleased, but they didn't realize all the hoops I had to jump through to get it to work.

It didn't take long for someone to figure out the problem with using the code on the PRE-FORM trigger. Users logged in to the application and never logged out. They left their systems up all night for days at a time. The pop-up list was not being updated when the equivalents of new departments were added. The quick solution was to implement a new policy that everyone must shut down his or her computer every night. This had the desired effect, and solved more than one problem because it seems that earlier versions of Windows required a nightly shutdown as part of system maintenance.

Another solution would have been to change the trigger that initialized the values for the pop-up list. I would have needed to modify the PL/SQL so that it destroyed the list before doing the CREATE_GROUP_FROM_QUERY. Otherwise, doing a CREATE_GROUP_FROM_QUERY on an already created group would have generated an error. Then I could have put it on a trigger that was fired more often, such as an ON-COMMIT.

The Traditional List

Management likes the form, but wants to be able to see all the available departments. This is an easy fix to make because you just need to replace the pop-up list with a traditional list. This change is a two-step process:

1. Change the List Style property to Tlist.

2. Change the height of the DEPTNO field on the form to accommodate the four department names.

The finished form should look similar to the one in Figure 8.13.

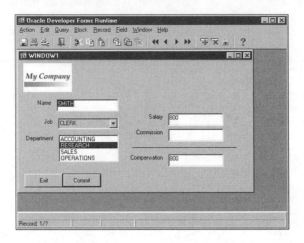

FIGURE 8.13
The form using a traditional list item to display the employee's department.

The same steps used to set up the static values in the combo list item work exactly the same way for the traditional list. So does the table-driven method shown with the pop-up list. With this information, you should feel comfortable using any of the three graphical elements.

Check Boxes

A check box is a graphical element used to show a Boolean value. The value is either true or false, depending on whether the box has a check or is empty. In the next example, you use a check box to display the contents of the gender column in the CONTACT table.

If you have not already done so, save the form that you have been working on. Now create a new form using all the columns from the CONTACT table. When the form is created, select the GENDER field and open the property list. Change the Item Type property from Text Item to Check Box.

Next, set the Value when Checked property to M and the Value when Unchecked property to F. When using check boxes, it is good practice to set the Initial Value property to one of the two choices. Without setting the initial value, there are three possible values for the gender field: M, F, and NULL, which is undefined. The only way to select the F value is to explicitly check the box and then uncheck it. Setting the Initial Value property reduces the possible values to just M and F.

The last thing to do is change the Prompt property to Male. This indicates that when the box is checked, the contact is male. Otherwise, the contact is female.

Now run the form and enter a few contacts to make sure that the check box is behaving correctly. After you have committed the new records, go into SQL*Plus and run the following query:

```
SELECT * FROM contact;
```

You should see the new rows displayed with an M for male contacts and an F for female ones.

Radio Buttons and Groups

Management is complaining. They would prefer to use radio buttons, rather than a check box, to indicate gender.

Radio buttons are used to indicate one of several choices. Only one radio button for a given database column can be chosen at a time. The way Forms Developer associates radio buttons with the column is through a radio group. Your form may contain several radio groups, and each radio group may contain several radio buttons.

In the sample form, the radio group will be associated with the gender column in the CONTACT table. There will be two radio buttons: one to represent male and the other to represent female.

Select the gender check box in the Layout Editor and change the Item Type property from Check Box to Radio Group. It should disappear from the form. Don't worry, the item is still in the Object Navigator and Forms Developer still knows about it.

Now create two radio buttons using the vertical tool palette. You are asked to specify the radio group to associate the button with, as shown in Figure 8.14.

FIGURE 8.14
The Radio Groups dialog used to associate radio buttons to a specific radio group.

Because the GENDER radio group is already created and selected in the dialog, click OK. After both radio buttons are created, set the properties for each radio button as shown in Table 8.6.

Table 8.6 Properties for the Male and Female Radio Buttons

Property	Male Button	Female Button
Name	MALE	FEMALE
Label	Male	Female
Radio Button Value	M	F

Run the form and test the radio buttons to make sure that they work. If you want, you can also unset the default value by clicking on the GENDER radio group in the Object Navigator and removing the value from the Property Palette.

Radio buttons should be used for only a small number of static selections. If there is a chance that the selection values will change, it is best to use a data-driven pop-up list instead. However, if you plan to use something that remains fairly constant, such as gender or age categories, radio buttons work well.

Save this sample form if you want to refer to it later. Otherwise, feel free to discard it.

Chart Wizard

In Chapter 4, "Oracle Reports Developer and Graphics," you were shown how to use the Chart Wizard with Reports. You also have the ability to use the Chart Wizard in Forms. However, the end result is much different than the anticipated result.

It seems that chart support still has a way to go before it is truly reliable and useful. Attempts to create charts using the Windows version of Forms Developer resulted in a chart being displayed for the first row of a query, but none of the subsequent rows displayed anything but a white box. Under Unix, the Chart Wizard was never enabled. Between the time that this chapter was written and the book goes to press, some of these problems might be fixed. Consult the release notes supplied with your version of Oracle Developer to find out whether these problems have been fixed.

Currently, the best way to incorporate charts into a form is to have the form call a report. Use the built-in PL/SQL function RUN_REPORT_OBJECT to run the report as shown in Listing 8.2.

Listing 8.2 PL/SQL Code to Run a Report from a Form

```
DECLARE
  repid REPORT_OBJECT
  rep_o VARCHAR2(100);
BEGIN
```

Listing 8.2   Continued

```
  repid := FIND_REPORT_OBJECT('graphreport');
  rep_o := RUN_REPORT_OBJECT(repid);
END;
```

Listing 8.2 can be called from a button or other trigger. From the report, you will have greater control over how the chart looks and behaves.

Running the Form in the Debugger

Your forms become more and more complex as you add PL/SQL code. At some point, your PL/SQL will not behave as you expect, and you will want to run your form in the debugger. It is similar to using the Procedure Builder as explained in Chapter 6, except for the fact that you now have to work with visual objects as well as code.

The compensation form created earlier in the chapter already contains some PL/SQL code that can be used for this example. If the compensation form is not already loaded in Form Builder, do so now. Run the form using the debugger. You can use the Run Form Debug button on the toolbar or Program, Run Form, Debug menu choice.

The client/server runtime starts and invokes the Forms Debugger. This allows you to set breakpoints and view code segments before the form is run. Figure 8.15 shows the Forms Debugger with the three panes used to help debug the form.

There are three panes in the debugger:

- **Code pane**—This is similar to Procedure Builder's code display pane. It is used to show selected PL/SQL code so that you can set breakpoints.

- **Object navigator pane**—This is used to select form objects. The code for any selected code objects will appear in the code pane. Non-code objects can be inspected to view values.

- **Command pane**—This is similar to Procedure Builder's PL/SQL Interpreter. Because forms include many visual objects, this pane is rarely used.

The best way to get a feel for the debugger is to actually use it. Expand the tree in the Object Navigator so that you can select the PRE-FORM trigger. First, expand the Modules object, and then expand the name of the form you have been using, and then the triggers. When you click on the PRE-FORM trigger, you should see the code displayed in the code pane.

Set a breakpoint on line 7 by double-clicking the line. You should see the familiar breakpoint dot to the left of the line. Now close the debugger using the big red X on the toolbar. The debugger allows the form to run, up to the first breakpoint. When the breakpoint is encountered, execution of the form stops and the debugger reappears.

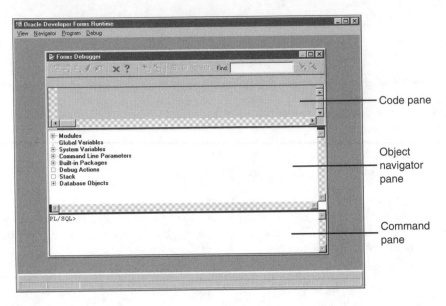

FIGURE 8.15
The Forms Debugger window used to help debug PL/SQL in forms.

When the Forms Debugger resumes, there is a new object, stack, in the object navigator pane. This allows you to inspect the variables in your PL/SQL code as the program runs. Also notice how the execution arrow is stopped at the left of line 7 in the code pane.

Click on the Step Into button on the toolbar to execute the current line of code. Now expand the stack objects to see what values are currently stored in the various variables. Continue to step through the code, making sure to notice that variables are being set, as expected.

You should be familiar with the functions of the buttons on the toolbar because most of them are found in the Object Navigator and the Procedure Builder. Take some time to play around with the debugger. If you have some experience with the debugger before you need it, using it when a problem occurs will be much less stressful.

Canvases

All the sample forms to this point have used a single canvas, but there will come a time in an application when you want to use different canvases in the same form. The purpose of this section is to introduce you to using multiple canvases in the same application form.

The example in this section uses the compensation form used with the Forms Debugger. At this point, there is only one canvas used by the form, and it has a default name of something like CANVAS2. Change the canvas name to something a little more descriptive, such as MAIN-CANVAS.

Now create a second canvas by selecting CANVASES in the Object Navigator and clicking on the Create Object tool in the vertical toolbar. A new canvas, with a default name, will be added to the form. Change the name to OTHERCANVAS. This canvas will be used to display the department information from the DEPT table.

Right-click on OTHERCANVAS in the Object Navigator and open the Layout Editor. You should now have two Layout Editors open: one for the MAINCANVAS and another for OTH-ERCANVAS. Use the Data Block Wizard and the Layout Wizard to populate the canvas. Because the canvas will be used as a lookup dialog, there is no need to create a relationship between the EMP block and the DEPT block. When you are asked to specify a relationship, simply click Next and no join condition will be created.

In the Layout Wizard, specify a tabular output style and display four rows with a scroll bar. When you are done, your OTHERCANVAS should look similar to the one in Figure 8.16.

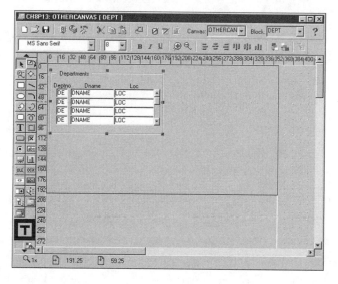

FIGURE 8.16
The department table will be used to show lookup information on the second canvas.

Now run the form. The original canvas is displayed until you click the Next Block button on the toolbar, and the original form is replaced with the department form. You can now execute a query to see information about the various departments. Clicking on Next Block or Previous Block returns you to the original canvas.

There are many reasons to use multiple canvases in the same form. Perhaps you are writing an application that asks the user additional questions based on the results of previous answers. This is a good case for hiding the various extra questions within the same form without having to display all the questions. As you experiment with canvases, you will come up with your own uses that fit your application.

List of Values

A list of values (or LOV) is a holdover from the days before GUIs, when pop-up lists weren't available. When you had only a character interface and didn't know the possible values for a text item, you could press the LOV key and it brought up a window with a list of possible values. The designers at Oracle have held onto the concept even though the functionality can be replaced by a simple pop-up list.

In defense of Oracle, there are several advantages of using LOVs. The first advantage is that LOVs are backward compatible with previous versions of Oracle's development tools. This is important if you are migrating an old SQL*Forms application to Oracle Developer.

Another advantage of LOVs is that they allow more information to be displayed because they use a pop-up window and can be larger than a pop-up list. A pop-up list generally contains just the department name, whereas an LOV can also contain the department location.

There is a LOV Wizard that you can use to help create a List of Values. Right-click on LOV in the Object Navigator and open the LOV Wizard. You will get a screen asking whether you want to use a previously created record group, or if you want to create a new one. This is the first LOV, so create a new one.

The next dialog asks for the SQL query to create the LOV. You could use the Query Builder tool or simply enter a SELECT statement in the text area provided. Enter the following query:

```
SELECT * FROM salgrade
```

This query creates a list of possible salaries for the employees. You can use this list to assign salaries for new employees as they are hired. After the SQL statement is entered, you can verify the syntax or click Next to continue.

You are now asked to enter the columns to display in the LOV. Select them all and click Next. The next dialog (shown in Figure 8.17) is very important. It is used to copy values from the LOV to fields on the form.

The value that should be copied is LOSAL and it should be copied into EMP.SAL. If you are not sure which field in the form to copy the value into, click the Look up return item button. Doing so will display an Items and Parameters dialog that you can select from.

The next LOV Wizard screen asks you to specify a title for the LOV pop-up window. Use Salary Grades for this example. The rest of the defaults in this screen will work just fine. Click Next.

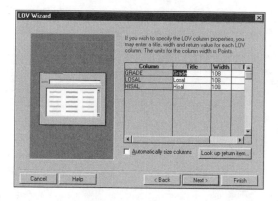

FIGURE 8.17
The LOV Wizard screen used to specify recipient form fields of LOV lookups.

You are now asked about some advanced LOV properties. Again, the defaults will work fine. After your first few LOVs, you might want to modify these values. For now, click Next. After the form is running, you might want to come back and experiment with some of these LOV properties.

The final action in the LOV Wizard is to signify that you actually want to use the return values provided by the LOV. Copy EMP.SAL to the assigned items list and click Next. There is one last screen saying that you are done. Click Finish.

Use the following steps to verify the assignment of the newly create LOV field to the SAL text item:

1. Click the SAL text item in the Layout Editor or Object Navigator.

2. If the Property Palette is not visible, open it.

3. Make sure that the List of Values property is assigned to the newly created LOV.

Now you are ready to test the form. Run the form and enter the information for a new employee. When you get to the Salary column, you'll see an indicator in the status line that tells you a list of values is available. Display the newly created LOV by choosing the Edit, Display List option. You should see a dialog similar to Figure 8.18.

LOVs are helpful for displaying long lists of information that can be used to populate text items in your forms. However, LOVs should be used sparingly. Generally, you can use a pop-up list to accomplish the same task. Most users are familiar with pop-up lists, and need to be trained to use a list of values dialog.

FIGURE 8.18
The newly created LOV dialog in action.

Dialog Boxes

Dialog boxes are useful for providing user feedback for error conditions or possible problems. One of the most common types of dialogs is known as a *modal* dialog box, which means that no other processing in the application can take place until the user responds to the dialog that has been presented.

In the next example, you will create a modal dialog box that provides some simple online help to the user about the form. First, create a new window. This is done by selecting Windows from the Object Navigator and clicking Create in the vertical toolbar. Assign the new window's properties as described in Table 8.7.

Table 8.7   Properties for the New Window

Property	Value
Name	HELPWIN
Window Style	Dialog
Modal	Yes

Now create a canvas with information that will be in the dialog. When you are done, it should look like Figure 8.19.

Use HELPCANVAS for the canvas name and DISMISS_BUTTON for the button's name. Also be sure to verify that Window property is set to HELPWIN for HELPCANVAS. The PL/SQL code to close the dialog when DISMISS_BUTTON is pressed is

```
go_block('EMP');
```

Now add a button to the MAINCANVAS to call the help window. The label on the button should be Help. The code to invoke the help dialog when the button is pressed is

```
go_item('DISMISS_BUTTON');
```

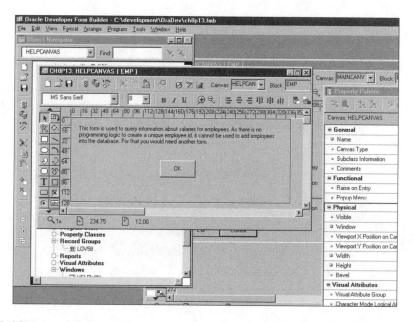

FIGURE 8.19
The finished dialog to provide users with online help if they need it.

The way that Form Builder shows and dismisses dialogs is by sending the cursor to an object on the form. That's why the calling button calls the GO_ITEM() procedure. Then the button on the dialog simply returns back to the EMP block.

Now run the form and click on the Help button. You should see your newly created dialog as shown in Figure 8.20.

There are many ways to use dialogs to provide important feedback to the user. The Oracle online documentation contains more examples of how to use dialogs with your forms.

Summary

This chapter has shown you some of the powerful features of Oracle Form Builder. You were given an extensive overview of the client/server default runtime environment. Then you were shown how to use all the many different types of graphical elements in your form. These include check boxes, radio buttons, pop-up lists, traditional lists, and combo lists. You were also shown how to create multiple canvases within a form as well as how to create dialogs.

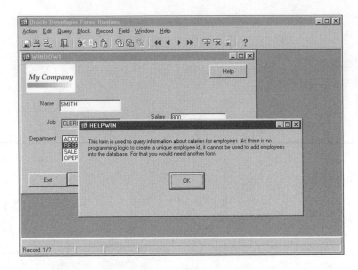

FIGURE 8.20
The completed form with a help dialog.

You should now have a good understanding of Oracle Forms running in client/server mode. Chapters 9, "More About Reports," and 10, "Graphics Development," will provide more in-depth discovery of Oracle Reports and Oracle Graphics. The rest of the book will concentrate on building a real application and moving it to the Web.

MORE ABOUT REPORTS

ESSENTIALS ———————————

- Reports Builder enables you to create the following kinds of reports: Tabular, Form-like, Mailing Label, Form Letter, Group Left, Group Above, Matrix, and Matrix with Group.

- Mailing Label reports are great for creating mail labels, but also can be used to print a small amount of information for a large number of database rows on a single page.

- Live Previewer mode is used to show how your finished report will look and includes live data. It is the mode you will use the most when creating reports.

- The Data Model mode shows the data relationships utilized by the report. It is most useful when you have a large number of tables joined together in creating your report.

- The Layout Model mode is used to fine-tune the layout of your report.

- Templates allow you to create a standard look-and-feel for all the reports for a given department or company.

- Parameter forms allow you to create a report driven by criteria specified by the user. This is a great way to limit the number of rows your report returns.

Chapter 8, "Using Graphical Elements in Forms," covered features of Forms Developer that were not included in Chapters 2, "Developer Basics," or 3, "Oracle Forms Developer." This chapter is similar and covers the details of Reports Developer that were not covered in either Chapter 2 or Chapter 4, "Oracle Reports Developer and Graphics."

The chapter starts by giving examples of the eight different types of report styles. It then covers the different views of the report used in Report Builder and how they help with report creation. The chapter provides an example for building a report template. Finally, it shows how to create and use a parameter form.

You should feel comfortable using the Report Builder tool. If not, take some time and run through some of the examples in Chapters 2 and 4.

Report Examples

Chapter 2 listed eight different styles of reports found in the Report Wizard. This section covers the different styles of reports, and provides examples on how to effectively use them. The styles are

- Tabular

- Form-like

- Mailing Label

- Form Letter

- Group Left

- Group Above

- Matrix

- Matrix with Group

It is important to have a good understanding of the capabilities of each report style before using it. This reduces the chance of you trying to get a style to do something for which it was not intended.

Tabular Reports

The Tabular report style uses headings at the top of the report with individual rows of data appearing below. This style is very useful for displaying a large number of rows on as few pages as possible. It is also useful for comparing column values between rows.

The drawback of the Tabular report style is that you are limited in the number of columns to display. Ideally, one row should correspond to one row of data. Although it is possible to have the data span multiple rows of the report, the report becomes difficult to read. At that point, you might be better off using a Form-like report.

Start Report Builder and use the Report Wizard to help create this report. Use the title Employees and make sure that the report style selected is Tabular.

Use the Query Builder to help build the SELECT statement to create the report. Figure 9.1 shows what the Query Builder should look like to create the proper query for the report. Remember that the relationship between MGR and EMPNO is explained in the previous chapter.

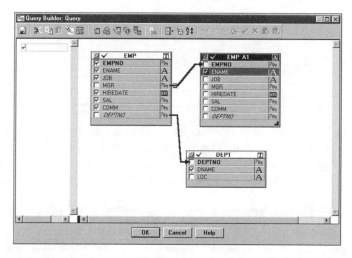

FIGURE 9.1
The Query Builder used to create the SELECT statement for the Tabular style report.

Remember that you will have to define the relationship between EMP and EMP_A1. This is done by using the Set Table Relationship button on the toolbar. Figure 9.2 shows how to properly fill out the dialog.

FIGURE 9.2
The Set Relationship dialog used to specify the relationship between EMP and EMP_A1.

When you are done with the Query Builder, click OK to see the generated SELECT statement. Give it a once-over to make sure that it looks correct, and then click Next. Now add all the columns from the query to the report using the >> button, and then click Next.

The next screen in the Report Wizard asks about total fields. This was done in Chapter 2, so you don't need to worry about it here. Click Next and set the field labels as shown in Table 9.1.

Table 9.1   Field Labels for the Report

Original Label	New Label
Empno	Emp #
Ename	Name
Hiredate	Date Hired
Sal	Salary
Comm	Commission
Dname	Department
Ename1	Manager

Click Next after the changes are made. Accept the defaults for the rest of the wizard and click Finish when you're done. The report looks pretty good, but it needs to have some of the columns adjusted. Widen columns whose data wraps to multiple lines and shorten any columns that are too wide. After everything is adjusted, the finished report should look like Figure 9.3.

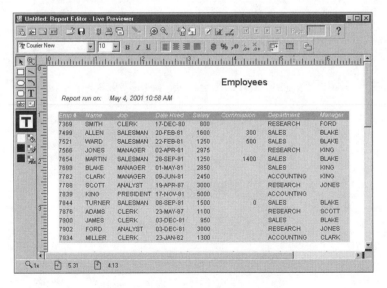

FIGURE 9.3
The completed Tabular report.

The Tabular report is quick and easy to complete. It does a good job of showing a number of rows close together for easy comparison.

Form-Like Reports

The Form-like report displays column headings to the left of column data. This is useful for displaying a database row that includes lots of columns. Generally, you would use this kind of report when you want a single page for each row in the database.

The drawback to the Form-like report is that it is very difficult to compare column data for different rows in the database.

The Form-like report example uses the same report information as the Tabular report. Rather than going through the entire Report Wizard, simply rerun it for the Tabular report making sure to change the style to Form-like. Also be sure to select the Draft template before finishing the Report Wizard.

The report is fairly unreadable in Live Previewer. You can try to move the columns around, but Live Previewer is not set up well to adjust the report layout. There is a Layout Model button on the toolbar that changes the view of the report. When in Layout Model mode, you can adjust the report to make it more readable.

Change to Layout Model mode and adjust the record cell to provide more room for the individual row. Then adjust the data fields to look like those in Figure 9.4.

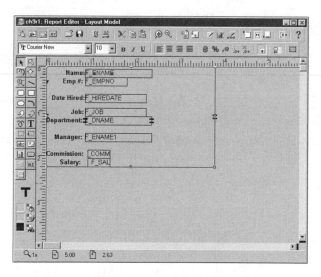

FIGURE 9.4
The Layout Model mode for the employee report.

After adjusting some of the columns to make the report more readable, change back to Live Previewer mode and look at the finished report. It should look similar to Figure 9.5.

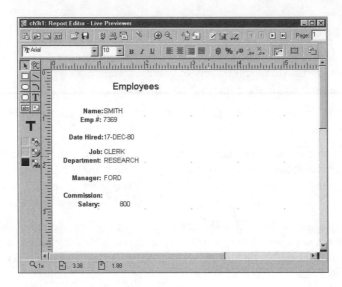

FIGURE 9.5
The completed Form-like report for employees.

Press the Page Down key and you will see that each employee is placed on a separate page. If you would like to add more employee records per page, do the following:

1. Select the record frame in the Layout Model mode.

2. Open the Property Palette.

3. Change the Maximum Records per Page property from 1 to the desired number.

The Form-like report works best when you want to display lots of information for each record in the database. When there is a smaller amount of information, the Form-like report allows you enough flexibility to include multiple records for each page of the report.

Mailing Label Reports

As the name implies, the Mailing Label style of report is used to create mail labels. However, it also has other uses. Perhaps you would like to print information about customers on 3×5 cards that you can take with you on the road to review before a sales call. This report style allows you to print the information in a grid style with four customers per page.

The Mailing Label example uses the customer information from the CUST table. If you have not already added several records to the CUST table, you should do that before continuing with the report.

ADDING SAMPLE DATA

The easiest way to add information to the CUST table is to build a simple form and add the information. If you skipped over creating forms, you can go back to Chapter 2 where there is a simple example on how to do this.

Here is the sample data you might want to enter so that your report looks like the example:

```
Customer #: 1
Seven Yachts
127 Jack London Drive
Alameda, CA 94072
Phone: (510) 555-1271
Fax: (510) 555-1272
Salesrep: 7499

Customer #: 2
Catalina Cycles
256 Sunnyside Drive
Los Angeles, CA 92035
Phone: (312) 555-2561
Fax: (312) 555-2562
Salesrep: 7521

Customer #: 3
Specialized Motors
5 Specialized Circle
Detroit, MI 32115
Phone: (800) 555-5001
Fax: (800) 555-5002
Salesrep: 7654

Customer #: 4
L4K, Inc.
11863 South 980 East
Salt Lake City, UT 84020
Phone: (801) 555-9516
Fax: (801) 555-9514
Salesrep: 7844
```

```
Customer #: 5
Island Packet Delivery
357 Grand View Way
Honolulu, HI 99872
Phone: (808) 555-3571
Fax: (808) 555-3572
Salesrep: 7521
```

With the data entered into the CUST table, you are ready to continue with the Mailing Label report.

Create a new report and start the Report Wizard. Be sure to select the Mailing Label report style. Use the following SQL query:

```
SELECT cname, addr, city, state, zip
FROM cust
```

There is a new screen for the Report Wizard to specify the mailing label text. Use the column names with the punctuation buttons to create the mailing label as shown in Figure 9.6.

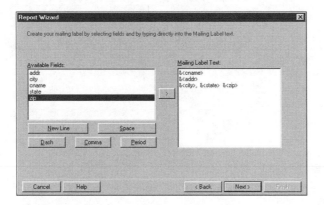

FIGURE 9.6
The Report Wizard screen to specify the text for the mailing label.

Use the Draft template because it is the simplest. The report is finished and you can print your mailing labels. You can use the Layout Editor to modify the output of the report if it does not meet your standards.

To change the number of columns per page, follow these steps:

1. Go into Layout Model mode.

2. Right-click on the address layout and make sure the pop-up menu shows that Flex Mode is selected.

3. Widen the area used to display the address label to decrease the number of label columns. Narrow it to increase the number of label columns.

You can also use the File, Page Setup menu option to set margins for the report. This should help create a Mailing Label report that works for your mailing label forms.

Form Letter Reports

The Form Letter report style is useful for creating form letters. It is also helpful for embedding dynamic data in English-like reports.

This example uses the CUST and CONTACT tables to create a form letter to each of the sales contacts. Enter some valid contact data into the CONTACT table. If you want to make sure that your example matches that in the book, use the information in Table 9.2.

Table 9.2   Sample Data to Be Added for the CONTACT Table

Contact #	Contact Name	Gender	Last Contact	Customer #
1	Tim Smith	M	10-OCT-2000	1
2	John Flynn	M	5-MAY-2001	2
3	David Johnson	M	5-MAY-2001	3
4	Natalie Rose	F	3-MAR-2001	3
5	Nathan Albion	M	25-APR-2001	4
6	Kathleen Tanner	F	27-APR-2001	5

After the contact data has been entered, run the Report Wizard and select the Form Letter report style. The next screen will ask for the query to use for the report. Use the address information from the CUST table with the contact name from the CONTACT table, as shown in Figure 9.7.

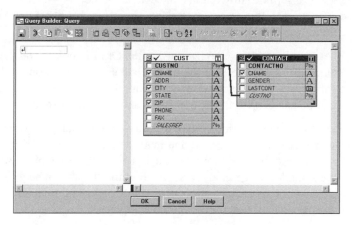

FIGURE 9.7
Query Builder showing the information that will be used to generate the Form Letter report.

Now you are asked to create the text for the form letter. Assume that the report will be printed on company letterhead and, therefore, you will not need to add your company name and address. The date for the report will be the day the report is generated. It will be added later in the report creation process.

The sample report will invite all the customer contacts to an open house to be held on January 4th between 10 a.m. and 4 p.m. You could include the salesperson information in the original query. However, to keep it simple, this message will be from the company president. Figure 9.8 shows the Report Wizard with the important information. The letter closing is not shown due to space limitations and contains a standard business closing.

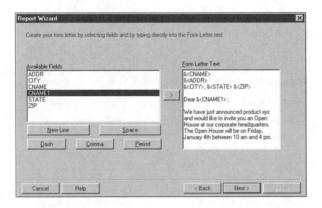

FIGURE 9.8
The text used in the Form Letter report.

Notice how both the customer and contact table have a CNAME column. Query Builder has automatically added 1 as a suffix to differentiate the contact name from the customer's company name. This can be a tough thing to keep straight. Therefore, I suggest that you use much more descriptive column names when you create your table.

Finish answering questions in the Report Wizard using the Draft template and then preview your work. Notice that there is no date. Use the Insert Date and Time button on the toolbar to add the date to the form letter. The dialog shown in Figure 9.9 will appear. Be sure to select the proper placement (that is, top left) for the date, as well as the proper format.

You might need to adjust the report margins, fonts, and Layout Model to fit your company letterhead. Then you are ready to print the report and mail out the invitations. You might even create another Form Letter report to print out the proper address on envelopes. Although you might be tempted to use the Mailing Label report, the Form Letter works better for envelopes. This is because your printer treats each envelope as a single page and it contains only a single address. Mailing Label reports are best used to print multiple addresses on the same page.

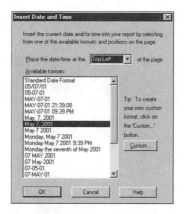

FIGURE 9.9
The Insert Date and Time dialog used to add the system date to your report.

Group Left Reports

The Group Left report style is a variation of the Tabular report. Instead of treating all rows equally, as in the Tabular report, the Group Left report allows rows to be grouped by specified criteria. The criteria information then appears to the left of the first row in the group. The grouping allows the reports to be read more easily.

An example using the Group Left report was demonstrated in Chapter 4. Therefore, a more advanced report will be shown in this section. To provide more data for the report, add the rows found in Table 9.3 to the CONTACT table.

Table 9.3 More Sample Data to Add to the CONTACT Table

Contact #	Contact Name	Gender	Last Contact	Customer #
10	Amanda Parson	F	10-JUN-2001	1
11	William Smith	M	15-MAY-2001	1
12	Ronald Jamison	M	3-JUN-2001	2
13	Katie Jensen	F	13-MAY-2001	3
14	Michael Yang	M	20-APR-2001	4
15	Catherine Shue	F	1-APR-2001	5

Now create a Group Left report using the Report Wizard. The title of the report can be something simple, such as Customer Contacts. Use the query shown in Figure 9.10 to help create the report.

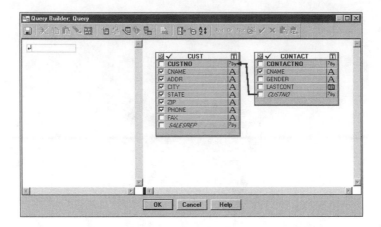

FIGURE 9.10
The query to use to help build the Group Left sample report.

Now modify the SQL generated by the Query Builder to concatenate the company name, address, and phone number into a single string. The SQL statement should look like this:

```
SELECT ALL cust.cname || chr(10) || cust.addr || chr(10) ||
       cust.city || ', ' || cust.state || ' ' ||
       cust.zip || chr(10) || cust.phone || chr(10),
       contact.cname
FROM cust, contact
WHERE (contact.custno = cust.custno)
```

This SELECT statement uses the || symbol to concatenate all the company name and address information into a single column. The chr(10) function prints a new line character.

In the next Report Wizard screen, use the CUST_CNAME_CHR... column as the group field. Then make sure that CNAME is also displayed on the report. There is no need for summary information in this report.

In the Labels window for the Report Wizard, change the long and confusing column name from Cust_Cname_Chr... to Company Information. Also change Cname to Contacts. Then click Next and choose the Draft template. When you are done, the report looks almost readable. Use the Layout Model view to fine-tune the information.

Group Above Reports

The Group Above report style is a variation of the Group Left report. However, rather than listing the grouping criteria on the left side of the report, it is listed above the rows of the group.

Chapter 4 contained an example of the Group Above report. However, that example was the result of using the Group Left report and then going back into the Report Wizard and changing the layout style. This example runs through the creation of a Group Above report from start to finish.

Create a new report using the Report Wizard. Set the title to Customers and be sure to select the Group Above layout. Use the following SELECT statement as the basis of the report:

```
SELECT ALL emp.ename, cust.cname, cust.city,
       cust.state, cust.phone
FROM emp, cust
WHERE (cust.salesrep = emp.empno)
```

The query will list all the customers for each sales representative. ENAME will be the field to group by and all the columns will be shown in the report. There is no need to display any totals. The headings Ename and Cname should be changed to Sales Representative and Company, respectively. Once again, use the Corporate 2 report template. The report is done and should look similar to Figure 9.11.

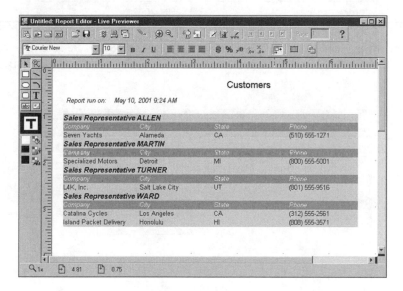

FIGURE 9.11
The completed Group Above report showing customers for each sales representative.

Matrix Reports

The Matrix or crosstab report is used to provide summary information when given two defining sets of characteristics. It looks very similar to a spreadsheet. The left column defines one set of characteristics, whereas the top row defines the second set. The summary information appears in the body of the report.

The best way to get an understanding of the Matrix report is with an example. The sample report will show the total number of customer contacts for a given company and a given state. Because all the contacts for a given company are in the same state as the company headquarters, the report will be kind of boring. Use the following INSERT command to add another row to the CUST table:

```
INSERT INTO cust(custno, cname, state, salesrep)
VALUES (6, 'L4K, Inc.', 'HI', 7844);
```

This has the effect of adding another office for L4K in the state of Hawaii. Now add another employee to that office by using the form from Chapter 8 and the information found in Table 9.4.

Table 9.4   Data to Add to the CONTACT Table Relating a Contact to a New Office

Contact #	Contact Name	Gender	Last Contact	Customer #
20	Bruce Kaaapa	M	15-JUN-2001	6

Create a new report with the title of Contacts by Company and State. Be sure to select the Matrix report, and then click Next. Figure 9.12 shows the query used with Query Builder for the report.

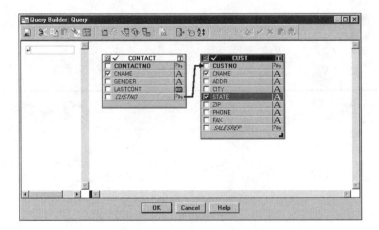

FIGURE 9.12
The Query Builder representation used to build the Matrix report.

Take a close look at the generated SELECT statement. Notice that the first CNAME to appear is from the CONTACT table. Also notice that the statement does not contain a COUNT() function or GROUP BY clause. They will be generated by the report.

Figure 9.13 shows the Report Wizard asking which field to use for the left column characteristic of the Matrix report. Use CNAME 1, as shown. Also notice that the icon on the left that helps to describe the choice you are making.

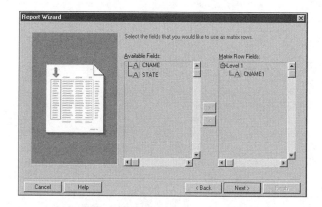

FIGURE 9.13
The Report Wizard screen used to specify the left column characteristic of the report.

Next you are asked to select the top row characteristic. Select the STATE field and move it into the Matrix Column Field list by using the > button. Click Next and you are asked to specify the matrix cell fields. There is only one remaining field: CNAME. Select it and add it to the list by using the Count > button. This will provide a total list of contacts for the desired characteristics to the report.

The next screen in the Report Wizard allows you to specify any column or row totals to appear to the right or bottom of the report. This report will not use any totals, so click Next to go to the next screen.

You now have the option of changing the field labels as they appear on the report. Change Cname1 to Company and Countcname to nothing. Then click Next and choose the Draft layout.

You are done with the report, but it is difficult to read. Select one of the state abbreviations and use the Center button on the toolbar. Do the same for the matrix cell data. The finished report should look similar to Figure 9.14.

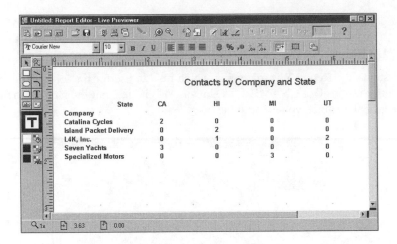

FIGURE 9.14
The finished Matrix report.

Notice that the company L4K, Inc. contains contacts in both Utah and Hawaii. If there are two L4K, Inc. entries, it indicates that there is some difference in spelling or punctuation of the company name as you entered it into the database. The report does a GROUP BY and if the two entries for the company name are identical, they will appear as a combined line item in the report.

Matrix with Group Reports

The Matrix with Group report is similar to the Matrix report, except that you are allowed to have a third characteristic to sort the data. Because three-dimensional charts are hard to output, a new spreadsheet or matrix is created for each of the third characteristics.

Creating a Matrix with Group report is very similar to creating a Matrix report. The only difference is the third grouping characteristic that must be added in the Report Wizard. Create a new report; specify a title of Contacts by Salesrep and the Matrix with Group layout.

The query will be the same as used with the Matrix report except that you will need to add the EMP table and select the ENAME column to add to the report.

The next screen in the Report Wizard will ask you to specify the field by which to group the various matrix reports. Select the ENAME column. The rest of the Report Wizard responses will be the same as the Matrix report, except for changing the Ename label to Sales Representative. When you are finished, the report will look similar to the one in Figure 9.15.

It is a bit difficult to read, but you can fix that by going into the Layout Model view and doing some adjustments. Save the report as groupmatrix; you'll use it again later in this chapter.

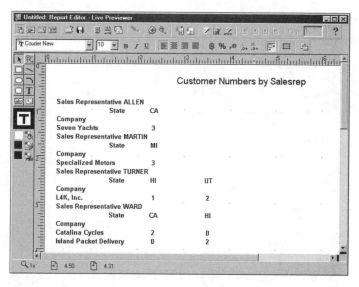

FIGURE 9.15
The finished Matrix with Group report.

Report Views

Throughout this chapter, as well as in Chapters 2 and 4, you have mostly used the Live Previewer view to see the results of your report. On occasion, you have gone into the Layout Model view to adjust the report to make it look more readable. The purpose of this section is to take a closer look at the three different views and how they can be used to help with report creation. The three views are

- Live Previewer

- Data Model

- Layout Model

Live Previewer

The Live Previewer view should be most familiar to you. It is used to preview how the final report will look, and it contains tools to help you manipulate the look of the report using real data. Although the Live Previewer does a good job of showing what the finished report will look like, it is different from the Runtime Previewer. The Runtime Previewer can be invoked using the View, Runtime Previewer menu option. The Matrix with Group report is shown in Figure 9.16.

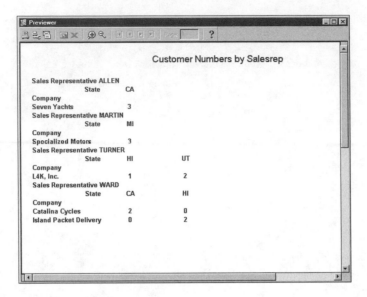

FIGURE 9.16
The Runtime Previewer differs from the Live Previewer view.

Notice the difference between Figures 9.15 and 9.16. The Runtime Previewer toolbar in Figure 9.16 contains only those tools that are useful while running the report. The Live Previewer, shown in Figure 9.15, contains a grid and tools useful to creating and modifying the layout.

You have already had experience moving and resizing data and fields in Live Previewer. You can also change the color of text. Select the field heading Sales Representative. Then click on the lowest color palette in the vertical tool palette on the left. This allows you to change the text color and make the field heading to stand out from the actual data.

You can also use the tool palette on the left to add graphical elements to your report. The tool palette was explained in Chapter 4. For completeness, the tools are described again and shown in Figure 9.17.

FIGURE 9.17
The tool palette with short descriptions of each tool.

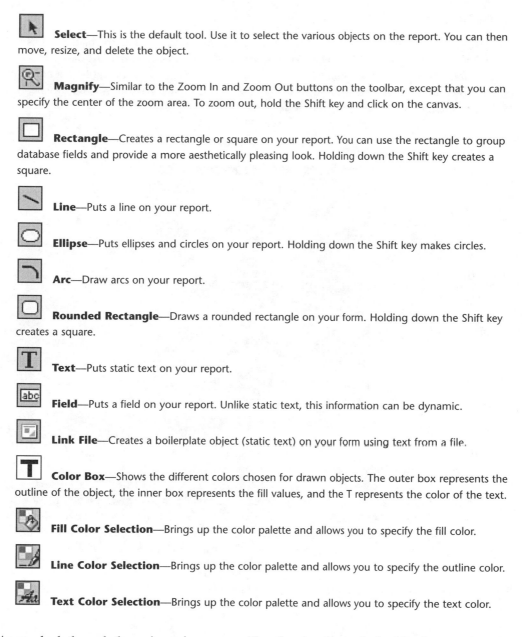

Select—This is the default tool. Use it to select the various objects on the report. You can then move, resize, and delete the object.

Magnify—Similar to the Zoom In and Zoom Out buttons on the toolbar, except that you can specify the center of the zoom area. To zoom out, hold the Shift key and click on the canvas.

Rectangle—Creates a rectangle or square on your report. You can use the rectangle to group database fields and provide a more aesthetically pleasing look. Holding down the Shift key creates a square.

Line—Puts a line on your report.

Ellipse—Puts ellipses and circles on your report. Holding down the Shift key makes circles.

Arc—Draw arcs on your report.

Rounded Rectangle—Draws a rounded rectangle on your form. Holding down the Shift key creates a square.

Text—Puts static text on your report.

Field—Puts a field on your report. Unlike static text, this information can be dynamic.

Link File—Creates a boilerplate object (static text) on your form using text from a file.

Color Box—Shows the different colors chosen for drawn objects. The outer box represents the outline of the object, the inner box represents the fill values, and the T represents the color of the text.

Fill Color Selection—Brings up the color palette and allows you to specify the fill color.

Line Color Selection—Brings up the color palette and allows you to specify the outline color.

Text Color Selection—Brings up the color palette and allows you to specify the text color.

As you look through the various views, you will notice that the vertical tool palette on the left adjusts to the environment. Even though a tool will be available in one view, it will not be available in another. Therefore, it is important to pay close attention to the view you are using and what it is capable of doing.

Data Model

The Data Model view is the least-used report view for simple reports like the ones used as examples so far in this book. The Data Model view is a work area to define the data used in your report. The view really becomes useful when you're trying to understand how a bunch of tables and columns have been combined to create a report. Figure 9.18 shows an example of a Matrix with Group report in the Data Model view.

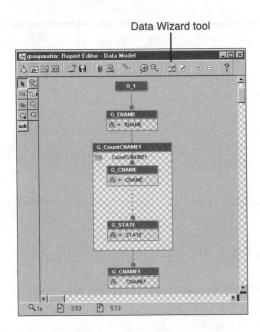

FIGURE 9.18
The Data Model view of the Matrix with Group report.

Notice how both the toolbar and the tool palette have adjusted for the environment. Most of the buttons on the toolbar should be familiar to you. As Figure 9.18 points out, however, the Data Wizard tool has been added. Most of the screens in the Data Wizard tool are derived from the Report Wizard and should look very familiar. You can use the Data Wizard to help create queries for your report.

The tool palette, as shown in Figure 9.19, should look completely different from any other in Report Builder.

FIGURE 9.19
The tool palette with short descriptions for the Data Model view.

Select—This is the default tool. Use it to select various objects on the report. You can then move, resize, or delete the object.

Magnify—Similar to the Zoom In and Zoom Out buttons on the toolbar, except that you can specify the center of the zoom area. To zoom out, hold the Shift key and click on the canvas.

SQL Query—Invokes the screen from the Report Wizard that is used to enter a query for the report. Multiple queries can be used in the same report.

Ref Cursor Query—Invokes the Procedure Builder with the stubs to build a ref cursor query. Ref cursors were introduced in Oracle 8i and are beyond the scope of this book. However, if you are familiar with ref cursors, you will find this feature very useful.

Data Link—Enables you to create relationships between two queries. The relationship can take the form of a query to query, group to group, or column to column link.

Summary Column—Creates a summary column in the Data Model view.

Formula Column—Creates a formula column in the Data Model view.

Placeholder Column—Creates a placeholder column in the Data Model view.

Cross Product—Enables you to create a cross product (one of each combination) of two groups.

When creating a report without using the Report Wizard, you would first go into the Data Model view and define the query and information to be used. In Chapter 8, however, you were shown how much work it is to create a form from scratch. The same is true for reports, so you should stick to using the Report Wizard when creating your reports.

Layout Model

The Layout Model view has been used in some of the previous examples to adjust the layout of a report. A report is made up of three parts: the header, the main, and the trailer. The Layout Model view allows you to edit all three parts, as well as modify margins.

You have been exposed to editing the body of a report using only the Layout Model view. Figure 9.20 shows the Layout Model view of the body of the Matrix with Group report that we completed earlier in the chapter. Notice the buttons that appear on the toolbar that are not present in the Live Previewer view.

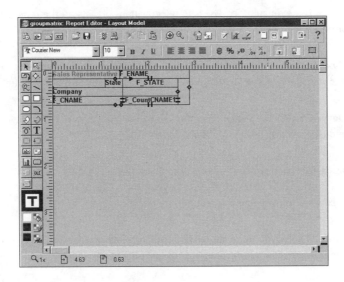

FIGURE 9.20
The Layout Model view of the Matrix with Group report.

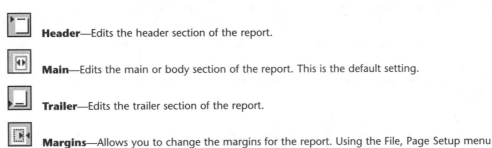

Header—Edits the header section of the report.

Main—Edits the main or body section of the report. This is the default setting.

Trailer—Edits the trailer section of the report.

Margins—Allows you to change the margins for the report. Using the File, Page Setup menu choice will adjust the margins for the printed page, but might truncate the report.

Some additions to the tool palette don't appear in the Live Previewer view. They include the following:

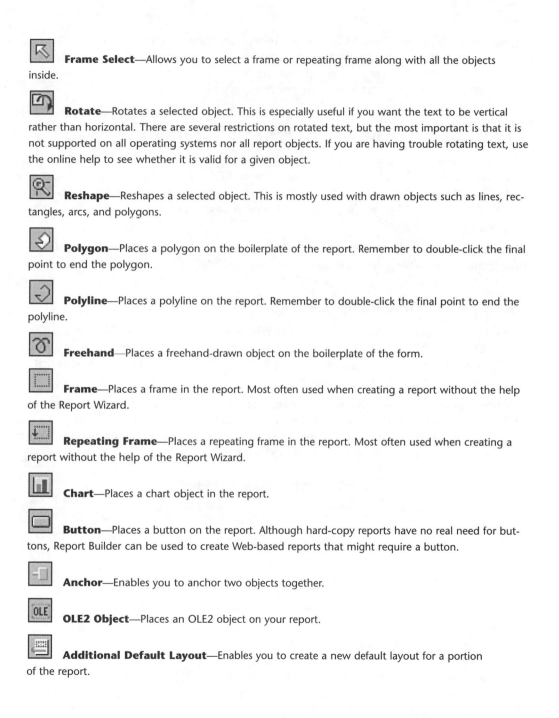

Frame Select—Allows you to select a frame or repeating frame along with all the objects inside.

Rotate—Rotates a selected object. This is especially useful if you want the text to be vertical rather than horizontal. There are several restrictions on rotated text, but the most important is that it is not supported on all operating systems nor all report objects. If you are having trouble rotating text, use the online help to see whether it is valid for a given object.

Reshape—Reshapes a selected object. This is mostly used with drawn objects such as lines, rectangles, arcs, and polygons.

Polygon—Places a polygon on the boilerplate of the report. Remember to double-click the final point to end the polygon.

Polyline—Places a polyline on the report. Remember to double-click the final point to end the polyline.

Freehand—Places a freehand-drawn object on the boilerplate of the form.

Frame—Places a frame in the report. Most often used when creating a report without the help of the Report Wizard.

Repeating Frame—Places a repeating frame in the report. Most often used when creating a report without the help of the Report Wizard.

Chart—Places a chart object in the report.

Button—Places a button on the report. Although hard-copy reports have no real need for buttons, Report Builder can be used to create Web-based reports that might require a button.

Anchor—Enables you to anchor two objects together.

OLE2 Object—Places an OLE2 object on your report.

Additional Default Layout—Enables you to create a new default layout for a portion of the report.

The primary use of the Layout Model view is to fine-tune the layout of your reports. It is also used to create additional templates. Even though Report Builder ships with several report templates, you will likely create additional templates specifically designed for your needs. How to do so is covered in the next section of this chapter.

Creating and Modifying Report Templates

The report templates included with Oracle Reports do a good job of showing you what is possible with Report Builder, but they will need to be modified to be useful for you and your company. The templates using the Oracle buildings on the report show that complex graphics can be added to reports. However, the graphic will need to be changed to incorporate your company logo or desired graphic.

This section contains two examples to help demonstrate templates. The first example shows how to modify an existing template and the second shows how to create a new one.

Modify an Existing Template

The Corporate 1 template is very well done and the reports that it produces look very professional. The only problem with it is that it includes a graphic that shows Oracle Corporation headquarters. If you could change that, the template would be perfect for some reports that management has requested.

The first step is to open the Corporate 1 template using the Template Editor. Select Templates in the Object Navigator and click on the Open icon found on the vertical toolbar. The Open dialog will appear and enable you to select the template file to change. Change the file filter to look for report template files only, as shown in Figure 9.21.

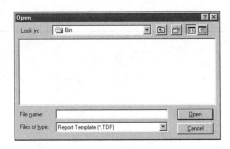

FIGURE 9.21
The Open dialog box to search for template files.

The predefined templates for Windows are found in the $ORACLE_HOME\Report60\ admin\template\Us directory. On Unix, they are found in $ORACLE_HOME/reports60/ admin/templates. The report template that corresponds to the Corporate 1 template is corp1.tdf. Select it and load it into the Object Navigator.

TEMPLATES ARE NOT AUTOMATICALLY ASSIGNED

Report Builder keeps your report and templates separate. Even though you might be editing a template and a report, the report is not required to use the template. After you have modified a template and saved it, you need to use the Report Wizard to reload the new template.

After you have loaded the template into the Object Navigator, you can modify it to meet your needs. In this example, you will remove the Oracle buildings graphic and replace it with My Company logo. To invoke the Template Editor, select the CORP1 template in the Object Navigator and right-click with the mouse. Select Template Editor from the pop-up menu.

The first change to make is to remove the graphic. Simply select the graphic and press the Delete key on your keyboard. Now replace the graphic by using the Link File tool on the tool palette. Remember to place the new object on the template by clicking and dragging the mouse to create a rectangle of the desired size.

The Link File area on the report is used to import a file and display it in the report. To link the file, you must open the Property Palette, set the Source File Format property to image, and set the Source Filename property to mylogo.bmp (be sure to include the proper path). If the graphic does not show up in the Link File area, you might need to make the area larger so that the graphic can fit. The finished template should look similar to Figure 9.22.

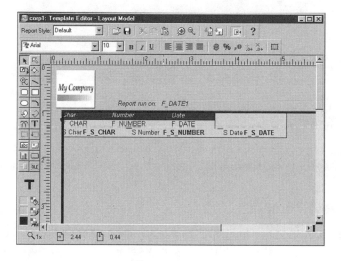

FIGURE 9.22
The completed Corporate 1 template with the new logo instead of Oracle Corporation's headquarters.

You can also take this time to modify the report's margins. The default margins for this particular template are a bit wide, and some printers have trouble printing that close to the edge. Simply adjust the margins (as indicated by the thick rectangle) to an appropriate size.

This is also a good time to change the color scheme, if you so choose. You must turn off the margin toggle found on the right of the upper toolbar, and then select the object you want to change. Bring up the Property Palette and make the modifications to the colors.

When you are finished changing the template, save the new template. You can use the same name and overwrite the predefined template, or you can choose a different name. After the template is saved, you can use it to create your report.

To change the template used to create a report, select the report name in the Object Navigator and open the Report Wizard. The last tab in the Report Wizard is where you define the template to use. If you have a template file for a report, select Template file and provide the full path to the template as shown in Figure 9.23.

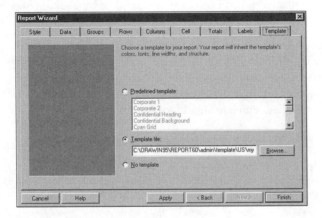

FIGURE 9.23
Selecting the newly created template for your report.

Your report should now display the company logo instead of the Oracle headquarters graphic. This satisfies the layout requests of management and you have quickly finished the job.

Creating a New Template

It is generally easier to modify something that already exists than to create something new. The same is true of templates. You should try using the existing templates and modifying them to fit your needs rather than creating one from scratch. If you do need to create a new template, however, it is not that difficult.

To create a new template, select Templates in the Object Navigator and click on the Create tool found in the vertical toolbar. The Template Editor will appear as shown in Figure 9.24.

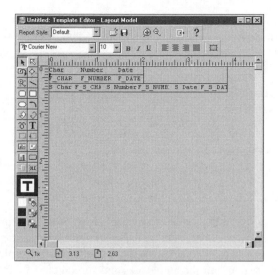

FIGURE 9.24
The Template Editor used to create a new report template.

Using the Margin Toggle button found on the upper toolbar allows you to add report boiler-plate information to the heading and footers. This information can include things such as the report name, the date the report was run, and the report page numbers.

Toggling back to the report data enables you to change the attributes for the data in the body of the report. The top row objects are used to specify the label attributes for character fields, numeric fields, and date fields. These attributes are found on the Property Palette and should be modified to meet your report needs.

The second row of objects in the Template Editor refers to the actual data fields. Again, you will want to modify them appropriately. One of the changes you might want to make is right justifying all the number fields so that they line up correctly in a Tabular report. This is done by selecting the F_NUMBER object, opening the Property Palette, and changing the Number Justification property to right.

The third and final row of objects in the Template Editor refers to the summary labels and data. You might want to change the color of the data and labels to be different from that of the report body.

Most of the work you do will apply to the entire family of reports. However, you can make special modifications to the report template for a Matrix report that will not be made for a Tabular report. This is done using the pull-down list in the upper toolbar. Simply change the report style from Default to the desired report style and make the change.

To get an idea of how each of the template areas affects the outcome of your report, play with the Layout Editor. Then modify one of the sample reports you have been working on in this chapter to use the new report template.

Template Summary

Report templates can be a powerful tool to help you provide a common look and feel for your reports. Although you have the option to create a new report template, I suggest that you modify an existing report template to fit your specific needs.

Parameter Forms

The reports used as examples in this book return a relatively small amount of data. In a production environment, this will rarely be the case. For example, sometimes you might want to see a list of employees only in the accounting department. Up to this point, you would have had to create a report that shows all the employees and sorts them by department. Now, I'll show you how parameter forms can be used to restrict the report query to provide only a subset of rows.

At the beginning of the chapter, you created a report to show all the employees in the database. The report was called groupmatrix. You will modify that report now to show employees for only a given department.

Start by opening the report that shows all the employees in the database table. If you did not save the report, re-create it now using the Report Wizard. By now, you should be pretty good at using the Report Builder and it should not take too long to create a simple report.

Next, define a user parameter to serve as a placeholder for the department in which the report will be run. To do this, expand the Data Model branch in the Object Navigator, click on User Parameters, and then click on Create in the vertical toolbar. The object should have a name like P_1. Change the object's name to P_Department.

Now select the Tools, Parameter Form Builder menu option and you should see a dialog similar to Figure 9.25. Scroll down to the last parameter and you will see P_Department. Change the label to Department, and click on the P_Department parameter name so that it is highlighted. Then click OK.

As you scrolled through the Parameter Form Builder's parameters, you probably noticed all the different system parameters that could be added to a parameter form. Normally, you will not need to add them to the form, but if you are not happy with the defaults, you can have them specified at runtime.

FIGURE 9.25
The Parameter Form Builder used to build a parameter form used by reports.

The Report Editor Parameter Form should now be displayed. You can modify any of the default labels to make them more explicit if you want. Select the PF_P_Department field from the form and open the Property Palette. To make the form more usable, take advantage of the List of Values property found at the bottom. Double-click the property value and you can specify a list of values. Use the following SELECT statement for this example:

```
SELECT deptno, dname FROM dept
```

Also be sure to click the Hide First Column option. Remember how the list of values works: The first column corresponds to the value stored in the database, and the second column refers to what is displayed.

The final step for the parameter form is to specify the limiting criteria in the report query. Open the Report Wizard and click on the Data tab. Modify the code in the WHERE clause so that it reads

```
WHERE ((EMP.DEPTNO = DEPT.DEPTNO)
      AND (EMP.MGR = EMP_A1.EMPNO(+))
      AND (EMP.DEPTNO = :P_Department))
```

Then click Finish and the report will be run. The parameter form should look similar to Figure 9.26.

Choose the department for which you would like to run the report, and click the Run Report button. Now, only those employees in the specified department are displayed in the report.

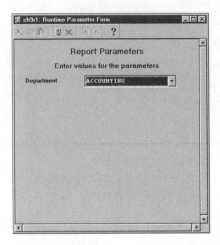

FIGURE 9.26
The completed parameter form used to limit the rows returned by the employee report.

THE ALL-IMPORTANT SELECT STATEMENT

On my first day at work at Oracle Corporation back in January of 1986, my boss called me into a meeting for a two hour training course on Structured Query Language or SQL. We spent fifteen minutes on INSERT, UPDATE, and DELETE. The rest of the short class was spent learning about the SELECT statement.

Query Builder is a great tool to help you build your SELECT statements for your reports. However, a true SQL expert will always double-check the SQL to make sure the generated query is correct. On occasion, he or she will even prefer to create the query without the help of Query Builder.

While it would be nice to have all reports using a single table, this is next to impossible to accomplish. Any application with any degree of usefulness will require the use of lookup tables. Understanding inner and outer joins is crucial. It is also important to be able to perform nested queries.

I have always seen building complex queries as a challenge and look forward to a particularly tricky SELECT statement. While at Network Computer, Inc. I was responsible for managing the team tasked with modifying our bug database. The development team did an excellent job fulfilling a complex set of system requirements but needed help with some of the reports.

On one occasion the team leader came to me with a question about how to create a complex report involving several lookup tables and a nasty join condition. The tables involved were several thousand rows long already and so we reduced the problem so it could be recreated using the scott/tiger example tables with some minor adjustments. I then created a first draft of the query to be used by the report.

The team leader ran the query and thought everything was fine. She then converted it from the scott/tiger tables to the real bug database tables and discovered some unique cases where the report was not providing the correct data. She then recreated those same cases in the scott/tiger tables and we worked together to create a SELECT statement that provided the correct results.

The whole process took about four hours to complete. In the end, the team leader had a report that worked the way she needed it to, I had fun creating another complex query, and neither of us had to waste time teaching or learning new data structures for an application.

Summary

You should now be very comfortable using Report Builder. This chapter showed you how to create a report using each of the eight different report styles. Each of the three different report views was explained. You were shown how to modify and create templates. Finally, you were also shown how to create a parameter form and integrate it into your report.

ORACLE GRAPHICS BUILDER DEVELOPMENT

ESSENTIALS

- Graphics Builder enables you to create the following kinds of charts: bar, line, pie, table, mixed bar and line, double-Y, scatter, and Gantt charts.

- Mixed bar and line charts might require a scaling factor with one set of values for the data to be displayed properly. Otherwise, the Y-axis values might be different enough to misrepresent the displayed data.

- A double-Y chart enables you to display two Y axes with differing values. This obviates the need for the scaling factor required with some mixed bar and line charts.

- Scatter charts require that both the X-axis and Y-axis use numeric values.

- Drill-down charts enable you to create a chart that calls another chart with more detailed information. This allows a user to click on one chart value, such as a pie slice, and see specific information about that slice.

In Chapter 4, "Oracle Reports Developer and Graphics," you used Graphics Builder to embed a chart in a report. This chapter goes into more detail about the various chart types available with Graphics Builder. Also, you are introduced to drill-down charts and shown how to create them.

Chart Types

Graphics Builder supports many different types of charts. To use them in your application effectively, you need to understand the strengths and weaknesses of each chart type. A bar chart is great for showing comparisons between data, whereas a pie chart is better for showing percentages.

This section of the chapter explains the various types of charts and how to use them effectively. Only so much can be done with the salary and commission values in the employee table, so be prepared to create a new table and to add data to it. You might want to review Chapter 5, "Query Builder and Schema Builder," and the Schema Builder if you have not already done so.

Graphics Builder supports the following chart types:

- Bar charts (both horizontal and vertical)
- Line charts
- Pie charts
- Table charts
- Mixed bar and line charts
- Double-Y charts
- Scatter charts
- Gantt charts

Bar Charts (Both Horizontal and Vertical)

Graphics Builder supports both horizontal and vertical bar charts. As I said earlier, a bar chart is great for showing comparisons between data. Perhaps you want to compare the differences between revenue for each salesperson. Another possible use (as shown in Chapter 2, "Developer Basics") is to show a comparison of salaries for each employee.

The example in this chapter builds on the example in Chapter 2 and shows how commissions can be added to salaries for comparison. Start Graphics Builder and run the Graphics Genie using the Chart, Create Chart menu option in the Layout Editor. Use the following SELECT statement to query the database:

```
SELECT ename, sal Salary, comm Commission
FROM emp
```

The name of the chart is Bar Example, and its title is Employee Compensation. Choose either the horizontal or vertical bar chart, depending on your preference (the example uses a horizontal chart). Then choose Bar with Stacked Bars as the subtype. When you are done, click OK. The finished chart should look similar to Figure 10.1.

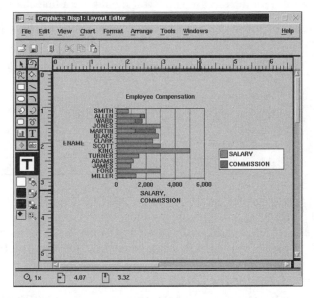

FIGURE 10.1
A stacked bar chart showing each employee's total compensation.

X AND Y AXES

In a horizontal bar chart, the X-axis and Y-axis are switched. The X-axis is now on the left, and the Y-axis is on the bottom.

Unfortunately, the X-axis and Y-axis labels are not very descriptive and should be changed. Use the following steps to make the changes:

1. Right-click on the X-axis description ENAME and select Axes from the pop-up list. Enter Employees in the Custom Label property.

2. In the Axis Properties dialog, use the pull-down list at the top of the dialog to select the Y1 axis. Enter Salary and Commission in the Custom Label property.

3. Click OK to close the Axis Properties dialog.

The horizontal bar chart is finished. You might want to play around with some of the other subtypes and see how they can be used with your application. When you are done, save the graph in case you need to refer to it again.

Line Charts

Line charts are very similar to bar charts. However, line charts are better at showing trends. If you want to compare sales for different months, you should use a line chart.

This next example requires you to create a new table and populate it with sales information. The SALES table to be created is shown in Table 10.1.

Table 10.1   Description of the SALES Table

Column Name	Data Type
CONTACTNO	Number
SALEDATE	Date
AMOUNT	Number
DESCRIPTION	Varchar2(50)

The CONTACTNO column relates back to the CONTACT table created in Chapter 5. The CONTACTNO and SALEDATE columns are used to form the primary key. In a production system, this table might require other constraints and columns, but it works well for the remaining examples in the chapter. After the table is created, enter the data from Table 10.2.

Table 10.2   Sample Data for the SALES Table

CONTACTNO	SALEDATE	AMOUNT	DESCRIPTION
1	15-JAN-2001	1000	Product A
1	15-FEB-2001	1000	Product A
2	5-JAN-2001	780	Product B
2	5-MAR-2001	1250	Product C
3	7-FEB-2001	1050	Product D
3	17-MAR-2001	950	Product E
4	1-JAN-2001	1000	Product A
4	15-FEB-2001	1000	Product A
5	2-FEB-2001	780	Product B
5	7-MAR-2001	950	Product E
6	31-JAN-2001	1000	Product A
6	30-MAR-2001	1000	Product A

You are ready to create the line graph after the data has been entered. If the bar graph from the previous exercise is still displayed in the Object Navigator, remove it using the Object

Navigator. Then create a new graph using the Navigator, Create menu choice in the Object Navigator, followed by the Chart, Create Graph option in the Layout Editor window.

Use the following query to select the information from the database:

```
SELECT saledate, amount
FROM sales
ORDER BY saledate
```

The name of the chart is Line Example and the title is First Quarter Sales. Then be sure to select the line graph with the default subtype. The graph is done, but it does not really accurately depict the sales for the three-month period. The chart makes it appear that an equal number of days have passed between each sale. This is not true and should be corrected.

Use the Tools, Queries menu choice to reopen the Query Properties dialog. Then change the query to the following:

```
SELECT to_char(trunc(saledate,'MON'),'MON'),
       sum(amount) Amount
FROM sales
GROUP BY trunc(saledate,'MON')
```

The trunc function truncates the date information so that all the sales look as if they took place on the first day of the month. The to_char function strips off the year and the day information to provide only the month name. If you clean up the axes using the method shown in the previous example, your finished line chart should look similar to Figure 10.2.

Pie Charts

Chapter 4 gave a pretty good example of how to use a pie chart to show the percentages of salary as broken down by department. The example in this chapter shows a percentage breakdown of sales by customer.

Close the previous graph, if you have not already done so, and create a new one. Use the Query Builder to create the query. Figure 10.3 shows the three tables to be used in the query. Select CUST.CNAME first followed by SALES.AMOUNT. Notice that none of the columns from the CONTACT table are used.

After the query statement is created, it must be modified slightly. In the current form, the query will return one row for every sale recorded. It should return only the sum of the sales for each company. This is accomplished by adding sum() around the field SALES.AMOUNT, and by adding GROUP BY CUST.CNAME as the last line in the query. Listing 10.1 shows the complete SELECT statement.

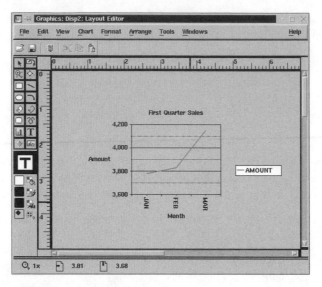

FIGURE 10.2
The completed line chart example using the newly created sales information. Save the chart to refer to in the future.

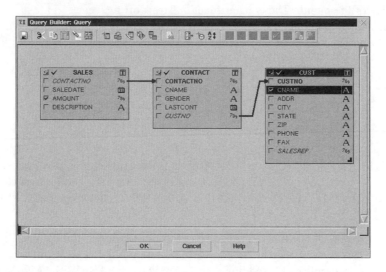

FIGURE 10.3
The tables used by Query Builder to help build the SELECT statement.

Listing 10.1   Query Used for the Pie Chart

```
SELECT ALL CUST.CNAME, sum(SALES.AMOUNT)
FROM SALES, CONTACT, CUST
WHERE ((SALES.CONTACTNO = CONTACT.CONTACTNO)
  AND (CONTACT.CUSTNO = CUST.CUSTNO))
GROUP BY cust.cname
```

Use Pie Example for the name of the chart and Sales by Company for the title. Use Pie with Depth as the subtype for the chart. The finished pie chart is shown in Figure 10.4. Feel free to discard the chart or save it for later reference if you think you might need it.

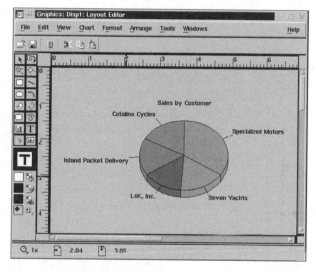

FIGURE 10.4
The completed pie chart, showing sales by company.

Table Charts

Table charts can be used to display information from a database table in a table format. This also could be done easily in a report. However, the advantage of using a table chart will be obvious when drill-down charts are discussed later in this chapter.

The table chart for this example shows the number of sales as well as the total amount of sales for the quarter. Close the previous chart and create a new one. The query to use is in Listing 10.2.

Listing 10.2   Query for the Table Chart

```
SELECT CUST.CNAME Customer,
       count(SALES.SALEDATE) Sales,
       sum(SALES.AMOUNT) Amount
FROM CUST, CONTACT, SALES
WHERE ((SALES.CONTACTNO = CONTACT.CONTACTNO)
  AND (CONTACT.CUSTNO = CUST.CUSTNO))
GROUP BY CUST.CNAME
```

Use Table Example for the name and Customer Sales Data for the title. Then click the Values tab in the Chart Properties dialog to specify the columns that should be displayed. The CUSTOMER column is already in the Chart Values column. Also add the SALES and AMOUNT columns or they will not be displayed. Click OK and your chart should look similar to Figure 10.5.

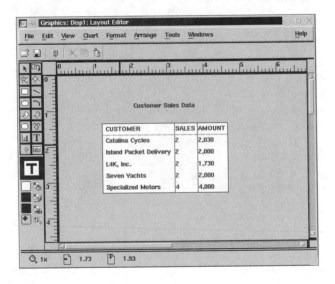

FIGURE 10.5
The completed table chart showing customer sales information.

Table charts are useful for showing information in a tabular format. The chart can be easily reproduced using a report. However, if you are building several charts and graphs using Graphics Builder and the table is not complicated, it is more efficient to use a table chart.

Mixed Bar and Line Charts

The data shown in the table chart also could be plotted using a mixed bar and line chart. The data for the number of sales must be modified slightly to account for the number of sales being three orders of magnitude smaller than the dollar amount for the sales.

Right-click on the table chart from the last example and select the Properties menu option. Select the mixed chart type with the default subtype. Click on the Categories tab and remove the second use of the CUSTOMER column from the Chart Categories list. Click on the Values tab and verify that SALES is selected for the column chart and AMOUNT is selected for the line chart. Click on OK and you should see only the line chart—the number of sales must be multiplied by a factor of 500 in order to be seen.

Use the Tools, Queries menu choice to bring up the query. Multiply the count(SALES.SALEDATE) column by 500 as shown in Listing 10.3.

Listing 10.3   Query for the Mixed Line and Bar Graph

```
SELECT ALL CUST.CNAME Customer,
       count(SALES.SALEDATE) * 500 Sales,
       sum(SALES.AMOUNT) Amount
FROM CUST, CONTACT, SALES
WHERE ((SALES.CONTACTNO = CONTACT.CONTACTNO)
  AND (CONTACT.CUSTNO = CUST.CUSTNO))
GROUP BY CUST.CNAME
```

Apply the changes and close the Query Properties dialog. The resulting graph should look similar to Figure 10.6.

It is probably a good idea to change the axis labels to avoid confusing the reader of the chart. You might use # of Sales * 500, Amount to remind the reader that the number of sales per customer is greatly exaggerated. You could also modify the query so that the value of the sales amount is divided by 500.

Mixed bar and line charts are useful for displaying two pieces of information that are somehow related. In this example, the number of sales can be correlated with the amount of sales for a list of customers. This information could be used to show that Specialized Motors is not just buying high-priced items, but it is also buying more of them.

Double-Y Charts

The previous example required you to multiply the number of sales by a factor of 500 in order to see the results for one set of data. The double-Y chart solves this problem by using two Y-axes with different scales.

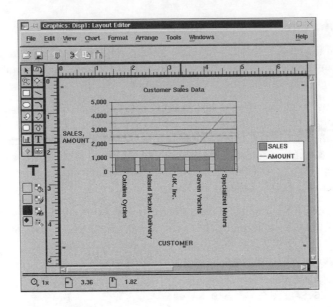

FIGURE 10.6
An example of a mixed line and bar graph.

Create a new chart using the query in Listing 10.4. Notice that this query is the same as the query in Listing 10.3, but without the multiplier.

Listing 10.4   Query for the Double-Y Chart

```
SELECT ALL CUST.CNAME Customer,
       count(SALES.SALEDATE) Sales,
       sum(SALES.AMOUNT) Amount
FROM CUST, CONTACT, SALES
WHERE ((SALES.CONTACTNO = CONTACT.CONTACTNO)
  AND (CONTACT.CUSTNO = CUST.CUSTNO))
GROUP BY CUST.CNAME
```

Use Double-Y Example for the name and Sales and Amounts for the title. Select the double-Y chart type with the default subtype. Use the Values table to verify SALES using the Y1 axis and Amount using Y2. The finished chart should look similar to Figure 10.7.

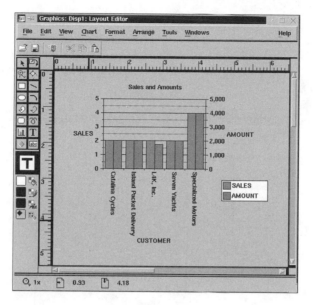

FIGURE 10.7
The completed double-Y chart shows the sales information using two separate Y-values.

Scatter Charts

Scatter charts are used to plot points using two numerical or value axes. This means that both the X-axis and Y-axis are required to be numbers. One case in which a scatter chart might be useful to analyze the dollar value of sales in relation to the day of the month on which the sale is made. If you notice that most people make large purchases toward the end of the month, you could offer discounts toward the beginning.

Create a new chart and invoke the Chart Genie. The query for this example is found in Listing 10.5.

Listing 10.5   Query for the Scatter Chart

```
SELECT to_number(to_char(saledate,'DD')),
       amount
FROM SALES
```

Use a title of Scatter Example and a title of Sales During the Month. Be sure to select the default scatter chart with no subtype. Click OK and you will see the chart completed. The X-axis label is a bit confusing and should be changed to Day of the Month.

Notice that the X-axis goes to 40. There are only 31 days in the longest months of the year, so the maximum value of the X-axis should be limited. Select the chart in the Layout Editor. Right-click on the chart and select the Axes menu option. Make sure that the upper pull-down list is set to the X-axis and click on the Continuous Axis tab. Set the Maximum value to 31 as shown in Figure 10.8.

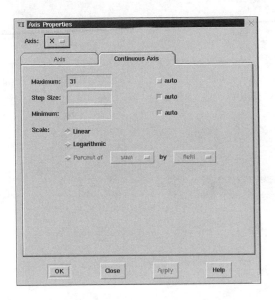

FIGURE 10.8
The Axis Properties dialog used to manually set the maximum values for an axis.

When you're done, you should have a fairly even scatter chart. Looking closely, you might see that most sales take place at the beginning of the month and not at the end.

High-Low Charts

High-low charts are most common to investors following the stock market. Throughout the day, a stock will have a high, low, and close value. High-low charts can be used to plot those values on a chart. With the sample data used for the charts in this chapter, a high-low chart can also be used to display the high and low purchases made by each customer.

Create a new chart and start the Chart Genie. Use the query statement in Listing 10.6 for this example.

Listing 10.6   Query for the High-Low Chart

```
SELECT ALL CUST.CNAME Customer,
       max(SALES.AMOUNT) Max,
```

Listing 10.6   Continued

```
      min(SALES.AMOUNT) min
FROM CUST, CONTACT, SALES
WHERE ((SALES.CONTACTNO = CONTACT.CONTACTNO)
  AND (CONTACT.CUSTNO = CUST.CUSTNO))
GROUP BY CUST.CNAME
```

Use High-low Example for the chart name and Maximum and Minimum Sales for the chart title. Select the High-low chart type and use the High-Low-Close with Fill subtype. Click on the Values tab; set the High column to MAX, the Close column to None, and the Low column to Min. Click OK and you will have a high-low chart similar to Figure 10.9.

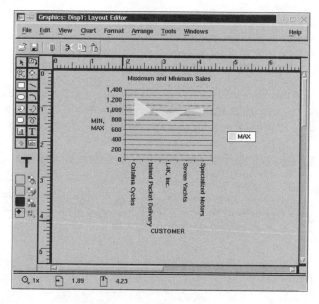

FIGURE 10.9
An example of a high-low chart showing the maximum and minimum sales per customer.

High-low charts can be used to display all sorts of useful data. Take some time to play around with the different subtypes and see what results you can come up with.

Gantt Charts

Gantt charts are most commonly associated with project management and resource scheduling. Three values are necessary for a Gantt chart: the task or description, the start date, and the end date. When the data is plotted, it becomes easy to see the relationships between tasks and potential scheduling problems.

The sales data used for most of the examples in this chapter has worked well up to this point. Unfortunately, that data will require a bit of massaging to get it to work with a Gantt chart. This example will plot the time between the first and last sale for each customer.

Create a new chart and start the Chart Genie. Use the query statement in Listing 10.7.

Listing 10.7   Query for the Gantt Chart

```
SELECT ALL CUST.CNAME Customer,
       min(SALES.SALEDATE) Min,
       max(SALES.SALEDATE) Max
FROM CUST, CONTACT, SALES
WHERE ((SALES.CONTACTNO = CONTACT.CONTACTNO)
  AND (CONTACT.CUSTNO = CUST.CUSTNO))
GROUP BY CUST.CNAME
```

Use Gantt Example for the chart name and Sales Timeframes for the title. Select the Gantt chart with the default subtype. Use the Values tab and verify that Min is used for the beginning date and Max for the ending. Click OK and you will have a Gantt chart similar to Figure 10.10.

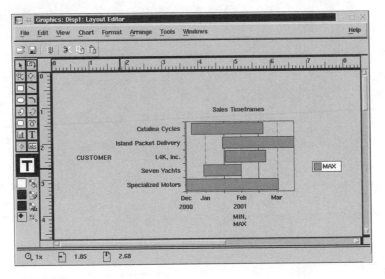

FIGURE 10.10
The completed Gantt chart.

The Gantt chart is a specialized chart; it would be rare that you would use it for anything other than project management. However, if you do need a Gantt chart, it is available in Graphics Builder.

Chart Type Summary

You have now seen an example of each of the different chart types provided by Graphics Builder. I hope this discussion gave you an idea of how to use each type effectively to present the information in your applications.

It would have been helpful to cover examples using each of the chart subtypes, but time and space do not permit it. With a little experimenting and the examples from this chapter, you will be able to figure out any problems you encounter.

WHERE IS THIS DOCUMENTED?

When I started writing this chapter, I had already used several of the chart types. However, there were several types that I had yet to use. Line, bar, and pie charts are commonly used and fairly easy to figure out. Others took a lot of experimentation and trial and error.

One problem with Graphics Builder is that an old product from Developer 2000 hasn't received a lot of attention. Even though the Chart Genie is nice, it is not the same as a Wizard and it is sometimes downright difficult to invoke. It would have been nice to have a toolbar icon to click to bring up the Chart Genie. Instead, I was required to right-click on the chart and open the properties sheet. After I discovered that trick, I could experiment more easily.

A second problem in using the Chart Genie was that I was required to go through each of the Chart Property dialog tabs and make sure that all the values were appropriately set. This became more confusing when the query information for the chart could not be found among the tabs. Of course, the query information is found in a different window.

Most of the problems were easily solved after I figured out all the right-clicking and picked the correct pop-up menu choices. However, there were several other occasions when that didn't help. I headed to Oracle's Web site at http://technet.oracle.com, and looked up the documentation for Graphics Builder. Unfortunately, it is buried in the Forms and Reports documentation. Even then, the new documentation is very cryptic and I could not find examples of the different chart types.

My next resource was to look through the online documentation provided by Oracle. There were a few useful pieces of information, but not enough to help me get through some of the more difficult chart types. To complicate matters, the Unix online documentation is incomplete and linked incorrectly. Clicking on a hypertext link should take me to the correct information. Instead, I was sent to a catchall placeholder that has no relevant information for the topic that you are researching.

Finally, I went into my basement and looked through all my old Oracle documentation. Graphics Builder has been around awhile (it used to be called Oracle Graphics), and I have many old manuals dating all the way back to Oracle version 4. Although it was the most helpful documentation I had found, I was still at a loss for help on one or two chart types.

In the end, through dumb luck and a lot of experimenting, I got the mixed chart to work correctly. Looking back at the text and examples in this chapter, I wonder why I had so many problems. It all looks so simple. I figure that if the charts were tough for me, they might be tough for others, and that is what makes a chapter like this rewarding.

Drill-Down Charts

Graphics Builder has a powerful capability to allow you to build master-detail or drill-down charts. Although it is nice to be able to combine multiple data sets into the same graph, it also can be desirable to keep them separate. Drill-down charts enable you to put two charts in the same display and to have the first one drive the data in the second.

A good example of this is the sales information for each of the customers. The main graph is good for showing the summary information, whereas the second graph can show the individual sales information.

The best way to see how this works is through an example. Create a new graph using Listing 10.8 for the query.

Listing 10.8   Primary Query for the Drill-Down Chart

```
SELECT ALL CUST.CNAME Customer,
        sum(SALES.AMOUNT) Amount
FROM CUST, CONTACT, SALES
WHERE ((SALES.CONTACTNO = CONTACT.CONTACTNO)
  AND (CONTACT.CUSTNO = CUST.CUSTNO))
GROUP BY CUST.CNAME
```

Use Drill-down Example for the name and Sales by Customer for the title. Select the simple vertical bar graph with no subtype. The master chart is done and should look familiar.

Select Parameters in the Object Navigator and click on the Create tool found in the vertical toolbar. You are presented with the Parameters dialog as shown in Figure 10.11. Name the new parameter P_Customer.

Use the Char data type and don't assign an initial value. After defining the parameter, click OK to dismiss the dialog. This will be filled in by the drill-down being performed by the user.

The next step is to create another chart. Use the Chart, Create Chart menu option to create a second chart in the same display. You are asked whether to use the existing query or create a new one. Create a new one and use the query in Listing 10.9.

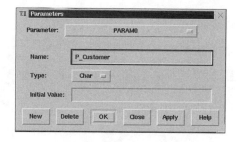

FIGURE 10.11
The Parameters dialog used to create user-defined parameters.

Listing 10.9   Second Query for the Drill-Down Chart

```
SELECT ALL SALES.DESCRIPTION Description,
       SALES.AMOUNT Amount
FROM CUST, CONTACT, SALES
WHERE ((SALES.CONTACTNO = CONTACT.CONTACTNO)
  AND (CONTACT.CUSTNO = CUST.CUSTNO)
  AND (CONTACT.CNAME = :P_Customer))
```

Use Detail Drill-down for the name and Sales Detail for the title. Select the pie chart with any of the three subtypes, and then click OK.

The Chart Genie places only the title of the pie chart on the display because there is no default value. The title represents the top of the pie chart and must be moved so that it does not interfere with the rest of the chart.

The last thing to do is wire up the drill-down functionality. This is done by selecting the actual graph values in the original chart and double-clicking. The Object Properties dialog for the actual graph values will appear. Select the Drill-down tab and fill it out as shown in Figure 10.12.

The P_Customer parameter you defined earlier will receive the name of the customer. The name will then be used by query1, which is the detail query defined second (the master query is query0). When you are done, click OK.

Now run the graph by clicking the Run button on the toolbar. You will be asked to save the graph and you should choose to do so. If the chart is running, when you click on one of the bars in the master graph, the detail information will appear in a pie chart elsewhere on the display. For example, clicking on the sales information for L4K, Inc. should provide information similar to Figure 10.13.

Congratulations, you have now completed a drill-down chart. Drill-down charts can help organize your data displays and make them more readable.

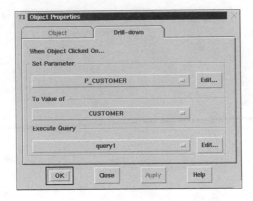

FIGURE 10.12
The Object Properties dialog that will allow the drill-down graph to function properly.

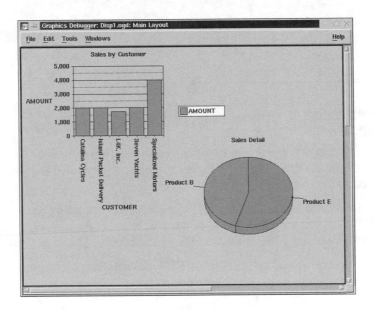

FIGURE 10.13
The drill-down chart showing detail information about the sales for L4K, Inc.

Summary

This chapter provided examples on how to use each of the chart types provided by Graphics Builder. You were introduced to drill-down charts and taught how to build them. You should now have a solid understanding of how to create charts using Graphics Builder.

A chart or graph often can be used to show information in an easy-to-read format. It is easy to bury numbers in a text report that all but the most careful reader will gloss over. If the information is something that you want your users to notice, be sure to use a chart or graph to illustrate your point. On the other hand, if you want to hide information, feel free to use Report Builder and maybe nobody will notice.

DEVELOPER
APPLICATION DESIGN

ESSENTIALS

- Application development begins by having a strong understanding of the business or organization for which you are creating the software.

- Create a document with all of the information you will need to create your application. This should include a synopsis of how the application will be used and its goals.

- Use the information in your design document to create an initial layout for your application interface. Be sure to include all of the forms, reports, and graphics that will be needed. Once these application interfaces are designed, show them to the customer and users to be sure the design meets the required goals and expectations.

- Distill the database objects from the application interface. Be sure to normalize data and use lookup tables when appropriate.

- Indexes can be used to help increase query performance. However, they have a tradeoff of slowing down data inserts and using database space.

This chapter takes the information you have learned about creating Oracle Developer applications and applies it to a real application. The EMP and DEPT sample tables are great for showing most of the features of Developer, but the real test of knowledge comes through building a real-world application.

Big Jim is a friend who promotes individual amateur sporting events. He started out promoting mountain bike events, but has now branched out to road cycling, running, and triathlon events. Many of the same people come to the events, and it would be nice to keep track of them all for future mailings and event promotion.

Chapter 12, "Making the Design a Reality," will take the sample application described in this chapter and create the forms, reports, and graphics. Chapter 13, "Deploying Developer Applications to the Web," will take the application and deploy it using the Web.

Application Background and Requirements

Big Jim owns a chain of furniture stores that specializes in items for the TV-watching sports enthusiast. His top-selling items are the All-Leather Reclining Chair and the Cooler on a Stand. Unfortunately, Big Jim loved them too much and gained a bit too much weight. His doctor told him to slim down a bit or he was in serious danger of having a heart attack.

So, Big Jim picked up a mountain bike and rode it on a trail near his home. Amazingly, he liked it. He liked it a lot, actually. Riding made him feel like a little kid again. He even started to look like a little kid. Some of his 300 pounds of weight came off, and although he is no lightweight at 175, he is a lot healthier.

To share his newfound enthusiasm for the sport of mountain biking, Big Jim started putting on fun races. At first, it was just a couple of friends and customers who heard about the races from the advertisements in his store. But soon the word was out, and lots of people started attending. Big Jim was so successful that other race organizers started asking for his help with their events. Now Big Jim puts on road cycling, running, and triathlon events almost every weekend.

When Big Jim started promoting mountain biking, all the record keeping could be done on paper. He left forms on the counters at all his stores, and people filled them out on the spot or mailed them back in. Now that he is running events every week, Jim needs a better system to keep track of everyone.

Jim has many volunteers who he can use to enter the information into the computer. He just needs a system that is easy to use and meets all his requirements.

Jim has noticed that a lot of the people that attend the mountain biking events also participate in the road cycling and triathlon events. He also has noticed that the triathlons are popular with the runners. Jim's first use for his information system is to create a list of participants who regularly attend his sporting events. This list can then be used by his volunteers to invite the regular participants to other races.

The next problem that Big Jim needs to solve is the number of people who come into his stores after an event, trying to find out how they did in comparison to all their friends. His current system is to type up everything by hand to create a report that people can look at. Unfortunately, he stays up all night after the day of an event putting the report together. Even though Jim does his best, there are often several errors in the report and that is starting to bother him.

If Big Jim can solve these two problems, he should be able to keep up with the demands of promoting all the races and events that he has planned for this season. He has come to you to ask for your help.

Application Interface

The main application interface will be used to sign up participants for an event. The following information needs to be recorded:

- First and last name
- Address, including city, state, and ZIP code
- Phone number
- E-mail address
- Birthday
- Gender

The address, phone number, and e-mail address are used to contact the participant about future events. The birthday and gender are used to sort the participants into categories for the race results.

People sign up for an event and the information associated with the event is

- Event name
- Event description
- Type of event
- Cost
- Date and start time

This information must be related back to the event participants, along with specific information for the individual taking part in the specific event. The specific individual participant information includes the following:

- Individual bib number
- Start time
- Finish time
- Date the individual registered for the event
- Payment information

It is important to record the bib number along with the start and finish times. Doing so enables Big Jim to streamline the results report at the end of the race or event. It is also important to record the payment information for each event that the individual participates in. Although the person might use a credit card for one event, he or she might use a check for the next. By recording the date of registration, the system can be used to provide a price discount to those who sign up early.

Looking over the information that will be stored in the database, it is apparent that several support tables must be added. The first table should store all possible event types. When Big Jim started promoting races and events, the table would have contained a single entry: mountain biking. Now that he is promoting other events, the table should contain road cycling, running, and triathlons. In the future, Big Jim might try to support other types of events such as swimming. He wants to be able to add those to his event list.

The second support table that must be added is for payment types. I mentioned earlier that a person could pay for one event with a check and another event with a credit card. Cash is also a valid payment method. In the future, Big Jim might offer coupons as part of his store's promotions. That would require "coupon" to be added to the database.

The third and final support table is used to keep track of credit card types. Big Jim's is set up to accept MasterCard and VISA as valid forms of payment. Big Jim is also working with Discover and American Express to be able to accept those cards for event registration. When that is completed, he wants to add those cards to the credit card list.

Keep in mind Big Jim's original goals for his database system:

1. Provide a system to keep track of former event participants so that they can be invited to upcoming events
2. Facilitate the report at the end of the event that lists the finishing places of all participants

The information being stored will meet Big Jim's original goals. Now it is time to design the forms, reports, and graphics used by the system.

Forms

The race application is made up of one primary form with several support forms. The support forms are used to maintain some of the lookup tables that provide such information as payment, event, and credit card types. A support form is also used to enter information about the events. The primary form is used to register the participants for the race or event.

All the forms for the three small lookup tables will appear similar. Each contains a field to enter the primary key and a field for the description. An example of one form is shown in Figure 11.1.

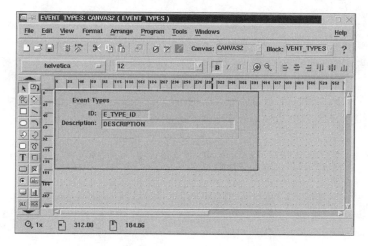

FIGURE 11.1
An example of one of the forms for the three simple lookup tables.

The event maintenance form is not much different from the other lookup forms except that it has more fields. Figure 11.2 is an example of what that form should look like.

The primary form of the application is much more complicated than any of the others. The person entering the participant must query the database to see whether the participant is already in the database. The participant's personal information is then linked to the event and event-specific information. Finally, the payment information must be recorded. If the payment is a check or cash, there is not much else to do. However, if the payment is a credit card, more information must be recorded. Figure 11.3 shows what this form must look like.

The credit card information field should be a button that brings up the information for the credit card transaction. This information includes the credit card type, card number, expiration date, name on the card, and billing information.

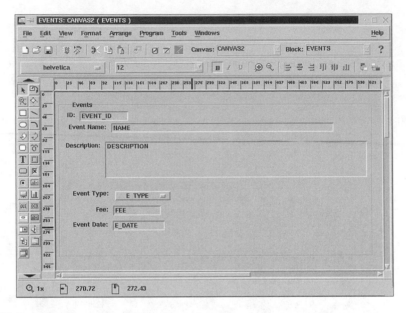

FIGURE 11.2
The form used to maintain the EVENTS table.

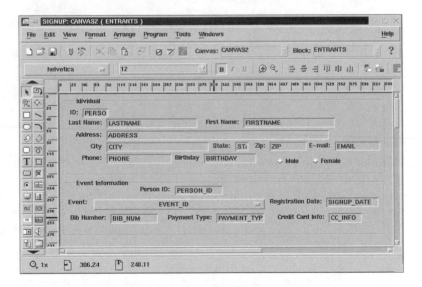

FIGURE 11.3
The primary form in the application used to add participants to races and events.

One additional form is needed. After the event is completed, Big Jim needs a form that he can use to enter the final results of the event. Although the primary form could be used to enter the results, it would be easier to have a form specifically designed for results entry. Figure 11.4 shows that form.

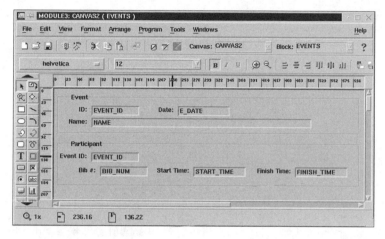

FIGURE 11.4
The form used to enter the result times at the end of a race or event.

The form queries the events so that the event closest to the system date is returned first. After the correct event is selected, the participants are queried in order of bib number. The finish sheets are then sorted by bib number, making it easier to enter the starting and finishing times.

You should now have an understanding of what is expected for the forms in the application. While you're building the application, do not be surprised if the finished form does not look exactly like the specification. As you build the form, it is not uncommon to swap out fields for other display objects (that is, pop-up lists, radio buttons, check boxes, and so on). An evolution always takes place during development.

Reports

The application must generate two reports. The first report is a form letter to let the participant know that he or she has signed up for the race or event. The second report is the event results divided into the various race categories.

The confirmation letter will be printed on Big Jim's Sport Promotion letterhead and will contain the following information:

```
<firstname> <lastname>
<Address>
<City>, <ST> <Zip>
```

```
Dear <firstname> <lastname>,

Thank you for signing up for the <event>. This letter is to confirm your
registration you submitted on <registration date> and to encourage you to
arrive at least 30 minutes before the start time so you will be ready when the
event begins. If you have any questions regarding this event, feel free to
contact us at (555) 555-1234.

Sincerely,


Big Jim
```

There needs to be a column in the database that is used to indicate that the confirmation letter has been sent out. After the report is run, the column will be updated so that a second letter is not sent out by mistake.

One of the advantages of having Big Jim put on all the sporting events is that he has consolidated all the different age categories. This reduces the complexity of the results report. The results should be separated for males and females. They should also be divided into the following age categories:

- 12 and younger
- 13 to 16
- 17 to 26
- 27 to 34
- 35 to 44
- 45 to 54
- 55 and older

The report should include the participant's place in the age category as well as the participant's name, bib number, and result time.

Graphics

Big Jim does not really need any graphics but after seeing what is possible, he thinks it would be nice to see the number of participants for each event that he promotes during the year. A simple bar graph is all he's looking for.

You should now have a rough idea of the forms, reports, and graphs that Big Jim is requesting for his event promotion application. Now it is time to distill that information into the database objects that must be created.

Review by Big Jim

The user interface is complete and should be put into a design document. Big Jim and his volunteers should be shown the document and be asked to provide some feedback on the design. They will be able to catch any problems before you have even started building the application. This has the potential to save you a tremendous amount of work.

Database Objects to Create

This application will use three types of database objects: tables, sequences, and indexes. The tables will be used to store the data. Sequences will be used to generate unique numbers used as primary keys by the tables. Finally, indexes will be used to decrease the amount of time it takes to search for information.

Other database objects could be created to ease application development (for instance, database triggers and procedures). However, the purpose of this book is to show how to create applications using Oracle Developer. Big Jim's application is simple enough that all the application logic can be contained within the forms, reports, and graphics elements and does not need to be encapsulated in the database. For larger applications, this would not be the case and special care should be taken to ensure that these other database objects are not forgotten.

Tables and Sequences

Looking at the data from earlier in the chapter that must be stored, there are seven tables that must be created. The following discussion describes each table as well as its relationship to other tables used by the application.

The first table is the PERSON table. It will hold the personal information for each participant in the various events. An individual can enter more than one event, and the information does not need to be duplicated for each event, so the personal info will be kept in a separate table. The PERSON table description is given in Table 11.1.

Table 11.1   The Definition of the PERSON Table

Column	Data Type
Person_ID	Number
Lastname	VARCHAR(20)
Firstname	VARCHAR(20)
Address	VARCHAR(50)

Table 11.1   Continued

Column	Data Type
City	VARCHAR(30)
State	CHARACTER(2)
Zip	VARCHAR(10)
Phone	VARCHAR(14)
Birthday	Date
Gender	CHARACTER(1)
Email	VARCHAR(50)

The Person_ID column will serve as the primary key for the table. There must be a sequence to generate unique numbers as people are added to the table. That sequence should be called PERSON_ID_SEQ.

The next table to create is the EVENTS table, and it will contain information about each of the events. The EVENTS table description is given in Table 11.2.

Table 11.2   The Definition of the EVENTS Table

Column	Data Type
Event_ID	Number
Name	VARCHAR(50)
Description	VARCHAR(500)
E_Type	Number
Fee	Number
Event_Date	Date

The Event_ID will serve as the primary key for the table. In addition to the date, the Event_Date column also will contain the start time. As with the PERSON table, a sequence will be used to generate unique numbers for the primary key. The sequence will be called EVENT_ID_SEQ.

The EVENTS and PERSON tables must be combined along with some additional information for each person in the event. This new table is called ENTRANTS and it should include foreign keys back to the EVENTS and PERSON tables. The ENTRANTS table definition is given in Table 11.3.

Table 11.3   The Definition of the ENTRANTS Table

Column	Data Type
Event_ID	Number
Person_ID	Number
Bib_Num	Number
Start_Time	Date

Table 11.3   Continued ———————————————————————

Column	Data Type
Finish_Time	Date
Payment_Type	Date
CC_Info	Number
Signup_Date	Date
Confirm	CHARACTER(1)

The Event_ID and Person_ID columns will work together to form the primary key. Remember that the date data type also works to store time as well as the date information. Rather than worry about using a VARCHAR column to hold the start and finish information, it is easier to put that information in a date column. Doing so enables you to use all of Oracle's SQL date and time functions in calculations. The CC_Info column is used as a foreign key into a table that contains the credit card transaction information (it will be described shortly).

There are three maintenance tables that will help to make the application dynamic. The first maintenance table is EVENT_TYPES and its description is found in Table 11.4. EVENT_TYPES contains the types of events that Big Jim promotes, such as mountain biking, road cycling, running, and triathlons. The E_TYPE_ID_SEQ sequence is used to generate unique IDs for each of the descriptions.

Table 11.4   The Definition of the EVENT_TYPES Table———————————————

Column	Data Type
E_Type_ID	Number
Description	VARCHAR(30)

The second maintenance table is PAY_TYPES and is described in Table 11.5. It contains descriptions for the different methods of payments such as cash, check, or credit card. The PAY_ID_SEQ sequence is used to generate unique IDs for each of the descriptions.

Table 11.5   The Definition of the PAY_TYPES Table ————————————————

Column	Data Type
Pay_ID	Number
Description	VARCHAR(15)

The third maintenance table is CC_TYPES and is described in table 11.6. It contains the different types of credit cards such as VISA and MasterCard. The CC_ID_SEQ sequence is used to generate unique IDs for each of the credit card names.

Table 11.6   The Definition of the CC_TYPES Table

Column	Data Type
CC_ID	Number
Name	VARCHAR(20)

The final table used in the sample application is CC_TRANSACTION, and it is used to store all the credit card transaction information. Because it is possible that children might use a parent's credit card to sign up for an event, some additional information must be stored in the table. The CC_TRANSACTION table description is presented in Table 11.7.

Table 11.7   The Definition of the CC_TRANSACTION Table

Column	Data Type
Transaction_ID	Number
CC_Type	Number
CC_Num	VARCHAR(16)
Exp_Date	Date
Name_on_Card	VARCHAR(30)
Address	VARCHAR(50)
City	VARCHAR(30)
State	CHARACTER(2)
Zip	VARCHAR(10)
Amount	Number

The Transaction_ID column serves as the primary key. The TRANSACTION_ID_SEQ sequence is used to generate unique numbers for the primary key.

All the tables and sequences for Big Jim's event promotion sample application have been described. The idea is to keep the application as simple as possible, but still meet the design requirement goals. The next step in database object creation is to look at the different types of indexes that must be created.

Indexes

Indexes decrease the amount of time it takes to query information in the database. However, an index has the disadvantages of taking more space in the database and increasing the amount of time it takes to add information to the database. Without those disadvantages, it would be easy to justify putting indexes on every column just in case the column is used in a query.

Another thought to keep in mind with indexes is when they are not used. If you have an index on a column that contains a string and you search using a substring function, the index will not be used to speed up the query. This is because indexes cannot be used when looking for modified data in columns.

Primary keys are good candidates for columns that should be indexed, especially when they are referenced by foreign keys. The only exception to this rule is with really small tables like the three lookup tables in Big Jim's application. The Oracle database has the ability to store small tables in a memory cache, making searches much quicker.

Indexes should be created on the tables and columns as shown in Table 11.8.

Table 11.8   Tables and Columns That Will Have Indexes

Table	Column
PERSON	Person_ID
	Lastname
	Firstname
EVENTS	Event_ID
	Name
ENTRANTS	Person_ID
	Event_ID
	Bib_Num
CC_TRANSACTION	Transaction_ID

Indexes are very flexible and can be added or dropped at any time. Therefore, if you find that an index on another column will help improve performance, don't hesitate to add it. On the other hand, if you find that an index is never being used, don't be afraid to drop it.

Now that you have the database objects for Big Jim's sample application, look over them to make sure that you have not forgotten anything. If you were building your own application, you might want to run the design by one of your colleagues. Often an associate will catch something that you have forgotten. After the review has been made, be sure to add the information to your design document. If everything looks good, you are ready to create the tables, sequences, and indexes.

THE DEVELOPMENT PROCESS

I was the Director of the Utah Development Center for Liberate Technologies and was responsible for managing a talented software development team. During that time, I immersed myself in the development process and was constantly looking for ways to increase productivity but, at the same time, decrease the number of software defects.

The software development process can be broken down into five phases:

- Analysis

- Architecture and design

- Implementation

- System test

- Maintenance

The cost of finding and fixing defects goes up for each stage of the development process. Therefore, it is best to find and fix problems as soon as possible. That led us to implement code reviews early in the design process and carry them through the entire development process.

A *code review* is basically a chance for a developer to run his code by a group of his or her peers and get some feedback. Sometimes the feedback turns out to be helpful suggestions on how to solve a problem elegantly. Other times the code review serves as sympathy when a developer is late getting a project done. The important thing is that other people get to take a look at what you are doing and provide feedback.

Doing a code review during the architecture and design process can greatly diminish the chances of problems occurring later. Although you might think that all contingencies are accounted for, you'll be surprised at what others will come up with. Making a few minor changes to the design is much easier than making major changes after coding has started.

Creating the Database Schema

The database design looks good, and now you are ready to create the database objects. This should be little more than re-creating the tables as described previously in the chapter. After the tables are created, relationships between the tables must be defined. Finally, the sequences and indexes will be created.

I recommend that you create another database login for Big Jim's sample applications. You might need to work with your database administrator to create the account. If you are the database administrator, you can create a new account using the system database login and the following command:

```
GRANT CONNECT, RESOURCE TO race IDENTIFIED BY events
```

The command will create a database login with a username of race and a password of events. If you do not have the ability to add a new database user and your database administrator is reluctant to add one, it is not a problem to create the objects in your existing account. Placing the objects in another account is a convenient way of keeping them separate and distinct from your other work.

All the tables to create are defined in Tables 11.1 through 11.7. Go ahead and create them, being sure to pay close attention to the column data types. Also be sure to define the primary keys for all the tables except the PARTICIPANTS table. PARTICIPANTS uses two columns to make up the primary key, and Oracle Schema Builder is not set up to do this. You might also want to leave off the primary key for the three lookup tables (EVENT_TYPES, PAY_TYPES, and CC_TYPES). Setting the primary key creates an index that has the potential to slow lookups for these tables. However, omitting the indexes requires that you create application logic to enforce uniqueness. Using a sequence to populate the primary key should be sufficient for such small lookup tables.

After defining the tables in Oracle Schema Builder, be sure to commit the changes. This ensures that the tables are created in the database. You are now ready to define the relationships between the tables. Table 11.9 lists the relationships to be created.

Table 11.9 Table Relationships to Be Added

Foreign Key	Primary Key
ENTRANTS.Person_ID	PERSON.Person_ID
ENTRANTS.Event_ID	EVENTS.Event_ID
ENTRANTS.Payment_Type	PAY_TYPES.Pay_ID
ENTRANTS.CC_Info	CC_TRANSACTIONS.Transaction_ID
EVENTS.E_Type	EVENT_TYPES.E_Type_ID
CC_TRANSACTIONS.CC_Type	CC_TYPES.CC_ID

When you have completed defining the relationships, the table definitions and relationships should look similar to Figure 11.5.

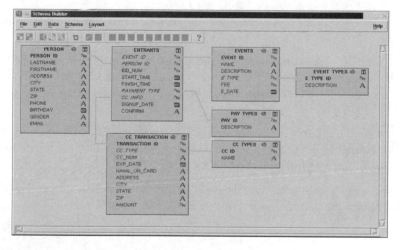

FIGURE 11.5
The schema definition for the database objects to be used by Big Jim's sample application.

You should create the indexes before you exit Schema Builder. Use Table 11.8 to remind you what indexes must be created. The indexes for columns that serve as primary keys will already be created. That limits the number of indexes that you need to create to six. When you are done, be sure to commit the schema changes.

The final step in database object creation is to create the sequences. Unfortunately, Oracle Schema Builder does not have the capability to create database sequences. Therefore, you must go into SQL*Plus and create the database objects by hand. Run the following code to create the necessary sequences:

```
CREATE SEQUENCE Person_ID_Seq;
CREATE SEQUENCE Event_ID_Seq;
CREATE SEQUENCE Pay_ID_Seq;
CREATE SEQUENCE E_Type_ID_Seq;
CREATE SEQUENCE CC_ID_Seq;
CREATE SEQUENCE Transaction_ID_Seq;
```

After running each line, you should get a message saying "Sequence Created." You have now created all the database objects for Big Jim's sample application.

Summary

In this chapter, you learned about Big Jim and his sporting event promotion hobby. He has been asked to help promote a series of cycling, running, and triathlon events, and needs an information system to make his job easier. The discussion in this chapter laid out the goals of the application.

The goals of Big Jim's application were combined with the information that Big Jim needed to keep track of. This was distilled into sample form prototypes that will be built in the next chapter. You were also given the necessary information to be contained in the reports and graphics.

Finally, you took all the information provided and were shown a plan for creating the necessary database objects. In the last section of the chapter, you created those objects in preparation for the creation of Big Jim's event application.

Chapter 12 will show you how to build the entire application for client/server deployment. Chapter 13 will take the application and deploy it using the Web.

MAKING THE
DESIGN A REALITY

ESSENTIALS ————————————————

- Forms to populate and maintain lookup tables are easy to create and should be kept as simple as possible.

- Use Display Items, not Text Items, to display and show primary keys derived from sequences. After the logic has been tested to ensure proper primary key assignment, the display item can be made invisible to the user during runtime.

- Date fields in forms do not contain time information. However, Date columns in the database do contain time information. To display time information on a form, change it to a datetime data type.

- Forms can be called from other forms using the CALL_FORM procedure.

- Reports and Graphics can be called from forms using the RUN_PRODUCT procedure.

- No application is ever complete. Therefore, it is best to define milestones and use those to release the application. Otherwise, it will never get done.

Chapter 11, "Developer Application Design," gave the history of Big Jim and his event promotion hobby. It also provided a brief specification of what the application should look like. This chapter takes that specification and turns it into a working application.

The forms used by the application will be created first. That will allow you to enter information into the system and test the functionality. Next will be reports and graphics. Finally, everything will be tied together using a menu created with Oracle Forms Developer.

Forms Creation

Big Jim's application requires six forms to be constructed. Four of these forms will be used to maintain lookup data, and the other two will be used to process information for the different events. The maintenance forms are the easiest to construct and will help to populate several tables used by the rest of the application. Therefore, they will be built first. Three of these forms are almost identical and will be constructed together. The last maintenance form will be created after that.

The last two forms, the information processing forms, are a bit more difficult to construct. However, they are very representative of the types of forms that make up most complex database applications.

Three Maintenance Forms

The EVENT_TYPES, PAY_TYPES, and CC_TYPES tables need a way to insert, update, and delete rows. If Big Jim had a dedicated database administrator employed full-time, that person could modify the contents of the table using SQL. Unfortunately, Big Jim doesn't have a full-time database administrator. To make it easier on Big Jim and his crew of volunteers, we will build a form to facilitate table maintenance.

Building a form for each of the three tables uses identical steps. Rather than repeating those steps for each table, I will show you how to create the EVENT_TYPES maintenance form and ask you to create the remaining two on your own.

The trick with maintenance forms is to not spend a lot of time putting them together. Therefore, use the Data Block and Layout Wizards to do most of the work. Use the following steps to create the EVENT_TYPES maintenance form:

1. Start Forms Builder if it is not already running.

2. Create a new block using the Data Block Wizard.

3. Use the EVENT_TYPES table and make sure that all the columns are included in the block.

4. Run the Layout Wizard and also include all the columns in the display of the form.

5. Change the prompt for E_Type_ID to be ID: and the prompt for Description to have a colon at the end.

6. Use the Form layout showing one record and a block heading of Event Types.

7. Finish the Layout Wizard and admire your handiwork.

8. Change the E_Type_ID field from a Text Item to a Display Item using the Item Type in the Property Palette.

9. Select the Triggers object under the EVENT_TYPES block in the Object Navigator, and click the Create Button on the vertical toolbar.

10. Select the PRE-INSERT trigger from the pop-up list of trigger types.

11. Enter the following code in the PL/SQL Editor:

```
SELECT E_Type_ID_Seq.nextval
  INTO :EVENT_TYPES.E_Type_ID
  FROM DUAL;
```

12. Click the Compile button, and then click the Close button (assuming that there are no typing errors).

13. Expand the Windows object in the Object Navigator and change the name of WINDOW1 to EVENT_TYPE_MAINTENANCE.

14. Save the form as Event_Types.

Your form is complete and ready to run. Try entering the following event types:

- Mountain Biking
- Road Cycling
- Running
- Triathlon

You can enter all the types and then commit them to the database, or commit each one immediately after entering it. Either way, the correct sequence number will be pulled from the database. The running form should look similar to Figure 12.1.

Now create maintenance forms for the PAY_TYPES and CC_TYPES tables. Be sure to use the correct database sequence to populate the primary keys for each of the forms. When you finish creating each form, save it using the same name for the form as the name of the table.

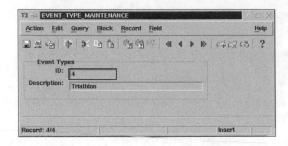

FIGURE 12.1
The running EVENT_TYPES maintenance form.

Add the following values to the PAY_TYPES table:

- Cash
- Check
- Credit Card

Add the following values to CC_TYPES table:

- VISA
- MasterCard

Now you are ready to move on to creating the Events form.

The Events Form

Use the following steps to create the Events form:

1. Start Forms Builder if it is not already running.
2. Create a new block using the Data Block Wizard.
3. Use the EVENTS table and make sure that all the columns are included in the block.
4. Run the Layout Wizard and also include all the columns in the display of the form.
5. Change the prompts to the values shown in Table 12.1.

Table 12.1   New Prompt Values for the Events Form

Field Name	Prompt Value
Event_ID	ID:
Name	Event Name:

Table 12.1   Continued

Field Name	Prompt Value
Description	Description:
E_Type	Event Type:
Fee	Fee:
E_Date	Event Date:

6. Use the Form layout, showing one record and a block heading of Events.

7. Finish the Layout Wizard and admire your handiwork.

8. Change the Event_ID field from a Text Item to a Display Item using the Item Type in the Property Palette. Remember that this value will be filled in from a sequence and does not need to be modified by the user. Changing it from a Text Item to a Display Item eliminates the possibility of the user accidentally modifying the value.

9. Select the Triggers object under the EVENTS block in the Object Navigator and click the Create button on the vertical toolbar.

10. Select the PRE-INSERT trigger from the pop-up list of trigger types. This trigger will execute the moment the user tries to insert a new record into the database.

11. Enter the following code in the PL/SQL Editor:

```
SELECT Event_ID_Seq.nextval
  INTO :EVENTS.Event_ID
  FROM DUAL;
```

12. Click the Compile button and then click the Close button (assuming that there are no typing errors).

13. Expand the Windows object in the Object Navigator and change the name of WINDOW1 to EVENTS.

14. Save the form as Events.

You now have a form that looks and behaves very similarly to the other maintenance forms in the application. However, the Events form is a bit different and requires some additional functionality. The first change is to make the Description field more usable. Use the following steps to accomplish this:

1. Select the frame surrounding the fields in the Layout Editor, and change the Update Layout in the Property Palette from Automatically to Manually. This will allow you to resize the frame without Forms Builder automatically trying to rearrange the enclosed fields.

2. Expand the frame to make room for the expanded Description field.

3. Select the Description field and change the Multi-Line property in the Property Palette from No to Yes. Then expand the height so that multiple lines can be seen. You might need to move some of the other fields to make room for it.

4. Save the form.

The next customization is to change the E_Type field into a pop-up list. Chapter 8, "Using Graphical Elements in Forms," gave you an example of how to do this. So that you don't have to go back, here is a summary of the steps to follow:

1. Change the E_Type field from Text Item to Poplist using the Item Type in the Property Palette.

2. Create a Pre-Form trigger using the following code (refer to Chapter 8 if you have forgotten how to do this):

```
DECLARE
   rg_name VARCHAR2(40) := 'Event_RG';
   rg_id   RecordGroup;
   errcode NUMBER;
BEGIN
   rg_id := CREATE_GROUP_FROM_QUERY(rg_name,
              'SELECT description, to_char(e_type_id) FROM event_types');
   errcode := POPULATE_GROUP(rg_id);
   POPULATE_LIST('events.e_type', rg_id);
END;
```

3. Select the E_Type field (the new pop-up list) in the Layout Editor and open the Property Palette.

4. Click on the Elements in List property so that it brings up the List Elements dialog. Enter a dummy element and value. The Pre-Form trigger will initialize this information when the form is run. Adding this information eliminates a compile warning.

5. Save the form.

The last change that must be made is to allow the event date to also hold the start time. This is done by changing the E_Date Data Type property from Date to Datetime. The Date data type in Forms Builder does not allow for the input of time information. However, the Date data type in the Oracle database does allow this. It is easy to forget this difference between the two Oracle products.

The Events form is now complete. Save and run the form, and it should look similar to the form in Figure 12.2. Enter the information shown in Figure 12.2 so that the EVENTS table has some information that can be used later in the application.

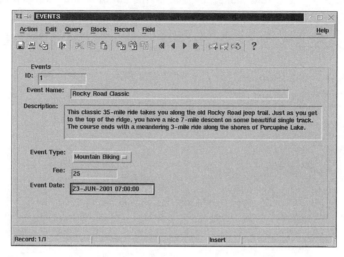

FIGURE 12.2
The Events form with some newly added data.

The Signup Form

The Signup form is the most complicated form in the application. It is comprised of two blocks referencing three separate tables. If the participant signs up for an event using a credit card, there is an additional block referencing another two tables. Normally a block would be associated to a single table, but pop-up lists allow a reference to a second table to be added as was shown with the Events form.

The first block is the PERSON block, and it serves as the master block for the form. The second block is the Event Information block and serves as a detail block. The third block will be used only if an individual pays the event entry fee using a credit card.

The PERSON Block

The PERSON block contains information about the individual participating in the event. When the volunteer signs up someone for an event, the volunteer will query the PERSON table first to see whether the participant is already in the database. If so, there is no need to reenter the information.

Use the following steps to create the PERSON block:

1. Start Forms Builder if it is not already running.

2. Create a new block using the Data Block Wizard.

3. Use the PERSON table and make sure that all the columns are included in the block.

4. Run the Layout Wizard and also include all the columns in the display of the form.

5. Change the prompts for the fields to those found in Table 12.2.

Table 12.2   New Field Prompts for the PERSON Block ————————————————

Field Name	Prompt Value
Person_ID	ID:
Lastname	Last Name:
Firstname	First Name:
Address	Address:
City	City:
State	State:
Zip	Zip:
Phone	Phone:
Birthday	Birthday:
Gender	Gender:
Email	E-mail:

6. Use the Form layout showing one record and a block heading of Individual.

7. Finish the Layout Wizard and admire your handiwork.

8. Change the Person_ID field from a Text Item to a Display Item using the Item Type in the Property Palette.

9. Select the Triggers object under the PERSON block in the Object Navigator and click the Create button on the vertical toolbar.

10. Select the WHEN-NEW-RECORD-INSTANCE trigger from the pop-up list of trigger types. This is a bit different from the PRE-INSERT trigger that was used earlier. Any master-detail form should use the WHEN-NEW_RECORD-INSTANCE trigger instead of the PRE-INSERT to ensure data integrity between the master and detail records. The disadvantage is that sequence numbers often will be discarded without being used. It is not a tragic problem, but it can cause some questions. You also run the risk of inserting records with all fields blank except for the one populated by the sequence. Handling this special case is an exercise left up to the user.

11. Enter the following code in the PL/SQL Editor:

```
SELECT Person_ID_Seq.nextval
  INTO :PERSON.Person_ID
  FROM DUAL;
```

12. Click the Compile button and then click the Close button (assuming that there are no typing errors).

13. Expand the Windows object in the Object Navigator and change the name of WINDOW1 to SIGNUP.

14. Save the form as Signup.

You now have a working block. However, the block takes up too much space on the form. Use the following steps to create room for an additional block:

1. Select the frame surrounding the fields in the Layout Editor, and change the Update Layout in the Property Palette from Automatically to Manually.

2. Move the Firstname field to the same line as the Lastname field. This enables you to move the other fields up as well. Remember to use the alignment tools on the toolbar to make sure that the two fields are vertically aligned.

3. Move the State, Zip, and Email fields to the same line as the City field. Once again, this adds more space and allows the other fields to be moved up.

4. Move the Birthday and Gender fields to the same line as the Phone field.

5. Resize the frame around the block so that it encompasses the fields in the block with as little extra room as possible.

When you are done modifying the form's layout, it should look similar to Figure 12.3.

The last thing to do with the PERSON block is to change the Gender field to a group of radio buttons. Use the following steps to do so:

1. Select the Gender field in the Layout Editor.

2. Change the Item Type property in the Property Palette from Text Item to Radio Group. The field will disappear from the form.

3. Set the Initial Value in the Property Palette to M.

4. Select the Radio Button tool from the Tool Palette in the Layout Editor and place it on the form.

5. Change the Radio Button's label to Male.

6. Set the Radio Button Value property for the new radio button to be M.

7. Repeat steps 4, 5, and 6 for the Female button. Be sure to set the Radio Button Value property to be F.

The PERSON block is finished. You are now ready to add the Event Information block to the form.

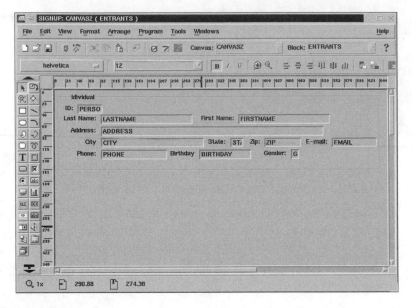

FIGURE 12.3
The PERSON block properly laid out in the Signup form.

The Event Information Block

The Event Information block contains information about the race or event for a specific individual. Utilizing a pop-up list to select the event information eliminates the need to include an additional block on the form. This greatly simplifies the form logic.

Use the following steps to create the Event Information block:

1. Create a new block by selecting PERSON in the Object Navigator and clicking the Create button on the vertical toolbar. Create the block using the Data Block Wizard. For the form to work correctly, you must make sure that the new block appears below the PERSON block in the Object Navigator.

2. Use the ENTRANTS table and include all columns in the block except for Confirm, Start_Time, and Finish_Time.

3. Click on the Create Relationships button and select the only defined relationship in the resulting dialog box. Close the dialog by clicking OK. Your master-detail relationship should be automatically defined and shown in the join condition field as ENTRANTS.PERSON_ID = PERSON.PERSON_ID.

4. Run the Layout Wizard and also include all the columns in the display of the form.

5. Change the prompts for the fields to those in Table 12.3.

Table 12.3   Values for Prompts in the Event Information Block ―――――――

Field Name	Prompt Value
Event_ID	Event:
Person_ID	Person ID:
Bib_Num	Bib Number:
Payment_Type	Payment Type:
CC_Info	Credit Card Info:
Signup_date	Registration Date:

6. Use the Form layout showing one record and a block heading of Event Information.

7. Finish the Layout Wizard and admire your handiwork.

8. Change the Person_ID field from a Text Item to a Display Item using the Item Type in the Property Palette.

9. Change the Event_ID field from a Text Item to a List Item.

10. Change the Payment_Type field from a Text Item to a List Item.

11. Create a Pre-Form trigger using the following code (refer to Chapter 8 if you have forgotten how to do this):

```
DECLARE
  rg_name1 VARCHAR2(40) := 'Event_RG';
  rg_name2 VARCHAR2(40) := 'Pay_RG';
  rg_1  RecordGroup;
  rg_2  RecordGroup;
  errcode NUMBER;
BEGIN
  rg_1 := CREATE_GROUP_FROM_QUERY(rg_name1,
            'SELECT name, to_char(event_id) FROM events');
  rg_2 := CREATE_GROUP_FROM_QUERY(rg_name,
            'SELECT description, to_char(pay_id) FROM pay_types');
  errcode := POPULATE_GROUP(rg_1);
  errcode := POPULATE_GROUP(rg_2);
  POPULATE_LIST('entrants.event_id', rg_1);
  POPULATE_LIST('entrants.payment_type', rg_2);
END;
```

12. Select the Event_ID field (the new pop-up list) in the Layout Editor and open the Property Palette.

13. Click on the Elements in List property so that it brings up the List Elements dialog. Enter a dummy element and value. The Pre-Form trigger will wipe this information out when the form is run. Adding this information eliminates a compile warning.

14. Repeat steps 12 and 13 for the Payment_Type field.

15. Save the form.

You now have a form that works fairly well for entering new participants and new events. Now it is time to adjust the layout to be more compact. Remember to turn off the automatic adjustment features of the frame using the Update Layout property. Adjust the layout so that it is similar to Figure 12.4.

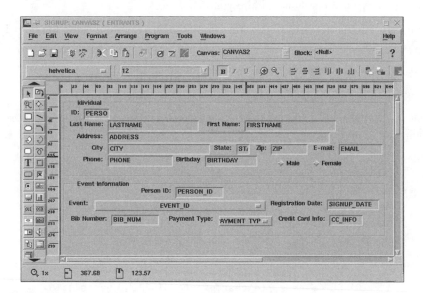

FIGURE 12.4
The Signup form after adjusting the layout to the Event Information block.

Form Navigation

Run the Signup form and use the Tab key to navigate around the form. You might notice that you start in the Event Information block instead of the Individual block. You might also notice that the field you think you should go to next is different from the field you actually go to.

This can be fixed by explicitly filling out the navigation information for each item on the form. The first place to start is with the blocks on the form. Select the Signup form in the Object Navigator and open the Property Palette. Look at the First Navigation Data Block property. On Unix, this value is left to Null. Null means that the starting block is undefined, so the first block to appear in the Object Navigator is used. Explicitly set value to the PERSON block. This corresponds to the individual's information.

Now select the PERSON block in the Object Navigator. Notice how there are navigation properties here as well. You might want to keep the Previous Navigation Data Block set to NULL and explicitly set the Next Navigation Data Block to ENTRANTS.

Unfortunately, there is no first navigation field that you can set at the block level. The first input element listed in the Object Navigator for the block is used. Display items are not input elements and therefore you cannot navigate to them. If you want to change the first item, you must rearrange the items in the block. On Unix, this means deleting and re-creating the object.

After the first field or item in the block is set correctly, navigation can be controlled using the field's navigation properties. Most of the time, the Data Block and Layout Wizards guess the navigation correctly. Sometimes it will be necessary to correct the navigation for each item manually.

Take some time to run through the form and correct any miscued fields.

The Credit Card Transactions Block

With navigation working correctly, you are now ready to create the Credit Card Transactions block. Unlike the previous two blocks, the Credit Card Transactions block will appear on a different canvas, so be sure to adhere to the following instructions closely:

1. Select the PERSON block in the Object Navigator and click the Create tool on the vertical toolbar. ENTRANTS should be the last block in the Object Navigator. Use the Data Block Wizard to create the new block.

2. Use the CC_TRANSACTION table with all its fields to create the block.

3. There is no need to create a relationship with any other block. It will be done manually later.

4. Use the Layout Wizard to help lay out the block.

5. Use a new canvas instead of placing the block on an existing one.

6. Show all the columns in the block.

7. Change the prompts using the values found in Table 12.4.

Table 12.4   Values for Prompts in the ENTRANTS Block ————————————————

Field Name	Prompt Value
Transaction_ID	Transaction ID:
CC_Type	Card Type:
CC_Num	Card Number:
Exp_Date	Expiration Date:

Table 12.4 Continued ─────────────────────────────────

Field Name	Prompt Value
Name_On_Card	Name on Card:
Address	Billing Address:
City	City:
State	State:
Zip	Zip:
Amount	Amount:

8. Use the form output with a frame title of Credit Card Information.

9. Change CC_Type from a Text Item to a List Item.

10. Change the Pre-Form trigger so that it populates the CC_Type pop-up list using the following code:

```
DECLARE
    rg_name1 VARCHAR2(40) := 'Event_RG';
    rg_name2 VARCHAR2(40) := 'Pay_RG';
    rg_name3 VARCHAR2(40) := 'CC_RG';
    rg_1  RecordGroup;
    rg_2  RecordGroup;
    rg_3  RecordGroup;
    errcode NUMBER;
BEGIN
    rg_1 := CREATE_GROUP_FROM_QUERY(rg_name1,
            'SELECT name, to_char(event_id) FROM events');
    rg_2 := CREATE_GROUP_FROM_QUERY(rg_name2,
            'SELECT description, to_char(pay_id) FROM pay_types');
    rg_3 := CREATE_GROUP_FROM_QUERY(rg_name3,
            'SELECT name, to_char(cc_id) FROM cc_types');
    errcode := POPULATE_GROUP(rg_1);
    errcode := POPULATE_GROUP(rg_2);
    errcode := POPULATE GROUP(rg_3);
    POPULATE_LIST('entrants.event_id', rg_1);
    POPULATE_LIST('entrants.payment_type', rg_2);
    POPULATE_LIST('cc_transaction.card_type', rg_3);
END;
```

11. Select the CC_Type field (the new pop-up list) in the Layout Editor and open the Property Palette.

12. Click on the Elements in List property so that it brings up the List Elements dialog. Enter a dummy element and value.

13. Change the Transaction_ID field from a text item to a display item.

14. Select the Triggers object under the CC_TRANSACTION block in the Object Navigator and click the Create Button on the vertical toolbar.

15. Select the WHEN-NEW-RECORD-INSTANCE trigger from the pop-up list of trigger types.

16. Enter the following code in the PL/SQL Editor:

```
SELECT Transaction_ID_Seq.nextval
  INTO :CC_Transaction.Transaction_ID
  FROM DUAL;
```

17. Select the frame surrounding the fields in the block and set the Update Layout property to Manually.

18. Lay out the block so that it is more readable as shown in Figure 12.5.

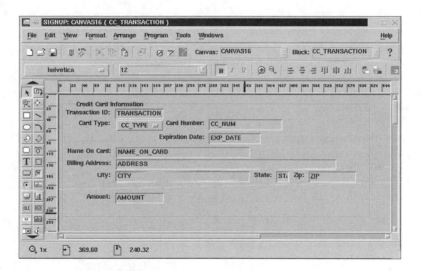

FIGURE 12.5
The CC_Transaction block laid out so that it is more readable.

The third block of the form is now created. All that remains is just the matter of being able to navigate to it when needed as well as making sure that the correct credit card information is stored with the individual and event information. Complete the block using the following steps:

1. Select the ENTRANTS block in the Object Navigator and set the Next Navigation Data Block property to CC_TRANSACTION.

2. Select the CC_TRANSACTION block in the Object Navigator and set the Previous Navigation Data Block property to ENTRANTS.

3. Select the AMOUNT field in the Object Navigator and click the Create tool on the vertical toolbar. This will create a new object in the block that looks like a text item. Change the name of the object to CC_CLOSE.

4. Double-click CC_CLOSE in the Object Navigator to open the Property Palette. Change the Item Type property to Push Button.

5. Set the Label property to Close.

6. Set the Canvas property to the canvas corresponding to the CC_TRANSACTION block. If you have been following the instructions exactly, it will be the canvas with the larger number after the word CANVAS.

7. The button should now appear on the proper canvas. Move it to the right of the Amount field. Make sure to size it properly as well.

8. Right-click on the button in the Layout Editor and select the Smart Triggers, WHEN-BUTTON-PRESSED menu choice.

9. Enter the following PL/SQL code:

```
:ENTRANTS.CC_INFO := :CC_TRANSACTION.TRANSACTION_ID;
PREVIOUS_BLOCK;
```

The first line copies the value from the field in this block to the corresponding field in the ENTRANTS block. The second line sets the focus to the previous block.

The last thing to do is add a button to the ENTRANTS block to be able to navigate to the credit card information block. Use the following steps to complete the form:

1. Save the form in case you make any mistakes or you experience an unplanned blackout.

2. Close the Layout Editor showing the second canvas.

3. Select the CC_INFO field from the ENTRANTS block in the Object Navigator. Click on the Create tool found on the vertical toolbar. Name the new object CC_BUTTON.

4. Double-click CC_BUTTON in the Object Navigator to open the Property Palette. Change the Item Type property to Push Button.

5. Set the Label property to Credit Card Info.

6. Set the Canvas property to the canvas corresponding to the ENTRANTS block. If you have been following the instructions exactly, it will be the canvas with the smaller number after the word CANVAS.

7. The button should now appear on the proper canvas. Move it beneath the PAYMENT_TYPE pop-up list. Make sure to size it properly as well.

8. Right-click on the button in the Layout Editor and select the Smart Triggers, WHEN-BUTTON-PRESSED menu choice.

9. Enter the following PL/SQL code:

```
:CC_TRANSACTION.NAME_ON_CARD := :PERSON.FIRSTNAME || :PERSON.LASTNAME;
:CC_TRANSACTION.ADDRESS := PERSON.ADDRESS;
:CC_TRANSACTION.CITY := PERSON.CITY;
:CC_TRANSACTION.STATE := PERSON.STATE;
:CC_TRANSACTION.ZIP := PERSON.ZIP;
SELECT fee
  INTO :CC_TRANSACTION.AMOUNT
  FROM EVENTS
  WHERE event_id = :ENTRANTS.EVENT_ID;
NEXT_BLOCK;
```

The first five lines of code simply copy information from the PERSON block so that it does not have to be retyped. This will work most of the time, and it eliminates the need for the volunteer to type in duplicate information. The SELECT statement pulls the credit card amount from the fee value found in the EVENTS table.

The form is now complete. Play around with the form by entering new participants and querying old ones to make sure that it works as designed.

The Signup form is relatively small and easy to reproduce. However, it does a good job at tying a large number of Forms Developer elements into a single interface.

The Results Entry Form

The Results Entry form is a basic master-detail form that lists the information for the event in the first block and the relevant information for the participant in the second. The volunteer entering the information into the database keeps track of start and finish times for every bib number that enters the event. Sorting the list by bib number will greatly facilitate data entry. The volunteer just queries the event and all the participants for that event will appear in the detail block and can be sorted by bib number. Data entry will then take a minimum amount of time.

Here are the basic steps to create the form:

1. Create a master block using the Event_ID, Event_Date, and Name columns from the EVENTS table.

2. Create a detail block using the Event_ID, Bib_Num, Start_Time and Finish_Time columns from the ENTRANTS table. You can use a form or tabular display type. The specification called for a form display type, but a tabular display might be more useful.

3. Change the Start_Time and Finish_Time columns to be Datetime data types. It will be a bit of work to type the date for the event, but is necessary for such long-term events as 24-hour mountain biking events. If you want to use the Time data type, the underlying field needs to be a VARCHAR2 field unless you want to write the data type conversion code yourself.

4. Set the ORDER BY property for the detail block to be Bib_Num.

5. Save the form as ResultEntry.

You now have a working Results Entry form that will save Big Jim and his volunteers countless hours in creating the final results.

Reports Creation

Only two reports are requested at this point in the application. Experience should tell you that there will be many more reports in the future. However, this section of the chapter concentrates on creating the confirmation letter and the event results report.

The Confirmation Letter

The confirmation letter is mailed out to participants who have registered for one of Big Jim's upcoming events. Ideally, the report will be run at the end of every day and print the letters to be mailed out. After the reports have been printed, the confirm flag in the ENTRANTS table needs to be updated to indicate that the letter has been printed. The next time the report is run, letters will be printed for only those entrants whose confirm flag is NULL.

Create the confirmation letter using the following steps:

1. Start Report Builder and use the Report Wizard to help create the letter.

2. Select the Form Letter report type.

3. Use the Query Builder to help create the report. Include the PERSON, ENTRANTS, and EVENTS tables with the columns shown in Figure 12.6.

4. Look at the query produced and then go to the next screen.

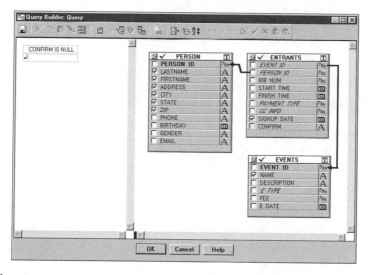

FIGURE 12.6
The Query Builder configuration showing the columns to use to create the confirmation letter.

5. Enter the letter as described in Chapter 11. It is reproduced here for your convenience:

```
<firstname> <lastname>
<Address>
<City>, <ST> <Zip>

Dear <firstname> <lastname>,

Thank you for signing up for the <event>. This letter is to confirm your
registration you submitted on <registration date> and to encourage you to
arrive at least 30 minutes before the start time so you will be ready
when the event begins. If you have any questions regarding this event,
feel free to contact us at (555) 555-1234.

Sincerely,


Big Jim
```

6. Select the Draft template.

7. Finish the report and admire the result.

8. Save the report as Confirm.

The form letter is done. There was no logic to update the ENTRANTS table's Confirm flag, but that will be done in the menu system created at the end of the chapter.

The Results Report

The event results report is the last difficult task in creating the application. It is difficult because of the various categories for the results. This leaves two options. The first option is to create a single report that breaks down all the results into the various categories and prints them as a single report. This is a very difficult task. It is much easier to create a single report for each category. However, this means creating 14 reports. A much easier way is to create one report that uses a parameter form to select maximum age, minimum age, and gender.

Use the following steps to create this report:

1. Create a simple tabular report using the Lastname and Firstname columns from the PERSON table joined with the Bib_Num, Start_Time, and Finish_Time columns from the ENTRANTS table.

2. View the report to see how it looks.

3. Add four user parameters (P_gender, P_minage, P_maxage, P_event_id) by selecting User Parameters in the Object Navigator and clicking on the Create button on the vertical toolbar.

4. Use the Property Palette to change the P_gender user parameter from a Number data type to a character.

5. Go back into the Report Wizard and modify the query to use the following SELECT statement:

```
SELECT person.lastname, person.firstname,
    entrants.bib_num,
    trunc(((finish_time - start_time)*3600*24)/3600 || ':' ||
    trunc(mod(((finish_time - start_time)*3600*24), 3600)/60 || ':' ||
    round(mod(mod(((finish_time - start_time)*3600*24), 3600), 60))
Time, rownum Place
FROM person, entrants
WHERE (entrants.person_id = person.person_id)
  AND (:P_event_id = entrants.event_id)
  AND (:P_gender = person.gender)
  AND (:P_minage <= trunc(start_time - birthday, 'YEAR')
  AND (:P_maxage >= trunc(start_time - birthday, 'YEAR')
```

6. Give thanks to the nearest person that you didn't have to figure out the date arithmetic in the previous SELECT statement.

7. Add the new columns to the report by filling out the rest of the values in the Report Wizard.

8. Run the report filling out proper values for the different event identifier, age, and gender categories. The sample data you have entered in your tables will determine the results of the report.

9. Save the report as Results.

You might now want to play around with the report and add such things as gender, minimum and maximum ages to the report results. Those additions will make reading the report much easier, but the steps to add them are left for you to figure out.

Graphics Creation

The chart asked for in this application is incredibly simple to build. Big Jim just wants to see the total number of participants for each event. In the future, he might want a breakdown of the various age and gender categories, but for now it is simple.

Build the chart using the following steps:

1. Start Graphics Builder if it is not already running.

2. Select the Chart, Create Chart menu option to invoke the Graphics Genie.

3. Enter the following query:

```
SELECT events.name, count(entrants.person_id)
FROM events, entrants
WHERE entrants.event_id = events.event_id
GROUP BY events.name
```

4. Enter Races for the name of the chart and Participants per Event for the title. Also select a simple bar graph for the chart type.

5. Use Name for the X-axis or chart categories.

6. Use Count(person_id) for the y-axis or chart values.

7. Save the chart as RaceNumbers.

Your chart is now completed. Although you might have only one or two races currently in the database, the chart will become much more interesting as Big Jim uses the application. Now it is time to tie everything together.

Creating a Menu

All the elements for Big Jim's event promotion application are in their first draft stage. No piece of software is ever complete, so it would be tough to say the elements are done. At any rate, the application is usable and can be shown to Big Jim for his approval.

A menu form that Big Jim can use to access the various forms you have created for him will make the application much more usable. The form will have three areas: one for the forms, one for the reports, and one for the graphics. Use the following steps to create the application menu for Big Jim:

1. Start Form Builder if it is not already active. You will not be using any data blocks, so there is no need to use the Data Block Wizard. Instead, create the form by hand.

2. Add the following text to the form: Big Jim's Event Promotion Application.

3. Add a button for each form associated with Big Jim's application. When you are done, it should look similar to Figure 12.7.

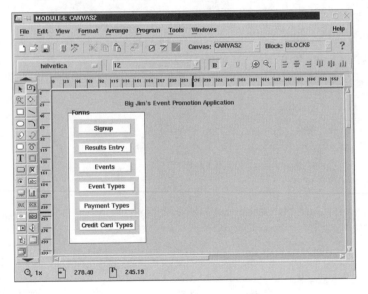

FIGURE 12.7
Big Jim's menu form after adding the buttons to call all the forms in the application.

4. Add the PL/SQL code to call the appropriate forms for each button. This is done for the Signup form by adding the following code to the WHEN-BUTTON-PRESSED trigger:

```
CALL_FORM('SIGNUP');
```

5. Add two buttons and a frame to call the two reports.

6. Use the following PL/SQL code to run the confirmation letter from the menu form:

```
DECLARE
  pl_id ParamList;
BEGIN
  RUN_PRODUCT(REPORTS, 'confirm', SYNCHRONOUS, RUNTIME, FILESYSTEM,
      pl_id, NULL);
  UPDATE ENTRANTS SET CONFIRM = '1' WHERE CONFIRM IS NULL;
END;
```

7. Add the button to call the graph.

8. Use the following PL/SQL code to run the graph:

```
DECLARE
  pl_id ParamList;
BEGIN
  RUN_PRODUCT(GRAPHICS, 'RaceNumbers', SYNCHRONOUS, RUNTIME, FILESYSTEM,
➥pl_id, NULL);
END;
```

9. Save the form as BJMenu and you are done.

Your menu form is complete and can be used to call all the other pieces of the application. You can set up an icon on the desktop or script to call the BJMenu form. On Unix, the runtime executable is called f60runm and takes the form name as the only parameter. You can set up a shell script called bjapp that executes the following command:

```
f60runm bjmenu
```

After logging in, you will see the menu form you designed earlier.

Possible Enhancements

I mentioned earlier that no software application is ever really complete. Some immediate enhancements that Big Jim might want to add to his application are as follows:

- Hiding all the ID columns and primary keys. Now that you know they are working correctly, you can set the Visible property to No. They will appear in the Layout Editor, but not while running the form.

- Creating KEY-NEXT-ITEM triggers for the last item in the block that moves the cursor to the next block on the form. That will reduce the amount of mouse navigation for the person doing data entry.

- Changing the Start_Time and Finish_Time columns in the ENTRANTS table to character columns. That will simplify data entry for events that are less than 24 hours and allow you to use the Time field data type.

As you develop your own applications, you will undoubtedly develop your own style and guidelines. At that point, you will also have a few more updates that you would like to see in Big Jim's sample application.

DEVELOPER DOCUMENTATION

I started working with the Oracle database while I was in high-school. To help pay my way through college, I started a consulting business specializing in taking over system development for companies that either lost their Oracle application development staff or discovered their development staff was inadequate. This meant I was often assigned to projects with little or no documentation. It was here that I discovered the importance of documenting the development process.

My most memorable client was a manufacturing company based in the Pacific Northwest. They had a consulting company that was tasked with creating an application to manage everything from inventory to payroll. The application was in mid-development when the owner of the consulting company disappeared. My task was to act as a database administrator as well as continue development of the unfinished yet critical applications.

I attacked the project and my first goal was to create some sort of development documentation. This was a long and involved process that I had to accomplish between emergency fixes and routine database administration. As I uncovered information, I created comprehensive notes and kept them in a central location. If something were to happen to me, my client would have a document to hand over to the next group of consultants and they would not have to rediscover this information.

I continued to work with the manufacturing company and maintained my notes. It was not long before I was going back and looking at my own notes to figure out what I had done to a particular form or report. As I would make changes and modifications, I would update the notes. This developer documentation became crucial in the maintenance of the system. When it came time for me to pursue my professional career, I was able to hand my documentation over to another consulting company and step out of the picture with a clear conscience.

Summary

In this chapter, you took the Big Jim sample application that was specified in Chapter 11 and turned it into a working application. This involved building six different forms with varying complexity. You also put together a signup confirmation letter and a somewhat complex report utilizing a parameter page. A graph was included to round out the application completeness. Finally, everything was tied together using a simple menu form.

Chapter 13 will now take the sample application one step further and show you how to deploy it on the Web.

DEPLOYING DEVELOPER APPLICATIONS TO THE WEB ———

ESSENTIALS ─────────────────────────────

- The Forms Server consists of three major components: the Forms Applet, the Forms Listener, and the Forms Runtime Engine. All these are used to help deploy your application in the Web environment.

- Forms Builder applications can be deployed in the Web environment simply by copying the form executable into the directory specified by the Forms Server.

- The Reports Server allows you to choose between a CGI and Java servlet architecture. If your Web server supports Java servlets, you will use the Reports Servlet. Otherwise, you will use Web CGI.

- Reports Builder applications can be deployed on the Web simply by copying the report's RDF file to the directory specified by the Reports Server.

- Stored procedures and functions written in Java can be called from within forms.

One of the distinct advantages of using Oracle Developer to create database applications is the ability to deploy them using either the client/server or Web method. This chapter shows you how to take the sample application developed for Big Jim and run it using the Web instead of the client/server runtimes.

The chapter starts with an overview of Oracle's Web deployment architecture. Following that are examples of deploying the three types of Developer objects (forms, reports, and graphics). The chapter closes by showing you how to integrate Java code with your application.

Understanding Web Deployment of Developer Applications

Big Jim loves the application developed for his race and event promotion hobby. He has managed to increase the number of events he is promoting and, therefore, has increased his volunteer staff. Some of his volunteers would like to be able to work from home, so Big Jim is asking for your help again. Working from home will allow his volunteers to put in more time helping out, as well as reduce the number of computers he has to install at his office location.

One of Big Jim's volunteers has suggested rewriting the application so that users can access the application from the Internet using a Java-enabled browser. Big Jim is apprehensive about doing that because he is afraid it will take a long time to rewrite his beloved application. What Big Jim does not realize is how easy it is to move the application onto the Web.

Oracle Developer 6i includes both the Reports Server and the Forms Server. The Reports Server includes the Graphics Server that allows you to display charts and graphs created with Oracle Graphics. The Forms and Reports Servers work as application servers, allowing the various pieces of your application to be moved from the client/server environment to the Web without any changes.

The Forms and Reports Servers are relatively similar in how they interact with the user, application, and database. However, there are some differences. The next two sections explain the architecture of the two servers.

Forms Server Architecture

The Forms Server consists of three major components:

- The Forms Applet
- The Forms Listener
- The Forms Runtime Engine

The Forms Applet is a thin Java-based applet used to render the application form in the user's browser. This applet is automatically downloaded from the Forms Server and cached on the user's local machine. The applet is responsible for handling all of the application's visual elements and interaction with the Forms Runtime Engine residing on the application server.

The Forms Listener acts as a broker between the Forms Applet and the Forms Runtime Engine. To maintain the highest levels of performance, the Listener utilizes a pool of running engines, thereby eliminating the time it takes start a new process when a new connection is requested.

The Forms Runtime Engine manages the application's logic and processing. It resides on the Forms Server machine and interacts with the Forms Applet through the Forms Listener. It also interacts with the database similarly to the client/server runtime.

The three components of the Forms Server work together in such a manner that forms in the application run without any modifications. No conversion needs to take place for the form to run in either the client/server or the Web environment. Simply copy the compiled form (with an .fmx extension instead of .fmb) to the proper directory on the application server. This is true regardless of form size or complexity.

Reports Server Architecture

The largest difference between the Reports Server and the Forms Server is that reports do not require complex user interaction. Therefore, the Reports Server architecture does not require an equivalent to the Forms Applet or Forms Listener. The Reports Server is able to handle all the processing for the report.

Forms Server allows for two configurations:

- Web CGI
- Reports Servlet

The choice of which configuration to use is determined by the Web server you are using with your application. If you are using a CGI-enabled server, use the Web CGI Reports Server. If you are using a Java-enabled server, use the Reports Servlet.

Both configurations behave in a similar manner:

1. The report request comes in from the client machine.

2. The request is converted to a command line to be executed by the Reports Server.

3. The Reports Server cache is used to create the report if proper flags indicate that the data is valid. Otherwise, a new request is made to the Reports Server Runtime.

4. The report is sent back to the requesting client.

As with Forms applications, reports need not be rewritten to be used with the Reports Server. This is true regardless of complexity or size.

Deploying Forms on the Web

Deploying Forms applications on the Web is actually fairly simple. The most difficult task is making sure that the Forms Server is installed and running correctly. After that is done, deployment is a three-step process:

1. Create a runtime executable for the form.

2. Copy the form executable to the proper machine and file location.

3. Make the form available using a link from an HTML page.

Creating a runtime executable is done every time you compile a form during the development process. The same FMX file used by the client/server runtime program is also used by the Forms Server.

CAUTION

FMX files are platform specific. If you build an application on Windows and want to deploy it on Unix, you will need to recompile the FMB file. This is done by moving the FMB file from the development platform to the deployment platform. You can then recompile using Forms Developer or running the Forms Compiler.

Copying the form executable to the proper machine and file location requires that you know how your Web deployment environment is set up. During the Forms Server installation, you specified the directory where FMX files are located. You might need your system administrator's help in locating this directory. After the FMX files are in place, your application is ready to run.

The last step is to create an HTML page that actually calls your form. Included with the Forms Server installation is an HTML file called runform.htm. Using the default install options and assuming that you have configured your Web server correctly, it should be called with the following URL:

```
http://<machine-name>/dev60html/runform.htm
```

The *<machine-name>* should be replaced with the name of your Web server. The runform.htm page is shown in Figure 13.1.

The easiest method for figuring out the URL of your forms is to use the runform.htm Web page and copy the URL it generates for you. The executables used to call application forms differ between Unix and Windows, so the URL will be different for each installation.

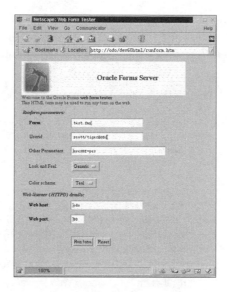

FIGURE 13.1
The runform.htm page used to test completed Forms applications.

Try running the signup form created in Chapter 12, "Making the Design a Reality," for Big Jim's event promotion. It should look similar to Figure 13.2.

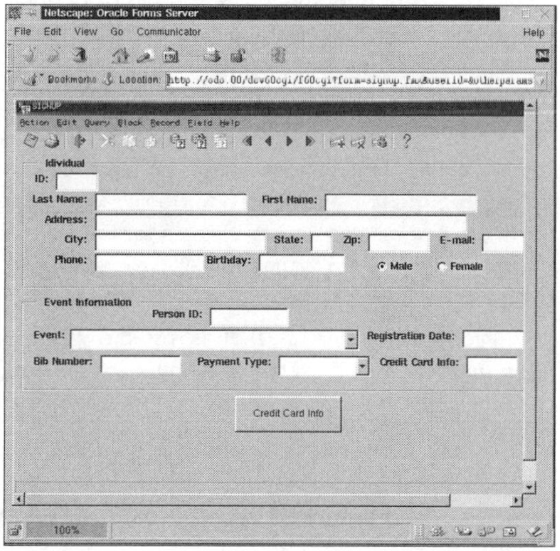

FIGURE 13.2
Big Jim's event signup form from Chapter 12 running on the Web.

Notice how the signup form is wider than the applet viewer's provided space. This can be adjusted by going into the formsweb.cfg file and modifying the applet's default width. Increasing the height will also allow the status lines to be appropriately displayed.

In the client/server deployment of the form, it was not necessary to provide a default login for the form. The same is true with Web deployment. If you omit the login information from the runform.htm page, the Forms Server will ask you to log in to the database using the familiar login dialog.

With the forms up and running on the Web, you are now ready to deploy Big Jim's reports using the Reports Server.

DEPLOYING THE FIRST FORM ON THE WEB

The first time I tried to deploy a Forms application on the Web, the only difficulty I had was setting up the Forms Server correctly. In vendor documentation, or a book like this, it is easy to direct the user to go talk to the database or system administrators to get help with environment and installation. When you are the highly paid consultant who is acting as the database administrator, comments like that don't help much.

The problem with Forms Server is that it relies on the system's Web server being properly configured. The first time I tried to run the runform.htm page, the Web server could not find the page. The problem was solved by correctly configuring the directory aliases. When this was solved, I could at least see runform.htm. I was happy and thought I had solved a major problem.

When I tried to run the test form from runform.htm, the resulting browser page just showed a bunch of garbage. To make things worse, it looked like the browser was giving me some sort of error message about ORACLE_HOME not being properly set. That sent me in the wrong direction for about an hour. Eventually, I decided to try executing a simple Perl script from the /dev60cgi/ directory (the same place runform.htm calls a CGI program to run the form). If everything was working correctly, the script should have printed out a simple message saying "This is a test." To my surprise, the Web server was listing the Perl script and not running it. I had not configured the Web server to run programs in the /dev60cgi/ directory, so it was listing them out to the browser as text.

I quickly modified the Web server's configuration file and was pleased to see errors from the Forms Server. Forms Server uses two files to help run the Java applet used to display forms. The first file is page.htm and it was not in the directory Forms Server expected. Doing a search for the file and symbolically linking it to the proper directory solved that problem. Next was the formsweb.cfg file. Again, it was not where Forms Server expected, so I performed another symbolic link.

I submitted the information in runform.htm to the server and crossed my fingers. Much to the amazement of the customer and myself, the application ran. It was a beautiful site. The most amazing thing was that no changes were necessary and the application ran as if it were in the client/server environment.

Deploying Reports and Graphics on the Web

Running reports using the Reports Server is just as simple as running forms using the Forms Server. The most difficult task is configuring the Reports Server to run correctly. It is not necessary to compile reports, so publishing reports on the Web is a two-step process:

1. Copy the report RDF file to the appropriate location.

2. Make the form available using a link from an HTML page.

When the Reports Server was installed, a location to store report definitions was specified. You might need your system administrator to help find this directory. After the directory is located, you simply need to copy the RDF files into it and you are ready to publish reports.

Unlike Forms Server, there is no runform.htm to help you figure out the proper URL to access your reports. However, reports can be accessed quite easily. Use the following URL as an example:

```
http://<web-server>/dev60cgi/rwcgi60?report=reportname.rdf&
     userid=username/password@database
```

The value *<web-server>* should be replaced by your Web server machine name. The report to be run is specified by reportname.rdf. Finally, the username and password are replaced with the appropriate values as well as the database identifier.

In the Big Jim example in Chapter 12, the form was used to call a report. As I stated previously, forms do not need to be modified when deployed on the Web. Therefore, you have two methods for publishing reports on the Web. You can continue to use the menu form created in Chapter 12, or you can create a new menu in HTML and call the forms as needed. The choice is up to you.

The graph requested by Big Jim to see how many people are participating in each event can also be called by the menu form created at the end of Chapter 12. If you decide to create an HTML menu instead, I recommend that you encapsulate the graph within a report. You will need to copy the report's RDF file as well as the graphic's OGD file to the same directory.

Using Java with Your Developer Application

There are several ways that you might want to use Java from within your Web-enabled applications. One way is to call stored procedures or functions written using Java. Another way is to include a Java component, such as a Java Bean, in your form. This section talks about how to use Java stored procedures and functions as well as the requirements for managing a Java Bean from within a form.

Using Java Stored Procedures and Functions

In Chapter 7, "Using Java with Oracle Developer and the Oracle Database," you were introduced to Java and how it can be used for stored procedures and functions in the database. It is worth noting that those stored procedures and functions can be called by your forms.

The example in Chapter 7 had you create a function called emplist_topemp( ). It basically returned the name KING as being the top employee in the EMP table. If you had a form with a text item named MANAGER, you could assign the top employee to the MANAGER item using the following line of code:

```
:MANAGER := emplist_topemp();
```

Using Java code with triggers in your Forms applications is slightly more complicated than using just PL/SQL. However, if you have a piece of Java code used throughout your application, it is much simpler to code it once and then call it when it is needed than to rewrite it multiple times.

Java Beans in Forms

Java Beans are graphical objects or components written in Java that can be used in your application form. Another example of a graphical object or component is the push button used on several of your forms. Unlike the push button, a Java Bean does not have a predefined behavior. This makes it difficult to manage from within your form or application.

Oracle Forms utilizes the IView interface to manage a Java Bean from within a form. If the Bean does not include the IView interface, you will require access to the source code to implement it. The oracle.forms.ui.VBean class provides an empty IView interface to simplify adding it to your Beans.

It is beyond the scope of this book to go into too much more detail about incorporating Java Beans into your application. However, after your application is created and deployed on the Web, all Java classes used by the application must be downloaded to the running browser before it will run properly.

Summary

Oracle Developer 6i does a fantastic job of creating a database application and being able to deploy it in a client/server or Web environment. Forms, reports, and graphical applications can be taken without any modification and run on the Web using Forms Server and Reports Server.

You should now be able to deploy any Oracle Developer application using either client/server or Web deployment. This chapter showed you how to publish forms, reports, and graphics on the Web. You were also shown how to include stored procedures and functions written in Java in your Forms applications. Finally, you were given the requirements for being able to manage Java Beans from a Forms application.

PROJECT MANAGEMENT AND SOURCE CODE CONTROL

ESSENTIALS ————————————————————

- Project Builder provides tools for the management of your application. These tools include a build environment, a delivery or deployment wizard, and integration with the RCS source code control system.

- Include source code files in your project only if you do not have the source to re-create an executable file.

- Project Builder provides support for a large number of source code file types that can be included in your application. If there are unsupported file types in your application, the Module Type Wizard provides a way to create rules on how to build the new source files into executables.

- Project Builder is integrated with RCS, but can be modified to work with any command line–driven source code control system.

- Source code control systems such as RCS allow you to check out code and make modifications. When those changes are completed, you can check them back into the system without worrying about someone overwriting your changes.

Big Jim's event promotion sample application from Chapters 11, "Developer Application Design," and 12, "Making the Design a Reality," is relatively small in relation to most real-world database applications. As applications grow larger, it becomes necessary to have tools to help manage them. This becomes even more true as more developers are assigned to the project.

Oracle Developer 6i includes Project Builder to help manage the development of complex database applications. The first tool, called Project Builder, is used to manage all the files associated with the application. This includes forms, reports, graphics, database object creation scripts, testing scripts, and developer notes. Project Builder enables the developer to compile and build all the files for the current project using a single command.

To help with source code control, Project Builder is integrated with Revision Control System (RCS). RCS is used to maintain versions of the different files associated with your application. This enables you to go back to a previous working version of the application if heinous bugs are introduced. RCS also can be used to track changes and limit access of the developer currently working on a piece of code.

Project Builder

Project Builder is provided to help manage all the files in your database application. These files need not be limited to forms, reports, or graphics files. They can also be executable files, Java code, testing scripts, and so on.

This section will show you how to use Project Builder to manage the files associated with Big Jim's event promotion application. A new project file will be created and the existing application files will be added to it. You can then use Project Builder to build all the necessary executables as well as to deploy them to a staging area. Before moving on to source code control, you will be shown how to customize Project Builder to work with atypical files in your application.

Creating and Adding Files to Project Builder

Start Project Builder by using the Start button menus on Windows or by running pj60 on Unix. You will see the Welcome to Oracle Developer dialog shown in Figure 14.1, and will be asked whether you want to run the tutorial or create a project. This section will show you how to create a project using the Project Wizard; make sure that it is selected and click OK.

The Project Wizard should present a dialog welcoming you. After reading through the information, click the Next button. The next dialog to appear asks you to specify a registry filename for the file that will be used to store information about the project. The dialog is shown in Figure 14.2.

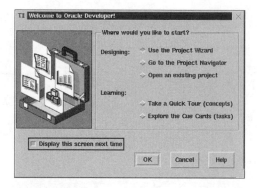

FIGURE 14.1
Welcome dialog for Project Builder.

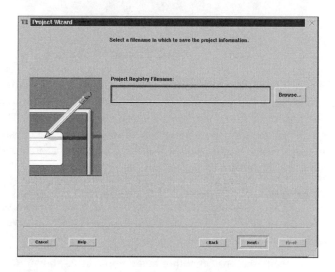

FIGURE 14.2
The Project Wizard dialog used to specify the project registry filename.

The project to be used with Project Builder is Big Jim's event promotion application. Use BigJim as the project registry filename and click on the Next button.

The next dialog is used to specify the title and the directory in which to store all the project files. It is shown in Figure 14.3.

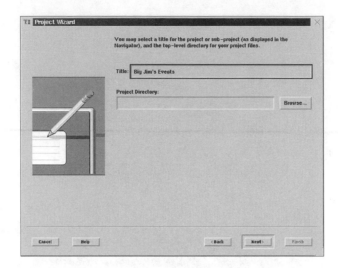

FIGURE 14.3
The Project Wizard dialog used to specify the project title and file directory.

The title for this project is Big Jim's Events. If you have already created a directory to hold all the files for Big Jim, fill in the full pathname. If you do not yet have a common file location for all of Big Jim's forms, reports, and graphics, you can specify one here. The Project Wizard will allow you to specify all the files to move into the directory after you answer a few more questions. If the directory does not exist, you will need to create it before continuing. When you are finished filling out the information, click Next.

The next dialog is used to specify a database connection for your application. This connection will be used to build your applications, and to ensure that database objects used by the project files exist. Figure 14.4 shows the database connection dialog. When you have filled out the connection information, click Next.

Next, you are asked to specify the project author and comments as shown in Figure 14.5. The author value is the author of the project and not necessarily of all the files in the project. Enter your name as the project author and any comments about Big Jim's application that you think are appropriate. When you are done, click Next.

The Project Wizard now gives you the opportunity to specify the files used in the project. Ideally, you would set up the project before creating any of the files used by the project. In this case, you would create an empty project and add files to it as they are created. In reality, most projects will have several files already created even before the project is declared. This is the case with Big Jim's application, and so you will want to specify files to add to the project as shown in Figure 14.6.

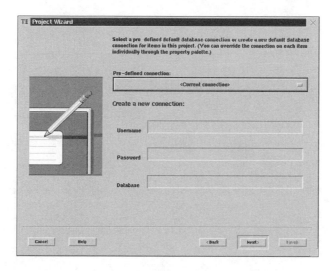

FIGURE 14.4
The Project Wizard dialog used to specify the database connection used for building the files in the project.

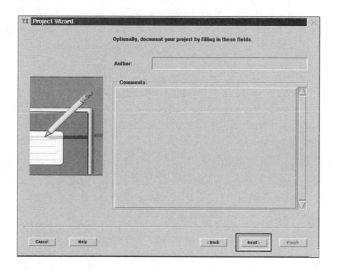

FIGURE 14.5
The Project Wizard dialog used to specify the author and project comments.

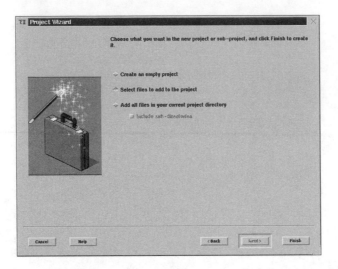

FIGURE 14.6
The Project Wizard dialog used to specify whether files will be added to the project at this time.

If you have kept all Big Jim's sample application files in one directory with no extra files, you can choose the third option and the files will be added automatically. This saves you from the tedious process of manually adding them one-by-one. For the purposes of this tutorial, make sure that Select files to add to the project is selected and click Finish.

This brings up the Add Files to Project dialog shown in Figure 14.7.

Add all the source files to the project that you created for Big Jim's sample application. You do not need to add any of the form's executable files. Doing so will confuse the Project Builder, as will be shown later in the chapter. Saving only source files should make logical sense in that all the executable files for Big Jim's application can be re-created from their sources.

Notice the pop-up list that limits the files displayed in the dialog. The first group of files is for forms. There are also limiting filters to show only reports, graphics, programming source code, and the Oracle Pro* language files. If you have other files to add to the project, you can specify them by turning the filter off and showing all files.

Use the file dialog section to navigate the directory tree. Use the Add button to add selected files to the project. Be sure to add both FMB and FMX forms files. When you have added all the files, click the Close button.

You are now done with the Project Wizard and should be at the Project View window. This is very similar to the Object Navigator used in the other Oracle Developer tools. If you expand Big Jim's Events, it should look similar to Figure 14.8.

FIGURE 14.7
The Add Files to Project dialog used to specify files for the project.

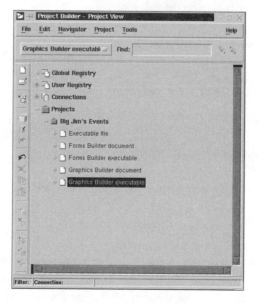

FIGURE 14.8
The Project View window with Big Jim's Events expanded.

There is a vertical toolbar on the left of the Project View window. These tools can be used to manage your project. The following list is a definition of the different tools:

New Project—Creates a new project to be managed by Project Manager.

Open Project—Opens an existing project.

Preview Actions—A toggle button used to turn on and off whether changes to the project should be viewed.

Project Wizard—Invokes the Project Wizard.

Module Type Wizard—Invokes the Module Type Wizard. It is used to create or modify an existing object type in Project Builder. This allows you to customize the Project Builder for your particular environment.

Delivery Wizard—Invokes the Delivery Wizard. It helps copy or FTP your files to the appropriate staging area.

Undo—Undoes the last project modification.

Cut—Cuts the currently selected object to the clipboard.

Copy—Copies the currently selected object to the clipboard.

Paste—Pastes the current clipboard object to the project.

Create—Creates a new object in the project.

Delete—Deletes the currently selected object from the project.

Add Files to Project—Invokes the Add Files to Project dialog.

Build Selection—Builds the currently selected object or group of objects.

Build Incremental—Builds the currently selected objects that have changed since the last build.

Most of these tools should be familiar from the Object Navigator in Forms and Reports Developer. The new tools are specific to Project Builder and are used to help manage the project.

After you have added all the necessary files to your project, you are ready to let Project Builder maintain your application. One of the primary tasks will be to build all the executable files, which is explained in the next section.

Building Files with Project Builder

Project Builder was specifically developed for Oracle Developer applications. Therefore, there is no need to explicitly tell it how to build executable versions for forms, reports, and graphics. This enables you to modify one or more of the application files and then to build them all simply by clicking on one of the build tools.

Selecting Big Jim's Events in the Project View enables the Build Selection tool. This will create executables of all the source code files in the project. If there are more than a few files, this could take a while.

Drilling down to various application objects (for example, forms, reports, graphics, and so on) enables the Build Incremental tool. This allows you to create executables for just one or two files in the project. Project Builder is also smart enough to know that only executable files older than the source files need to be built.

Unfortunately, Big Jim's sample application does not use any non-Oracle Developer source files. However, if Big Jim decided to add some features that required the use of Java or another development language, Project Builder would allow you to create rules to compile or build those objects as well.

After your application objects are created and built, it is time to deploy them for the users. The next section will show you how.

Using the Delivery Wizard

One of the benefits of the Web deployment method is that you only have to copy the application files to a central location and they are accessible by all users. The Delivery Wizard can be used to deploy the application files to the proper location. If the Forms or Reports Server expects the executables on a machine that is different from your development machine, Project Builder will use FTP to copy the files across the network.

Project Builder uses the Delivery Wizard to copy files. Working through an example will help you understand how to use it. Click on the Delivery Wizard tool found on the vertical toolbar. You are immediately greeted with a welcome dialog to let you know that the Delivery Wizard has been invoked. Click the Next button and you are shown the dialog shown in Figure 14.9.

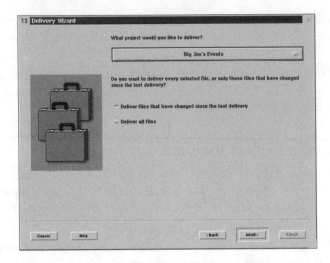

FIGURE 14.9
The Delivery Wizard dialog asking you to specify delivery of all files or just the ones changed since the last delivery.

You are asked to specify whether to deliver the file changes since the last delivery or all files. Because this is the first delivery, both choices produce an identical result. Accept the default and click Next.

The next dialog asks you to specify how the files will be delivered, as shown in Figure 14.10.

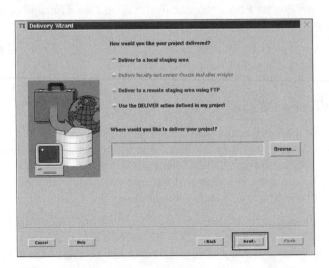

FIGURE 14.10
The Delivery Wizard dialog asking you to specify how you want the files delivered.

The first option is used to deliver the files to a staging area on the local machine. If you are developing applications on the same machine your users will use to access the application, choose this option. You can use the location text area to specify the full path of the location to which the executable files should be copied. If you are unsure of the path, the Browse button will open a file dialog and let you find the proper directory.

The second option is unavailable in Figure 14.10. It is used when you want to copy the files to a staging area on the local machine and use the Oracle Installer to install the applications on client machines.

The third option is to copy the files to another machine using FTP. If you are developing on one machine and using an application server on another machine, you would select this option. Specify the name of the machine to copy the files to in the location text area.

The final option is to use the deliver action specified by the project. This can be used when your project has special deployment requirements.

Big Jim's sample application will use either the first or the third deployment option, depending on your development environment and configuration. After your selection is made, click Next.

The next dialog asks you to specify the files to deliver for this release, as shown in Figure 14.11.

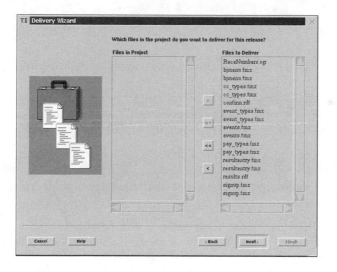

FIGURE 14.11
The Delivery Wizard dialog asking you to specify the files to deliver for this release.

Notice how Figure 14.11 shows two form executables for every form in the application. This is because both the form source (FMB) and executable (FMX) files were specified when the project was created. This was not necessary, and Project Builder does not understand that the two executables will be derived from the same source. The only reason to include executable files in your project is if you do not have the source files to re-create them.

List all the files in the Files to Deliver list, and then click Next to specify the directories to which the files will be copied, as shown in Figure 14.12.

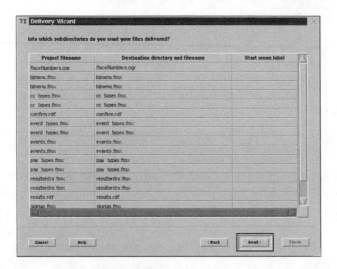

FIGURE 14.12
The Delivery Wizard dialog asking you to specify the directory to which the files should be copied.

Make any appropriate changes for the files in Big Jim's application. Remember that the Forms Server might keep files separate from the Reports Server. When you are done, click Next to see the Delivery Wizard confirmation dialog shown in Figure 14.13.

Click the Finish button and the actions will be performed. If you added both the form executable files and the form source files to the project, you will get a dialog asking whether it is okay to copy one executable over the top of another. Although this is not a problem, it is an inconvenience and should be avoided.

This completes the Delivery Wizard. Each time you make changes to the application and create new versions of the project, you will need to rerun the Delivery Wizard after the build.

Customizing Project Builder with the Module Type Wizard

Big Jim's event promotion sample application used only forms, reports, and graphics source files. Although a lot was accomplished, there will be occasion to use other types of source files in your application. Project Builder has an extensive list of other types of files to be included, but also provides a way for you to add your own through the Module Type Wizard.

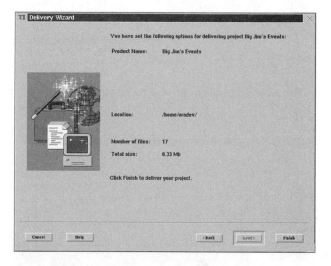

FIGURE 14.13
The Delivery Wizard dialog asking you to confirm the delivery choices.

This example will show you how to use the Module Type Wizard to add new application file types to your project. Click on the Module Type Wizard button on the vertical toolbar in the Project View. You will see the welcome dialog for the wizard. Click the Next button, and you will see a dialog similar to Figure 14.14.

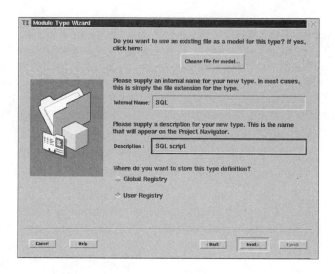

FIGURE 14.14
The Module Type Wizard dialog to describe the new file type.

You can select a file to use as a model for the new file type. If the file does not yet exist (as is the case with Big Jim's), you can create an internal name using a filename extension. For this example, use SQL. Type "SQL script" for the description and select the User Registry radio button before clicking the Next button.

The next dialog asks some questions about how to recognize the new file type. This dialog is shown in Figure 14.15.

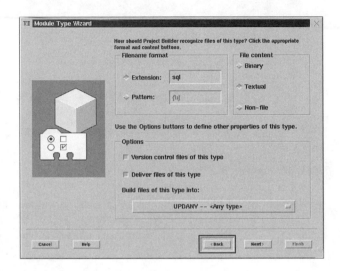

FIGURE 14.15
The Module Type Wizard dialog to define the characteristics of the new file type.

Filename extensions are probably the easiest to recognize and the most common. In Big Jim's example, you add a SQL script to the project and it is denoted with a `.sql` extension. The File Content is Textual. You will also want to select both choices in the Options section so that you can use Project Builder's version control and deliver the files when you deploy the application. Click Next and you will see the dialog shown in Figure 14.16.

This dialog is used to define actions for the new file type. SQL script files can be edited, viewed, printed, and so on. All these actions are valid, so click the Next button.

Now you can select an icon for the new file type as shown in Figure 14.17. This icon will be used in the Project View, so it is best to choose an icon that uniquely identifies your file. If none of the icons provided accurately matches your file, you can use your own icon from a file. This is done by checking the From File box and navigating to the appropriate graphics file.

For the example in this section, use one of the existing icons provided by Project Builder and click the Finish button.

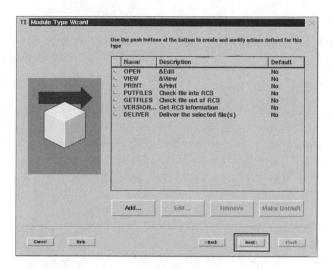

FIGURE 14.16
The Module Type Wizard dialog to define actions for this file type.

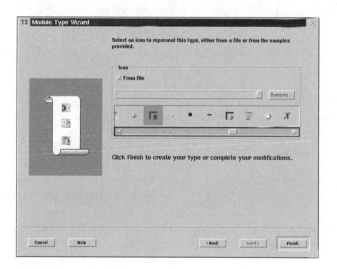

FIGURE 14.17
The Module Type Wizard dialog to select the icon associated with the new project file type.

The new file type is added to the Project View window under the User Registry tree. If you go back and look at the file types in the Global Registry, there is an entry for SQL*Plus scripts, but not for SQL scripts. In reality, they are nearly the same thing. This serves as a good check to make sure that you answered all the Module Type wizard questions correctly.

While you're in the Global Registry tree, look at some of the other file types. This will give you an idea of the different source code files you can use with Project Builder.

Source Code Control

Project Builder is useful for helping you manage and build files for your application. The most useful feature, however, is integration with a source code control system. Source code control systems are like complex software backup utilities. When used properly, they keep track of previous versions of your application source code. If you make changes to your application and break something, you can use your source code control system to help you go back to a working version.

SOURCE CODE CONTROL CAN SAVE YOUR PROJECT

I have always been a believer in backup systems, but it wasn't until I was managing a team of software developers that I came to appreciate the power of a source code control package.

My team was responsible for building operating system software for a new breed of computers. The project was divided in two parts, with one section being done by developers in California and the other in Utah. My team was located in Utah and consisted of a bunch of developers I trusted completely. My team's first recommendation was to install a source code control system, and we made a recommendation to use Concurrent Versions System (CVS). The team in California was reluctant to use CVS because it was new to them; they preferred something that was not as robust and was available only for the Windows environment. Unfortunately, our development systems were Unix-based. Therefore, it was not possible to use the Windows-based product and upper management mandated that we use CVS.

Naturally, the team in California was not happy. This became especially true when the team's inexperience with CVS caused them to lose several important files. My response was to send one of my CVS gurus to California to educate that team on how to use the source code control system. California was not happy, but they continued to use the system.

Things progressed quite steadily for the next several months. As always happens, something went wrong and a developer introduced a critical defect that caused all sorts of programs to stop working. To compound matters, we were critically close to hitting a milestone and needed the software to work for a rapidly approaching demo. There was no time to trace the defect, so we simply backed up to a working version of the software.

The demo went well and we were given the green light to continue with the project. Although the California developers were initially reluctant to implement the source code control system, they were glad it was in place when the problem occurred.

It is easy to pay lip service to source code control systems and not really bother to use them. After all, how would a non-technical manager know whether it is being used? However, if the system is embraced and developers use it as intended, it might just save your project.

The process for using a source code control system is to check in source code files at specific milestones in the project development. This can be after adding and verifying a particular feature or completing a version. After the code is checked in, other developers are free to check it out and make modifications. When those modifications are checked back in, the source code control system keeps track of the changes. This allows you to go back to previous versions of the code that have been checked in to the system.

The key to effectively using any source code control system is to check in software that has been tested and verified to work. If you constantly check in untested code, the source code system will not be able to help you restore an earlier working version of the code. You also want to be sure to check in your code often.

Sample Source Code Control Systems

There are lots of examples of source code control systems. Here is a list of some of the more popular ones:

- SCCS—Source Code Control System. One of the first source code control systems available for Unix.

- RCS—Revision Control System. The source code control system built into Project Builder.

- CVS—Concurrent Versions System. A popular source code control system built on top of RCS.

- PVCS—INTERSOLV's Polytron Version Control. A source code control system that was included with earlier versions of Oracle Developer.

Project Builder comes set up to work with RCS. This can be changed to work with any number of command-line drive source code control systems. Whichever source code control system you use, be sure to use it religiously.

Source Code Control Using Project Builder

The RCS source code control system is freely available for most platforms. Therefore, Oracle has included it as the default for Project Builder. It works quite well, and I encourage you to take advantage of it.

Unfortunately, the default is to leave source code control turned off for all the documents in your application. All Oracle Developer projects should take advantage of source code control, and Oracle would encourage this more by setting the default to Yes. To turn on source code control, open the Property Palette for one of the documents in your project. The Source Code Control property is set to No. Set it to Yes. If you expand the Actions properties, you will see the Check in and Check out properties filled out with RCS commands.

Right-clicking on the source object in the Project View brings up a menu with the option to check in the file or check it out. Checking in the file creates a second file in the project directory. This new file serves as the repository for all your changes.

Check In

The first step in using a source code control system is to check in your code to a repository file. The repository file contains a base copy of the code and all changes throughout the source code development. RCS uses the following command to check code into the repository:

```
ci <filename>
```

The command adds the file or changes to the repository and then deletes the file. Deleting the source file could be annoying if you plan to continue working on it. Project Builder uses the -u option to keep from deleting the source file. If you look at the Property Palette for the check in command, you will see the following:

```
ci -u {1}
```

The reference to {1} is to be replaced by the name of the file you are checking in.

You check in a file to RCS by right-clicking on a project file in the Project View and selecting the Check-in menu option. This will bring up a window to add comments about the changes that you made to the file. It is important to provide as much detail as possible. Although you understand all the changes you have made when you check the file in, those changes will be much more difficult to remember as time goes on and more check-ins are performed.

Check Out

Checking out a file from the source code control system copies the file from the repository and puts it in your directory to edit. RCS uses the following command to check files out of the repository:

```
co <filename>
```

One advantage to using a source code control system like RCS is that you can lock specific files. This tells other developers working on the same project that someone else is working on the file. If you check out a file, make changes to it, and try to check it back in, RCS will give you an error saying you have not locked the file. Use the -l option to lock a file when checking it out. Project Builder uses the following command for check out:

```
co -l {1}
```

{1} is replaced by the name of the file you are currently checking out. You can check out a file in Project Builder by right-clicking on the file in Project View and selecting the Check-out menu option.

For some reason, if you have checked out a file without using the `-l` option, you can lock it using the following command:

```
rcs -l <filename>
```

Using Project Builder to do your check-ins and check-outs will eliminate having to explicitly lock files.

Version Numbers

Every time a check-in is performed in RCS, it automatically assigns a version number to the changes. The first check in of a file is given 1.1 as the version number. The second and subsequent numbers increment until explicitly told otherwise.

There will come a time when you have added enough features to warrant the change of the major version number. The major version number can be changed using the following check in command:

```
ci -r2 <filename>
```

The `-r2` will change the major version number from 1 to 2. If you wanted to change it to version 3, you would use

```
ci -r3 <filename>
```

If you need to check out a specific version of the file, that is accomplished using the following check out command:

```
co -r2.1 <filename>
```

If you are not sure of the latest release for a particular major version, you can omit the second number and RCS will check out the latest version.

Branching

Software development often leads to a case in which you deploy one version of the project, but continue development of new features. Sometimes a user will expose a bug or defect that must be fixed immediately. You will want to make the change to only the version in which the user reported the bug. Although you will want to make the change in future versions of the software, you don't want to ship a bunch of unfinished changes for the next version of your software. To allow bug fixes on previously released code, RCS uses a feature known as a *branch* to accomplish this.

First, you check out the version of the code your user discovered the bug in and fix the problem. Then you check in the new code as a branch by assigning a branch number. If the bug was found in version 1.3 of the original code, you would check in the branch using the following command:

```
ci -r1.3.1 <filename>
```

A branch will be started at number 1 and assigned the version number 1.3.1.1.

Summary

Project Builder is a useful tool to help manage the source files in your application. This chapter introduced you to Project Builder and showed you how to use it to manage your application project. You were shown how to add files and build the entire source code tree. You were also shown how to use Project Builder to deploy your application.

Project Builder is a robust tool and can handle many different types of source code files. If you have a new type of source code file, Project Builder can be expanded and customized to handle it.

The RCS source code control system can be integrated tightly with Project Builder. You were shown how to perform check-ins and check-outs as well as create new versions and branches. Proper use of the source code control system will help reduce the number of potential software development problems.

GUIDELINES FOR BUILDING GREAT DEVELOPER APPLICATIONS

ESSENTIALS ————————————————————

- Follow look-and-feel guidelines created by your company, work-group, or site as you develop applications. If these guidelines are not formally written down, use previous applications to serve as a template.

- Throughout the development process, ask for feedback from the eventual users of the application.

- Performance tuning is an important part of any application. Start with tuning benefits that will provide the greatest speed increase, and work your way down to those that provide the least.

- A large number of environment variables exist that can be used to help in developing multilingual applications. If you plan to create applications to run in multiple languages, familiarize yourself with these environment variables and learn how they can help with your application.

- Oracle Developer allows you to create applications that will run on a variety of platforms. Even if your initial deployment environment might be homogeneous, you will want to follow the portable application guidelines. This will alleviate any problems with changes in future deployment architectures.

This chapter covers topics that help complete your application. Hints are given on tuning the look and feel so that your applications will have a finished look and not just be functionally driven. Some quick tips are also given on how to increase performance for slow applications. Developing multilingual applications can pose some interesting problems, and this chapter gives you some things to keep in mind. Finally, the chapter ends with some hints on creating portable applications to be distributed across a variety of runtime platforms.

Tuning the Look and Feel

It is easy to slap together a user interface (UI) that you think will work for the application. You might be satisfied with the visual design without realizing there is a simpler or better way to lay out the application object. Enlisting the help of a graphic designer and some simple guidelines can greatly enhance the application.

You can control some visual aspects of your application to provide a high-quality look. The look and feel also deals with the usability of your application. Paying close attention to both of these details will provide a successful experience for your application's users.

Many sites have established a set of guidelines for look and feel. If your company or site has developed applications previously, check to see whether these guidelines exist. If not, you will want to copy the look and feel of existing applications. It is very important that look-and-feel guidelines are followed on existing production systems.

Visual Aspects

The first thing users will notice about your application is how it looks. You can include wonderful algorithms and complex data processing behind the screens, but if the application does not look good, it can be considered a failure or at least unsuccessful. A graphics designer can be used to polish the application, but there are some things that you can do to help provide that finished look.

This next section will concentrate on the visual aspects of your application and how to control your user's experiences. Explicitly specifying colors and fonts will go a long way toward making your application look customized for your specific users. Choosing an appropriate coordinate system will help to provide a common look and feel across various machine displays. Finally, creating reusable components, such as warning message dialogs, will tie the individual pieces of your application together and make it look unified.

Colors and Fonts

Big Jim's sample application never explicitly specified colors or fonts to be used by the forms, reports, and graphics. Instead, the defaults were used. Although this is an acceptable practice for a sample application trying to be written as quickly as possible, it should be avoided for a real production application.

Using undefined colors and fonts has some unpredictable behavior in Oracle Developer. The Unix version of Forms uses a Helvetica font to display the form in the Layout Editor, but uses a serif font in the runtime. Explicitly specifying the font will eliminate the problem. There is a similar problem relating to colors. Therefore, you will want to always specify fonts and colors for objects in your application.

Many companies have developed internal guidelines for colors to be used for application development. Don't hesitate to specify these using appropriate properties such as foreground color and background color.

Coordinate System

Oracle Developer enables you to use different units for your coordinate system. The default is to use points, but there are other choices as well. These include

- Points
- Inches or Centimeters
- Pixels
- Characters

You should be familiar with the point coordinate system as the size of fonts used in word processing documents. Point coordinates should be the coordinate system of choice.

Using inches or centimeters has a higher precision than points, but is more difficult to compare the size of objects to text. Oracle recommends using this unit of measure with SVGA or better.

You are strongly discouraged from using pixels as the coordinate system unless you are absolutely sure that users will be using identical screens and resolutions. Remember that not all pixels are created equal; this setting can have a dramatic effect from machine to machine.

Use the character coordinate system when you are deploying applications in character mode only. Otherwise, it is too difficult to get the resolution required for GUIs.

The coordinate system is defined in the Property Palette at the form level. Clicking on the Coordinate System property value invokes the Coordinate Info dialog shown in Figure 15.1.

Creating Reusable Components

Remember that Big Jim's sample application was meant to be small. There was very little need to create a common set of components used by forms or reports throughout the application. As your applications become larger, however, you will want to look for common components.

FIGURE 15.1
The Coordinate Info dialog used to specify the coordinate system for your form.

Here are some examples to think about:

- You might have a dialog that asks the user to confirm or cancel changes. If this dialog can appear more than once in the application, be sure to create it in such a way that the same dialog can be used.

- Look for common data displayed throughout the application. Perhaps there are several places in which the user sees a customer's address information. Rather than re-creating the layout each time the information is shown, copy the layout exactly for each display instance.

- Consider creating a reference module with standard objects already created and ready to be used as an example. This will help to ensure a standard look and feel for all objects displayed in your application.

Creating reusable objects ensures that your application has a common look and feel. It also has the added benefit of reducing the amount of coding to complete your project.

Usability

Think about the user as you build your application. This will help you to design and create an application that does more than just allowing a user to enter information in a database. Instead, you will create a solution to a problem.

Here are some guidelines to help you:

- Define user requirements and interview potential users.

- Plan the user interface and show it to colleagues and potential users.

- Use common elements throughout.

- Test prototypes and don't be afraid to change them.

Take the time to define the user requirements before starting to design your applications. These requirements can be distilled from an earlier version of the application. They can also be formulated from the goals and expected benefits. Don't forget to spend time with the expected users of the application. If they are experienced with the problem and have used other solutions, they will be invaluable in helping you define requirements.

After you record the requirements, create a UI design document. This document can be as simple as hand-drawn pictures of the forms and reports. The important thing is to record your ideas in a format that can be reviewed. It is helpful to have access to a graphics designer who can make the application elegant and usable. You should also get input from other developers. Most importantly, show the design to potential users. Although they might not be able to tell you how to improve the UI, they will be able to tell you whether it will be usable.

Don't try to re-create an element that is used multiple times throughout your application. It is obvious that creating one dialog or form is much faster than creating multiple copies of the same object. Using the object multiple times might involve adding some extra code to the object. However, it should be easier than creating multiple copies of the same thing. The users will also appreciate the consistency.

It has been pointed out that software is never complete. Don't be afraid to put together a prototype and test it with your potential users. Making changes to an existing prototype is always easier than doing it right the first time. Software revisions should be expected.

Performance Tuning

Performance tuning is an important part of any application. The desire to tune the application should be adequately balanced with the required amount of work to do so. For instance, if only one person uses the application on an intermittent basis, it does not make sense to spend months fine-tuning the performance provided the rarely done task does not interfere with other system users. On the other hand, if many people use the application all day long, you want to make sure that it runs as fast as possible.

This next section will discuss several areas in which you can make changes to increase performance. The categories are as follows:

- All applications
- Forms
- Reports
- Graphics
- Web deployment

All Applications

Several performance adjustments can be made to all applications, regardless of whether they are forms, reports, or graphics. These ideas might be assessed before looking at anything else because they have a tendency to speed up the entire application and not just one aspect of it.

Upgrade Software

You should always make sure that you have the latest versions of the Oracle database and Oracle Developer. In addition to including new features and enhancements, Oracle often includes performance improvements. The Oracle Technology Network can be used to find the latest versions of software and what performance enhancements have been included.

Your hardware vendor might have included a performance increase in the latest version of the operating system. Of course, you want to be sure that it is compatible with the version of Oracle you are running.

Also be sure to check for the latest versions of other software used by your application. If you are using any Java or C components, remember to check for any speed improvements available in the latest releases of the software.

Upgrade Hardware

Upgrading hardware is much more difficult and expensive than upgrading the software. Generally, it should be considered only when absolutely necessary. However, there are one or two things that don't require a lot of system downtime or expense and can provide a dramatic performance increase.

Always make sure that you have enough system memory. Read the Oracle installation guide and make sure that you have enough memory for the database and Developer components. If your systems contain the minimum, you might be surprised by the performance increase from adding more RAM.

Look closely at network connections. If you are running using standard 10 megabit per second Ethernet with many users on the network, you might notice a significant performance increase by moving to 100 megabit per second Ethernet. Be sure to consult your network administrator who can help you determine whether this really is a bottleneck in application performance.

Use Array Processing

Forms and Reports Developer runtimes are both able to take advantage of array processing. The default is to fetch records from the database one at a time. This results in a large number of database accesses. Array processing allows the application to fetch records in blocks, reducing the number of database calls. This is done by increasing the ARRAYSIZE runtime parameter for either the Forms or Reports runtime.

Improve the Data Model

The data model for your application can have some significant performance implications. It is not uncommon to discover database designs with overly normalized tables. Although it is important to normalize your table structures and leverage the use of lookup tables, it is also important not to become overzealous. Joining the lookup table information can be complex and require a lot of extra processing time.

You will also want to be sure to use indexes to reduce the number of full-table scans. If you discover that your application is consistently qualifying data from a query using a specific column, make sure an index for the column exists.

Other General Improvements

Many other general improvements can be leveraged to increase your application performance. Be sure to consult with your database administrator and other application developers for ideas about how to increase the speed with which your application runs. There are also conferences, documentation, and Web sites that specialize in performance issues.

Forms

There are many different performance suggestions specific to forms that can be applied in addition to the general suggestions. These ideas have an advantage in that they can be applied to specific forms that don't meet your expectations.

Array Processing Specifics

Array processing was mentioned earlier as a method of increasing application performance. Forms Developer allows you to specify this value at the block level using the Query Array Size and Number of Records Buffered properties. Don't hesitate to adjust these properties if you discover performance bottlenecks associated with specific blocks in a form because of a high number of rows being retrieved.

Stored Procedures for Data Blocks

Basing a data block on a stored procedure can be a performance advantage when you want to move processing from the client back to the server. Foreign key lookups and calculations often require post-query triggers to execute for every row in a query. This causes additional database calls and can negate the benefits of using array processing.

Not all blocks can be based on a stored procedure, so it is necessary to look closely at your application and find those data blocks that are used in queries. The stored procedure can then return a ref cursor or table of records to be used by the application.

Inserts, updates, and deletes can also be performed on blocks based on a stored procedure that returns a table of records. You will need to write a specific procedure to handle each insert, update, or delete.

Using LOBs Instead of LONGs

If you are using version 8 or greater of the Oracle database, it is more efficient to use the LOB data type than the LONG data type.

Control Inter-Form Navigation

It is more efficient to divide a large form into smaller ones. However, opening and closing these smaller forms creates a lot of overhead. It is best to open the smaller forms and hide them when they are not being used rather than closing and reopening them.

Erase Global Variables After Use

Each global variable in your application requires 255 bytes. If you have a large number of global variables, it is best to erase them when they are no longer needed.

Reports

The best way to improve the performance for reports is to optimize the database and the queries used by the reports. There are one or two other things you can do to improve performance, but the most effective speed increases will happen at the database level.

Link Your Tables

Reports returns rows much faster from a query that accesses multiple tables than from multiple smaller queries. Therefore, you will want to be sure to use a single query to retrieve all the report information.

Turn Off Debug Mode

Make sure that you do not deploy your reports with debug mode turned on. Although debug mode can be helpful during the development process, it can dramatically slow down the production report.

Graphics

The same major performance improvement recommended for reports is also recommended for graphics: Optimize the database and query. There are one or two other things that will help with a performance increase, such as preloading graphics files and updating the display only when necessary. However, the largest performance improvement will come from making sure that the query and database are tuned appropriately.

Web Deployment

All the performance enhancements listed earlier will also help to increase the speed of your application in the Web deployment environment. Several other additional considerations also can help increase performance, and they are discussed in the next sections.

Increase Network Bandwidth

It is possible to run Developer applications using a 28.8Kbps modem, but this will seem unbearably slow to the user. One of the best performance enhancements to make is to increase the speed of the connection between the user's machine and the application server.

Minimize Changes to the Runtime Interface

Forms Developer allows you to change the user interface while the form is running. This can involve something as simple as changing the description text for fields from English to French or another language. However, this creates an extra burden on the network connection from the application server to the client's machine. If your network connection is limited, you will want to limit the number of interface changes.

Keep the Display Size Small

The amount of information that must be sent down the network connection to the client machine from the application server should be minimized. This can be accomplished by reducing the number of graphics that appear on the form. You also should limit the number of layers on the form and create objects programmatically. Finally, you will want to take advantage of stored procedures for data-intensive displays.

A Final Note on Performance

There are many other small things that can be done to increase your application's performance. Oracle's documentation lists many more than were discussed in this section. Remember to concentrate on those fixes that will create the greatest performance increase.

Amdahl's Law states that the performance improvement to be gained by using some faster mode of execution is limited by the fraction of the time the faster mode can be used. In other words, work on decreasing the execution time of lengthy bottlenecks rather than smaller ones. Once the large bottlenecks are taken care of, then feel free to take care of the smaller ones.

SOMETIMES IT'S THE LITTLE THINGS

There are many large things you can do to tune your database and applications. These are often documented in multiple locations and talked about at all the Oracle trade shows. Sometimes, however, it is the little things that will produce the largest speed increases.

I spent one summer in Seattle doing some consulting work, and I discovered a little-known tuning trick with the Oracle database. When I was back at the Oracle offices, I met with some performance tuning experts and asked them about the trick I had stumbled on. They hadn't heard of it before, and didn't think it would provide enough of a speed increase to warrant documenting it. However, I ran a report in four hours that used to take eight hours, and it was all because of a tiny little adjustment.

The customer had a single table that was 95% of the database. The table was huge. Every night, statistics were gathered from information stored in the table and used to create a report. This involved lots of sorting as well as the need to create some rather large internal temporary tables.

I was working as an application developer, but also was given the task of analyzing the table structure to see whether there was anything we could do to reduce the size of the massive main table. In looking at the database, I discovered that the temporary table space created an initial extent that was incredibly small. When I altered the tablespace so that the initial extent was larger by a factor of 10, the report execution time was cut in half.

Never have I seen that fix documented anywhere. When I talk about it with other Oracle experts, some smile knowingly, but most don't see it as a huge performance boost. All I can say is that it worked for me.

Developing Multilingual Applications

Most application developers will plan to deploy their applications using a single language. However, some developers will need to create applications to be deployed using multiple languages. This is one of the strengths of Oracle Developer, and it should be leveraged when needed.

Oracle Developer includes a list of national language support (NLS) environment variables to create applications in other languages. If French is your native language, and you would prefer to develop Forms applications with a French IDE using the WE8ISO8859P1 character set, you should set the NLS_LANG variable as shown:

```
NLS_LANG=French_France.WE8ISO8859P1
```

When you invoke Forms Builder, you will see your first welcome dialog in French rather than English, as shown in Figure 15.2.

FIGURE 15.2
Forms Builder's welcome dialog in French rather than English.

Here is a list of other NLS environment Variables and their uses:

- **NLS_CALENDAR**—The calendar system used.
- **NLS_CREDIT**—The string to indicate a positive monetary value.
- **NLS_CURRENCY**—The currency symbol.
- **NLS_DATE_FORMAT**—The default format for dates.
- **NLS_DATE_LANGUAGE**—The default language used for dates.
- **NLS_DEBIT**—The string to indicate a negative monetary value.
- **NLS_ISO_CURRENCY**—The ISO currency symbol.
- **NLS_LANG**—The language to use in Forms and Reports Developer.
- **DEVELOPER_NLS_LANG**—The language for the Builder component.
- **USER_NLS_LANG**—The language for the runtime component.
- **NLS_LIST_SEPARATOR**—The character used to separate items in a list.
- **NLS_MONETARY_CHARACTERS**—The decimal and thousands separators for monetary values.
- **NLS_NUMERIC_CHARACTERS**—The decimal and thousands separators for numeric values.
- **NLS_SORT**—The type of sort used for character data.

Remember to set the environment variables for the runtime systems as well as for the development machines.

Considerations

Developing multilingual applications requires a bit more advanced planning than single-language projects. It is almost mandatory to have the screens laid out long before you start coding them. This will allow you to have translations made of all static strings before you start coding. You also will need to know the lengths of all your variables, especially ones that will store text and strings. Finally, you must be sure that you understand local conventions where the application will be deployed.

Screen Real Estate

Laying out your forms and reports before developing them will give you an idea of how much information will be displayed. You will need to have all the boilerplate text translated correctly. Then you will need to make sure that you leave enough screen real estate. Boilerplate text in

English might take up less space than its French equivalent. If you don't have enough screen real estate, there will be problems.

Variable Sizes

Not all character sets are eight bits or a single byte. Unicode is two bytes and certain character sets use eight. Therefore, you might need to quadruple the size of character variables to accommodate the fatter strings. If you plan to deploy the application using an Asian language, you will probably need to expand strings by a factor of four.

Local Conventions

There are countless stories about how applications have been translated into other languages only to have the translations be horribly wrong. Even though the text might be literally correct, there could be hidden meanings that are not conveyed and cause confusion.

English is read from left to right. Other languages are read in the opposite direction. Also remember that certain languages are read from the bottom up. This might require a complete rewrite of your user interface, but doing so will help to eliminate any misunderstandings by your users.

Choose your icons carefully. Certain graphics will look perfectly normal and understandable to you. However, those same graphics could be offensive to other cultures. Make sure that all graphics and icons are approved by end users from the country and culture in which the application will be deployed.

Multilingual Application Caution

Countless resources are devoted to the building and deployment of NLS applications. The preceding section covered only one or two potential problems. It was meant to get you thinking about all the potential problems you might encounter, but it was not an exhaustive list.

The key to working with NLS applications is to involve the users of the system. Getting them involved early in the development process will help to eliminate recoding and re-layouts.

Writing Portable Applications

Oracle has always been known for developing cross-platform application development tools. Although Oracle tries to minimize the amount of trouble you will encounter, there are one or two things to keep in mind when developing applications that will be deployed on several different platforms. This next section will cover some of those issues.

Colors

Colors are one area that should be treated with caution. Just because you have the capability to display thousands or millions of colors does not mean you should. Pick four or five colors that work together in your application and stick to them. This will make the applications appear more uniform as you move them from platform to platform.

Fonts

It is interesting to note the different fonts available on various platforms. Although one font might be available on your Unix system, it might not be installed on Windows. Therefore, you will want to pick standard fonts that appear on all systems that will be using your application.

Key-Specific Messages

It is also interesting to note the various differences between keyboards for the different development platforms. Even though Windows and Linux use the same style of keyboard, there are differences in the key mappings. This makes it difficult to create help text or error messages with recognizable key names. Instead of saying something like Press the F1 key to continue, you will need to say Press the Execute Query key to continue. It will be difficult for your users to understand at first, but with a little training, they will figure out which keys to use.

Summary

This chapter was written to help you complete your application development. You were given some guidelines on how to tune the look and feel of the application to be the most usable for your application audience. You were given some simple guidelines for tuning the performance of your application. Multilingual application development was touched on lightly. Finally, the chapter ended with some quick ideas about how to make your application portable across various runtime platforms.

This is also the end of the book. You should now have a good idea how to develop applications using Oracle Developer 6i. Although there is not enough room to cover all the features in a single volume, the high points were covered and you should feel comfortable creating complex applications.

INDEX

A

Add Files to Project dialog box, 301

adding

calculations, 102-103

check boxes, 176

combo lists, 172

dialog boxes, 184

pop-up lists, 173

push buttons, 168

radio buttons, 177

radio groups, 177

traditional lists, 175

adjusting columns, 80

alerts, 36

aligning objects, 63-64

appearance

Interpreter, 124

Procedure Builder, 121

Program Unit Editor, 123

Query Builder, 95

applications, 242-243

amateur sports tracking example, 242-243

building, 317, 321-324

colors and fonts, 319

forms, 323

manually, 163

multilingual, 326-328

performance, 321, 325-326

point coordinates, 319

portable, 328

reports, 324

reusable components, 320

visual guidelines, 318

deploying, 292

deploying forms, 288

examples, 252

forms, 260-275

interface, 243-253, 260

Java, 291

portable, 328

array processing (performance), 322

assigning

LOV fields to SAL text items, 183

templates, 213

Axis Properties dialog box, 223, 232

B

backgrounds (applications), 242-243

bandwidth (performance issues), 325

bar charts, 222-223

horizontal, 222-223

mixed with line charts, 229

vertical, 222-223

beans. *See* Java

building

applications, 317, 321, 324

colors and fonts, 319

forms, 323

multilingual, 326-328

performance, 321, 325-326

point coordinates, 319

portable, 328

reports, 324

reusable components, 320

upgrading software, 322

visual guidelines, 318

files (Project Builder), 303-306

forms, 31, 34-36

reports, 41

built-in exception handling, 138-139

buttons, Lock Record, 161

C

calculated fields, 166

calculations, adding, 102-103

calling stored procedures, 147

canvases (multiple), 180

tools
client/server runtime environment, 158
Data Model, 208-209
forms, 15
Interpreter (PL/SQL), 126
Layout Editor, 59, 64-67
Layout Model view (reports), 210-212
Live Previewer view, 207
Object Navigator, 87
Project Wizard, 302
Report Editor, 84-86
reports, 15
Results window, 106
Tools menu
Data Block Wizard commands, 52
Report Wizard command, 77
tracking application example, 243-253, 260
traditional lists, 171, 175
Translation Builder, 17
triggers, 36
databases, 137
Event forms, 263
PRE-FORM, 174, 264
selecting, 169
Triggers dialog box, 169

U - V

UI (visual guidelines), 318
undoing mistakes (client/server runtime environment), 159-160
Unix
installing on, 27
obe60, 94
upgrading software and hardware, 322
usability (in design), 321
user parameters, 41
user-exits, 120

variables
declaring, 128
NLS, 327
PL/SQL, 129-130
verifying push buttons, 170
vertical bar charts, 222-223
views
reports, 205
Data Model, 208-209
Layout Model, 210-212
Live Previewer, 207
Schema Builder, 116
visual attributes, 36

W

Web, deploying forms to, 290
Web CGI (Forms Server), 287-288
Web Wizard, 13
Web-based applications, 8
WHILE-LOOP statement (PL/SQL), 134
width (columns), 80
windows
Forms Debugger, 179
Query Builder, 95
Schema Builder, 109
wizards
Chart, 12-13, 88, 90
Data Block, 11, 31, 34, 50
Layout, 12, 34
LOV, 12, 182
Report, 13
Web, 13